Tango™

web application construction kit

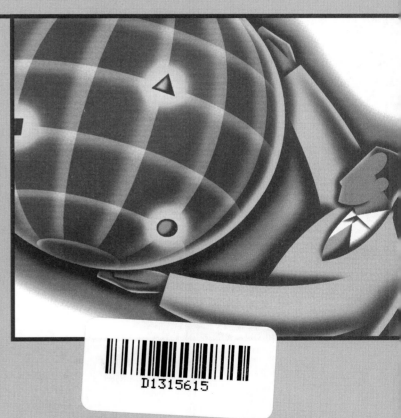

Ron Davis

SAMS

A Division of Macmillan USA
201 West 103rd St.,
Indianapolis, Indiana, 46290 USA

D1315615

Tango Web Application Construction Kit

Copyright ©2000 by Sams Publishing

International Standard Book Number: 0-672-31948-9

Library of Congress Catalog Card Number: 00-101481

Printed in the United States of America

First Printing: August 2000

03   02   01   00   4   3   2   1

Trademarks

Warning and Disclaimer

Acquisitions Editor
Jeff Schultz

Development Editor
Scott D. Meyers

Managing Editor
Charlotte Clapp

Project Editor
Elizabeth Finney

Copy Editor
Michael Henry

Indexer
Erika Millen

Proofreaders
Katherin Bidwell
Juli Cook

Technical Editor
Klaus Sonnenleiter

Team Coordinator
Amy Patton

Media Developer
Jason Haines

Interior Designer
Gary Adair

Cover Designer
Alan Clements

Production
Gloria Schurick

Overview

Contents

Dedication

To Doug Doe, the best manager I ever had.

Acknowledgments

I'd like to thank all the people at Pervasive Software who made this book possible: Greg Hemstreet, Gerardo Dada, Doug Doe, Gary Allison, John Daub, Joe Janakovic, Renata Rubinsztajn, Rob Haskett, Manoj Patwardhen, Jeremy Bower, Dan Ivanisevic, and Ramon Acosta. Not only did they support the production of this book, but also they created the coolest Web app development environment out there. Alex Kac deserves thanks for being not only my Tango guru inside Pervasive, but also my ASP with his Tango hosting service (http://www.webis.net/), where most of this book was tested. Also thanks to my tech editor, Klaus Sonnenleiter, who pointed out often where I was screwing things up, and my acquisitions editor, Jeff Schultz, for putting up with my newbie questions. I also couldn't have done this without the support of my family and friends, especially my wife Suanna and my sons, Elijah and Micah.

About the Author

Ron Davis is a Senior Lead Software Engineer on the Macintosh Tango IDE for Pervasive Software. He worked with the team coding the Tango 2000 product and is involved with design for future versions of Tango. Before Pervasive, Ron Davis worked for Metrowerks on its CodeWarrior IDE. He's programmed a variety of Macintosh software products, from anti-virus to version control. Ron Davis has also published articles in *MacTech* magazine and the *Tango Developer's Journal*, and presented at the Mac Hack conference.

Tell Us What You Think!

As the reader of this book, *you* are our most important critic and commentator. We value your opinion and want to know what we're doing right, what we could do better, what areas you'd like to see us publish in, and any other words of wisdom you're willing to pass our way.

You can email or write me directly to let me know what you did or didn't like about this book—as well as what we can do to make our books stronger.

Please note that I cannot help you with technical problems related to the topic of this book, and that due to the high volume of mail I receive, I might not be able to reply to every message.

When you write, please be sure to include this book's title and author as well as your name and phone or fax number. I will carefully review your comments and share them with the author and editors who worked on the book.

Email: `webdev_sams@mcp.com`

Mail: Mark Taber
         Associate Publisher
         Sams Publishing
         201 West 103rd Street
         Indianapolis, IN 46290 USA

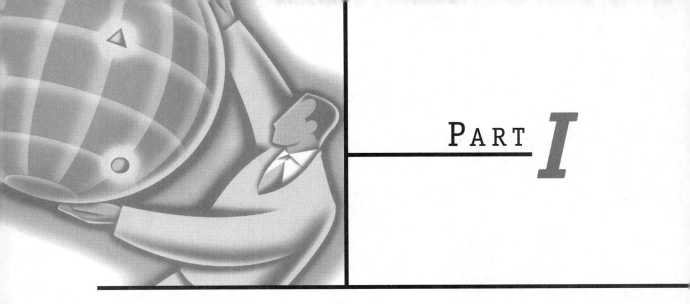

PART I

Introduction to Tango

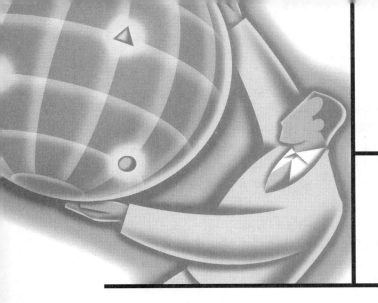

CHAPTER 1

Introduction

What We'll Learn

Tango is a program that enables you to create Web applications. In this chapter, you are introduced to the following concepts:

- What a Web application is
- How a Web application works
- How Tango creates and executes Web applications
- How this book is organized

Why Use Tango?

When the Web was born, it was strictly a static, textual process. People coded pages in straight text HTML, and then they uploaded those pages to a Web server for the public to consume. But things have changed so rapidly over the years that the term *Internet time* has come to be synonymous with rapid change. The need for rapid change of Web sites has led to a new kind of software, called Web applications.

Web applications are programs that run on a Web server and dynamically create HTML for Web sites on the fly. Using programmer's logic along with standards for interfacing with databases, Web applications are changing the Web. Most major Web sites are Web applications. Although millions of static Web pages are still out there, they are mostly confined to smaller sites. A portal site is one example of a specific class of Web application. It tracks the user and lays out the Web page according to that user's preferences.

Tango is an environment for the creation and deployment of Web applications. It consists of two parts: the Tango Integrated Development Environment and the Tango Application Server. The Tango IDE provides an easy-to-use editor for creating the files that make up the applications for your Web site. The Tango Application Server actually interprets these files and generates the HTML or other content for the site.

Tango started out as a way to take data out of an SQL database and generate a Web page from it. It has grown into a full-fledged application-building environment for the Web, interfacing not only with databases, but also with email programs, scripting environments, and component architectures. It is a true cross-platform development environment, enabling you to develop application files on a Windows or MacOS machine and to deploy not only to those two platforms, but also to Solaris and Linux.

Web applications vary in complexity just as computer programs do. Often all a person wants to do is the simplest of tasks, such as sending an email or slightly changing the format of the page for a specific browser. However, a developer might want to do really complex things such as generate a portal page. Many people use scripting languages such as Perl and PHP to do simple tasks on their Web sites. The problem comes when they need the sites to do more complex things, such as tracking users or keeping values associated with a user through multiple Web page requests. These functions can be done in scripting languages, but they become very complex. Tango makes the creation of even the most complex sites easier. The IDE's drag-and-drop interface creates Tango application files that can replace hundreds of scripting files, without you writing a single line of code.

Here's an easy, although not foolproof, way to tell whether you are asking for a simple file or a Web application. If the server part of the URL looks like a file path, ending with a filename with the .html extension, it probably is a simple file request. Other file extensions give away the fact these files need interpretation before they are usable by your Web browser. Extensions such as .jsp, .asp, and .php indicate files that are handled by an application server and whose output is returned to your browser.

If the URL contains a ? after the file with the non-HTML extension, with a bunch of word pairs like something=4 *or* something=tom%20hanks, *the URL is even more likely to be pointing to a Web application. The question mark begins the parameters passed to the Web application file.*

How Tango Works

Here's what happens when you request a simple Web page from a Web server. Assume your URL is <http://www.macmillanusa.com/newbooks/index.html>. Your Web browser looks up the server www.macmillanusa.com and connects to it. It then sends the URL to the server and waits for a response. On the server is a program running to handle Web requests. There are a number of different Web server applications, such as Apache and WebStar. The server takes the rest of the URL and parses out the path to the file you want; in this case, /newbooks/index.html. The Web server program looks at the file's extension to determine whether it needs to do anything special with the file. In the case of .html files, it knows no special processing is needed. The server program opens the requested file on its internal drive and sends the contents of the file back to your Web browser. Your browser then interprets the HTML in the file and displays the Web page.

Here's what happens when you request a file from a Tango Application Server. Just as earlier, the browser sends its URL to the specified Web server. The Web server application—for example, Apache—finds the requested file in the URL. It looks at the file's extension and compares it to a table of extensions telling it about other programs that can handle specific extensions. In the case of Tango, if the Web server sees a file with a .taf extension, it knows the Tango Application Server can handle the file. So, the Web server passes the URL to the Tango Application Server for the file and waits to get some HTML back. The Web Application Server interprets the file, using any parameters that appear after the filename in the process. Then the Web Application Server generates HTML based on the logic in the file and returns it to the Web server application, which passes the HTML back to the browser for display.

It should be noted that Tango doesn't have to return HTML. It can return any kind of text, from straight unformatted ASCII to XML. As a matter of fact, Tango makes the generation of XML pages quite easy.

The Tango Application Server runs in one of two ways on the Web server machine—either as a plug-in to the Web server application or as a separate CGI program. If the application supports a plug-in architecture, Pervasive ships a version of the Tango Application Server in plug-in format. For all the supported server platforms, Pervasive ships a CGI. CGI stands for Common Gateway Interface, which is a standard means of communicating between a Web server application and some other piece of code. Most Web server applications can be configured so that when you request any file with the extension .taf, the file is passed to the Tango CGI. If the server doesn't support a plug-in, the URL must look like this:

```
http://your.web.server/tango2000.acgi$/path/to/app/file/yourfile.taf
```

In either case—and I will assume the plug-in case for the rest of the book—the .taf file is sent to the Tango Server, which interprets the actions or instructions in the TAF. The result of these actions should be an HTML page, which is passed back to the Web server application.

What is a .taf file, and how do you create one? A *Tango Application File*, or TAF, is the output of the Tango Integrated Development Environment. It contains a series of Tango actions that defines a flow of control for a Web application. Tango uses a graphical, drag-and-drop editing environment for TAFs. Figure 1.1 shows what a sample TAF looks like in the Tango IDE.

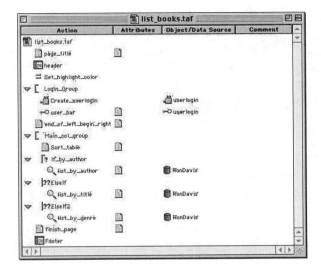

FIGURE 1.1   *A sample TAF screen shot.*

Although the editing of a TAF is graphical, it is saved as XML. XML stands for Extensible Markup Language, and it is an international standard for representing hierarchical data structures using text. XML is a cousin to HTML and you will see the similarity in their structures. Because a TAF is saved as text, it is extremely easy to transfer between platforms. This enables you to develop on a Macintosh and deploy to a Linux server without any special conversion of files, as long as there is a Tango Application Server running on your target platform.

How Tango Development Works

Here are the steps you go through when developing a Web application with Tango.

Installation

You must install the Tango Server on your Web server and the Tango IDE on your development machine. These machines can be the same, but in most cases, they are not.

TAF Creation

You run the Tango IDE and create a new TAF document. Then you use the features of the Tango IDE to create the logic inside the TAF. The logic is created by dragging and dropping Tango actions into the TAF window and configuring those actions.

Deployment

Now you've saved your TAF file on your development machine, but you need to get it on your Web server. The process of getting the TAFs on your Web server is called *deployment*. Most often, deployment is done by FTPing the files to the server; in fact, Tango even supports this method in the Tango IDE. You could also mount your Web server's drive on your development machine using the services of your OS and transfer files that way.

Execution

Now that you have your file on your Web server, you can execute it by pointing your Web browser to the file. Point your Web browser by entering a URL that corresponds to the location of your deployed TAF.

Debugging

Tango 2000 provides simple debugging features that enable you to see how a TAF was executed. By using these tools and elements you can add to your TAFs, you can determine what went wrong if your TAF doesn't do what you expect. TAFs specifically created for debugging can also assist you.

Editing

If you find a problem with your TAF, you go back to the Tango IDE and edit the TAF file. Then, you go back to the deployment step and repeat this process until the TAF is working the way you want.

Completion

After you have the TAF generating the Web page or pages you want, you are done. You'll find this whole process goes very quickly and easily with Tango.

How the Chapters in This Book Are Structured

You're going to take a slightly different approach to learning about Tango in this book. Instead of introducing a concept, such as Tango actions or using data sources, and then creating examples showing how to use that concept, you will create an entire Web site through various Tango applications. This means you're going to start with a problem and develop a solution using Tango. Along the way, you'll learn different concepts about how Tango works. At the end of this book, you'll have a complete Web site with lots of features.

This approach means you could just skip to the chapter on the module you want to learn. That is fine after you understand Tango. If you've completed the book once, or are an experienced Tango user, you can immediately skip to the chapter you are interested in. If you are new to Tango, you need to go through the chapters in order to learn the concepts of each chapter because I assume you already know how to do things that were taught in previous chapters. You can find out what was taught before by looking at the "What We'll Learn" section in each chapter.

Chapter Schema

A couple of introductory chapters in the book have their own structure, but most of the book is made up of what I call module chapters. Each module chapter creates a new piece of our Web site and each of these chapters has the same structure. Here are the specific sections.

What We'll Learn

A bulleted list of new areas of Tango covered in this chapter.

Purpose

The purpose of the module we are creating in a short, one-paragraph description.

Planning

Feature List

A list of all the features of the module.

Database Schema

A discussion of the data used in the module with the layout of the database tables. All the databases are SQL databases, and the layout is expressed in this section in two ways: as a table diagram and as a CREATE TABLE statement.

Creating the TAFs

This is the core of the chapter, with detailed, step-by-step descriptions of the creation of the Tango files used in the application. Chapter 2, "Web Application Planning," explains in depth the process you go through to plan out a module, but the short version is that most TAFs implement functionality either for the user of the site or for the site's administrators. There are two main subsections to the "Creating the TAFs" section of each chapter: "User TAFs" and "Admin TAFs."

What You Need to Understand to Use This Book

HTML

You need to have a basic understanding of how HTML works. This book will not teach you how to create HTML that bolds text or creates a table. In many cases, the HTML will be generated for you by Tango, but you will often need to create it yourself or modify the output of Tango, so you must understand how HTML works.

If you are completely unfamiliar with HTML, you might be able to do many of the things in this book by following the step-by-step directions, but you will not completely understand what Tango is doing.

SQL Databases

Although Tango supports some non-SQL databases such as FileMaker, we will use Pervasive.SQL as our database. You can use any ODBC-compliant database for most of the examples.

I assume that you understand SQL, and that you know how to create your own database and tables.

Also, you should have your database installed and configured correctly on your Tango machine. Any connection between the machine you are developing on and the database server needs to be active and in working order.

Tango Installation

I also assume that you have installed Tango according to the documentation that comes with your Tango IDE and Server. Although the process of installation is quite easy, attempting to cover it here would be time-consuming.

After the server is installed, you need a means of getting files from your development machine to the Tango Application Server. You should ensure that this means is also working.

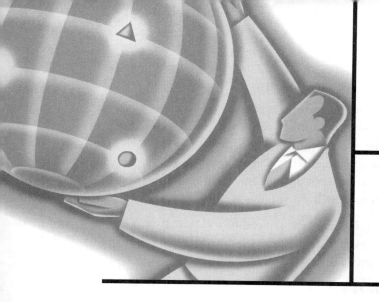

CHAPTER 2

Web Application Planning

Almost every project benefits from planning, and Web applications are no exception. In some ways, using Tango to create a Web site makes things easier. For example, because one TAF can create many pages, you don't have to worry about the consistency of the site's look across hundreds of pages. On the other hand, Web applications have more functionality than straight HTML and that can add complexity. For example, you now have to set up your database as well as lay out your HTML.

It is rare that a Web application is only a few Web pages. If your Web site can be done with only three pages, it probably doesn't need a powerful backend such as Tango, so almost by definition Web applications are complex enough to really require planning.

Planning is also critical when you are doing a project for someone else. Before you drag in a single action, you must know what your client expects of you. Having a clear list of requirements can affect your bottom line, and your customer's satisfaction.

How to Plan a Web Application

The start of any project is very high level. It generally can be summed up in one statement. For example, "I want a Web site to sell my widgets," or "I want a Web site to allow all lovers of Clint Howard movies to congregate," or "I need an intranet that allows people to access our customer leads database." These are the missions of your project. They are the statements you check against to make sure you aren't moving off into something other than what you intended. If you are creating an e-commerce site and someone wants to put a game or a stock-trading application on it, your core statement will tell you this isn't needed.

At the beginning of the project, it is a good idea to codify and actually write down a statement of what your project is supposed to do. This statement will help you as you move through the planning process.

Break It Down into Pieces

After you have a mission statement, you need to break down your project into smaller pieces. These pieces will help you to define the specific features or requirements of your project. For example, if you are building a community site, you might break it down into pieces such as member registration, forums, chat, and so on.

There are a number of ways to go about this breakdown. One way is to just do it off the top of your head. But that can lead you to miss things. One of Steven Covey's *Seven Habits of Highly Effective People* is to begin with an end in mind. You need to think about what you want at the end of the project, including what the site will look like and function when you are done. Think of it like this: You are going to start coding your Web site, and are working furiously. When do you stop? When is the site done and ready to deploy? That is literally the *end*.

You can determine the end either from the top down or from the bottom up.

Top Down

This is the page approach. The idea is to create or visualize the Web site as it will be seen from the browser. Think about the ways user will want to use your site. You can create storyboards of the site, drawing out rough markups of specific pages and connecting them with lines. As the ideas crystallize, you might want to create actual HTML mockups of the site. You can put dummy static data into each page representing the data you will ultimately draw from database.

After you have an HTML mockup, you can take it to your client or end user and get their feedback. I can't stress too much how important user feedback is early in the process. When working on any coding project, we often get too close to the code and easily miss things that the average user would see right away.

As part of the breakdown process, you need to look at what data you want to display. The top-down approach works well when you don't already know the specifics of the data you want to display. For instance, if you are creating a Web site to display book reviews, doing an HTML mockup will tell you what data your users want to see. And, it will often tell you about data that you might miss, such as a book's ISBN number so that you can link to an external bookstore. After you know the data you are displaying, you can intelligently design your database tables. You might even find that your data doesn't lend itself to tables and columns, and you need to use a hierarchical data store or XML.

Bottom Up

Sometimes your project is to put some existing data on a Web site. What you are doing is creating a Web interface to a database. In this case, you might want to take a bottom-up approach. Look first at the database and determine what data you want the user to view and change. Now think about how you want to display this data and how the user needs to access it. Does the user want to drill down to a specific record from higher views of the data? Or does she just need to enter a specific part number and find that one record for editing? Does the user need to change more than one record at a time? What data is related? Are there links you want to display between records or tables?

As you answer these questions, a web of HTML pages will begin to emerge until you have covered all your data. At that point, you have a complete Web site.

This approach also works with external objects. Tango has the capability to call COM objects and JavaBeans. If your client has a set of JavaBeans that calculate something and the client wants to let people access those calculations over the Web, you can look at the parameters of the objects and design pages to get the data for those parameters. You then look at the output of the function calls and determine what needs to be displayed and how.

Two Viewpoints on a Web Application: User and Admin

In addition to mapping out the look of the site and the makeup of the data, it is important to examine the functionality your Web application is going to have and make sure all of it is covered. There are normally two views on a Web site: the view of the user and the view of the administrators of the Web site. The user view is all the parts of the Web site that are publicly accessible. The admin sections are those parts that require getting through some kind of security to access. The admin sections are also the pages that can make changes to the Web site or database that you don't want everyone able to make.

For instance, you probably allow the user to post to a public discussion, but you don't allow everyone to delete messages. But because you might get messages on your discussions that must be edited or deleted because they violate the rules of the area, you do allow administrators to delete messages.

So when you are breaking down the functionality of your Web site, think in terms of user functionality and administrator functionality. Throughout this book, we actually break up our TAFs into user and admin TAFs. Putting all the admin functionality of a specific module into a single TAF enables you to put that TAF in a different, and secure, place on your Web site.

Sometimes you can reveal certain options on a page only if the currently logged-in user is an administrator. Going back to the discussion example, it would be a pain for the administrators to have to remember some reference to a specific message, go to the admin TAF, and enter that reference. Instead, it is better to add a delete link that is displayed on the page only if the person looking at it was an administrator. Tango allows you to do this easily.

Integration with Other Parts

Before you finalize a module's design, you must think about how it will interact with other modules. This sometimes shows you where you've missed a database column that you might need. There are a couple global modules in this book that you should take special care in thinking about: user and find.

Many modules will use the user system for security and display of personalized information. Because of that, you need to think about what data you need to hook a module into the user system. For instance, when a user suggests a URL in the Web directory, you want to give him user points, so you need to make sure you have his username.

Another global system is the find system. You need to think about what data you need to search and display. For instance, you will want to be able to search the Web directory, including the name and description.

A Step-by-Step Approach

Let's take these principles and put them in a step-by-step process that we can use when creating modules of our Web site.

1. Know What You Want to Do

The first thing you need to do is know what you want the module to do. This is our mission statement.

2. List Functional Requirements

The next step is to list functional requirements. A *functional requirement* is a specific feature or bit of functionality that the application is supposed to have. By listing functional requirements, you know when you are done. If you think you've done everything, you can go through your list of requirements and determine whether they are all fulfilled.

It is important that a functional requirement is testable. Don't create a requirement that says, "Write a cool navigation bar." *Cool* is something that is hard to test. Instead, give specifics about the navigation bar, "Write a navigation bar that enables the user to jump to the starting points of the previously defined sections of the Web site." If you have a separate quality assurance department, it can use the functional requirements to test that the app does what it is supposed to do.

Functional requirements are also important when dealing with a client. Functional requirements are often contract points—they are the things the client is paying you to do. After you and the client agree on what your functional requirements are for a project, they should be very hard to change. Changing requirements can cause your schedule to slip and the project to come in late and over budget.

Functionality is of primary importance in a project. Don't be sidetracked early on by laying out your Web page. Because most of us come from a background of static HTML pages, the presentation is the thing of which we are most conscious. In a Web application, the presentation is secondary to the logic. Develop your application and get the data on the page, and then go back and "gold plate" the page to make it look the way you want it to look. Often you can have a separate designer do the layout and you, the programmer, do the data generation.

3. Divide and Specify Functionality by Admin and User

After you know the functionality, start thinking of it in terms of user and admin. This might cause you to change the functional requirements as you think of new things that must be included. When you know the differences in functionality, divide it into two lists.

4. Design the Database

At this point, the data will follow out of the site. You should be able to create the tables for your data. You can look at how it will be used and figure out whether you must have data in separate tables that you can search with a join, or if the data can go in one table.

5. Create the TAFs and TCFs

You are now ready to start coding. Create the TAFs you will use and implement the requirements you have specified.

6. Test the Code

You will do two kinds of testing. First, make sure that the code works, meaning that there are no errors. Did you create a TAF that searched a database column that wasn't there? Do you access a variable that isn't there anymore?

The other type of testing you must do is to check whether the functional requirements are met. The code might "work," but not do what it is supposed to do. It could incorrectly perform the functionality, or it could just miss a requirement.

7. Repeat as Needed

After you've tested the code, you will have to fix some bugs. If there are no bugs, you are ready to release the code. If there are bugs, go back to step 5 and fix the code. Repeat step 6 and test the code again. Fixing a bug might introduce new bugs into other parts of the application.

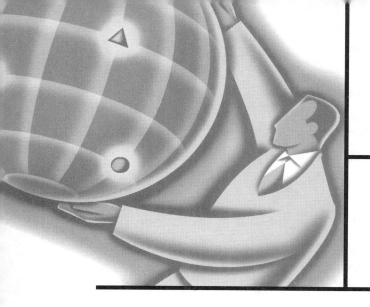

CHAPTER 3

The Coming Soon Page

What We'll Learn

- Result HTML action: how to put simple HTML into a TAF
- <@ARG> meta tag: how Tango processes forms
- Data sources: how Tango represents databases
- Email action: sending email from a TAF
- If, IfElse, Else actions: basic flow control
- Insert action: putting data in a database
- Search action: getting data out of a database
- <@VAR>, <@ASSIGN>: introducing variables in Tango

Purpose

Since we will create an entire Web site through the course of this book, you should put up a notice on your Web site letting people know it is coming. It is doubtful that people are waiting with bated breath for your site to go up and you don't want people to have to keep coming back to see whether your site is there yet. The solution is to provide a way for the user to be notified when your site goes up. We do this using an HTML form to gather each visitor's name and email address, which we will store in a database.

Planning

Feature List

- Have a coming soon message
- Create a form for users to enter a name and email address for notification when the Web site is up
- Put the submitted information in a database
- Allow the admin to send messages to everyone on the list

Database Schema

The data in this example is very simple—just the name and password that the user enters in your form. So, we need only a single database table with two columns.

Database Table Name: Notify

Column Name	Data Type	Size
username	Char	50
email	Char	255

```
CREATE TABLE notify (
    username char(30) PRIMARY KEY,
    email char(30)
)
```

Creating the TAFs

We are creating two TAFs for this module, following our methodology of dividing the user and admin functionality. This enables us to put the admin TAF in a secure location—not doing this would enable anyone who types the URL in his browser to send email to all the people in your database. As the project progresses, we create our own TAF security that does not require you to put TAFs in a secure location.

User TAFs

Let's start with the user TAF. Two pages are generated by this TAF to take care of all the functionality in the module. The first is the main welcome page. This is the page the users see when they come to your site for the first time. Most of the functionality in this TAF is on this page, with the welcome message at the top and the registration form at the bottom.

The second page this TAF generates is a thank you message when the user registers to be notified.

Using Arguments

Because a TAF's actions are executed from top to bottom, how do we know which page to generate? We'll use the Tango convention of the _function argument. This works by adding an argument to the URL for the TAF. An *argument* is a name and value added to the URL. A URL for a TAF file is just like any other URL for a specific file. Arguments are added by putting a question mark after the filename, followed by the argument's name, an equal sign, and the value of the argument. For instance, the URL to point to the TAF we are creating is

`http://www.yourdomain.com/index.taf`

If we want to add the argument _function with the value of insert, the URL becomes

`http://www.yourdomain.com/index.taf?_function=insert`

Adding arguments to URLs doesn't just apply to URLs you enter in your browser by hand; it also applies to links in your HTML. You'll see this more as we go through the creation of this TAF.

Creating Tango Application Files

Open the Tango Editor and choose File, New, Tango Application File from the menu to create a new Web application. Save it as index.taf.

You'll see an empty TAF window. TAFs are organized in a hierarchical fashion. There is a root node, which has the name of the TAF. You see it when you first create the TAF. You can add Tango actions by dragging them from the Actions palette into the TAF. When you drag in your first action, it can go in only one place: right under the root action. You will notice that as you are dragging the action, a line appears in the TAF display showing you where your action will be in the hierarchy. At the left end of this indicator line is a triangle. This triangle indicates where—from left to right—you are in the hierarchy. It is important to watch this triangle because where an action is in the hierarchy can affect how it is executed.

Some Tango actions are considered to have subactions. Subactions appear below and to the left of their parent. An action with subactions has a disclosure triangle next to it; you can click on it and hide all the action's subactions. Often, a parent action determines whether its subactions are executed. An If action is a great example of this, and it is the first thing we need to create for our Coming Soon page.

The If Action

The first thing we must do in the TAF is determine whether it is being called when the user first visits the site, or if it is being called after the user fills out the registration form. We do this by checking the _function argument and executing the correct set of actions. Drag an If action into the TAF; when you do this, a new empty If action window opens that looks like Figure 3.1.

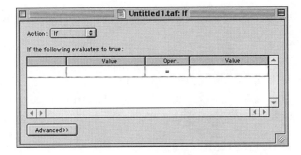

FIGURE 3.1   *An empty If window.*

An If action evaluates some expression and if the expression evaluates to true, the actions following it are executed. If the expression evaluates to false, the next action at the same level in the TAF as the If action is executed. Sometimes when an If action evaluates to false, it is said to fail. Likewise, when it evaluates to true, it is said to succeed.

You set the expression by filling in the two Value columns in the If action window and setting the Oper. column to how you want the values compared. You can also add multiple comparisons by using the Insert menu item. Each row is one comparison and you can choose whether they are ORed together or ANDed using the first column of the table.

The If action has two sister actions: Else and ElseIf. Sometimes you want a specific set of actions to execute if an If action succeeds and a different set of actions to execute if it fails. That is the purpose of the If action's sisters. Without them, you would have to put another If action after the first one with the opposite expression. An Else action is executed only if the If preceding it fails.

An ElseIf action is like an Else in that it is executed only if the preceding If action fails, but it contains a new expression to be evaluated like an If action. Combining these three actions enables you to set up logic to execute sets of actions for a number of possibilities.

Now we need to fill out the columns of the If action. Tango uses a meta tag (named, aptly enough, <@ARG>) to get the value of an argument. In this first If action, we want to handle the welcome message case and then the insert case. So, in the Value column of the If action window, enter <@ARG _function> to get the value of the _function argument. What is the value of _function when the user first comes to the Web site? There is no value because there is no ?_function in the URL. So, in the Operator column of the If action window, select Is Empty. When you've done this, your If action window should look like Figure 3.2. Close the window.

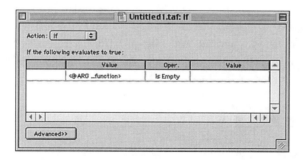

FIGURE 3.2   A finished If window.

If you like, you can rename any action by clicking the action name and editing it. I renamed this If action to IfEmpty.

Creating the Welcome Page

Now we want to add the functionality of the empty if; namely, displaying the welcome page. What we need to do is have a bunch of standard HTML to create the page. I want to do it in two parts to keep the welcome message in its own Result action. So, let's first drag a Result action under the IfEmpty action. Make sure that the insertion point is indented and the Result action appears inside the If.

You are now presented with an empty Result action window. You can enter any text you want in this window and it is passed directly on to the Web server after any meta tags in it are evaluated. In our case, we want a simple HTML page template with some welcome text. You can use the Page Template Snippet to create the basics of an HTML page, and add your welcome message to the page. I entered the HTML in Listing 3.1 and renamed the Result action to WelcomeMessage.

Listing 3.1   Welcome Page Message Result Action

```
<!DOCTYPE HTML PUBLIC "-//W3C//DTD HTML 3.2//EN">
<HTML>
<HEAD>
    <TITLE>Welcome</TITLE>
</HEAD>
<BODY>
Thank you for visiting our web site.  We are in the process of creating
a great dynamic site with lots of cool features right now. Please be patient.
```

Now we need the second part of the main page, which is the form the user fills out to be notified when the Web site goes public. To create this, we use another Result action. Drag it in under the WelcomeMessage action and enter the HTML from Listing 3.2.

Listing 3.2   Welcome Page Form Result Action

```
<FORM METHOD="POST" ACTION="<@CGI><@APPFILE>
?_function=insert&<@USERREFERENCEARGUMENT>">
<TABLE>
<TR VALIGN=TOP ALIGN=LEFT>
    <TD>
        Name:
    </TD>

    <TD>
        <INPUT NAME="username" TYPE=TEXT SIZE=40 MAXLENGTH=255>
```

```
    </TD>
</TR>
<TR VALIGN=TOP ALIGN=LEFT>
    <TD>
        Email Address:
    </TD>

    <TD>
        <INPUT NAME="email_address" TYPE=TEXT SIZE=40 MAXLENGTH=255>
    </TD>
</TR>
</TABLE>
<INPUT TYPE=SUBMIT VALUE="Save"> <INPUT TYPE=RESET VALUE="Reset Values">
</FORM>

</BODY>
</HTML>
```

If you are familiar with HTML, you understand the syntax here for a form inside a table. I'm not going to go into that part in detail, but let me explain the Tango-specific stuff in the HTML.

First is the beginning FORM tag itself. The form is submitted via the POST method, which means its values are passed as arguments.

Second, we see the ACTION portion of the FORM tag. The ACTION attribute is the URL or HREF to which the form data is passed. It is the file that handles the form data. In our case, we want the current TAF file to handle it. We could put the actual URL of our TAF in there, but what if we moved the TAF? We would have to come back and change the HTML. Luckily, Tango has a better method for handling this case: a meta tag called <@APPFILE> that returns the path to the current TAF.

When you were setting up your Web server, you learned you can use either a CGI or Tango plug-in for the Application Server. If you use a CGI, you have to include the CGI application in all your URLs that refer to a TAF. So, in the CGI case, just using <@APPFILE> by itself wouldn't work because it doesn't include the CGI application. Tango provides the <@CGI> meta tag to add the CGI application to the URL. If you use the plug-in, <@CGI> resolves to nothing. It is good Tango-programming practice always to include the <@CGI> tag, even when you aren't using the CGI. You might use the CGI in the future or you might give your TAF to someone who does.

Continuing on through the ACTION attribute, we see the setting of the _function argument to insert. This flag tells the Tango server to perform the database insert when the index.taf is called after the form is filled out.

Handling the Signup Form

Let's go on to the handling of the form. From the ACTION attribute of the form, we know our current IfEmpty If action doesn't execute the actions inside of it when the form is posted because the _function argument has a value. So, we need to handle the case where the value is insert. To do this, we need to add another If action to the TAF, so drag in an ElseIf action. It must be at the same level as the other If action, so watch the indent level. An ElseIf action works just like an If action, but is called only if the matching If action fails. So enter the value as <@ARG _function>, and the operator as =. For the value, enter insert. Your completed ElseIf window should look like Figure 3.3. I renamed the action ElseIfInsert.

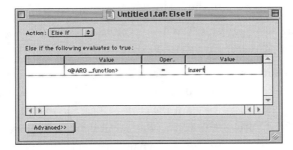

FIGURE 3.3 *An ElseIfInsert window.*

When the user fills out the form and the TAF is executed, we need to do a couple of things. First, we must insert the form information into our database. We do this with an Insert action. Drag one in under the ElseIfInsert.

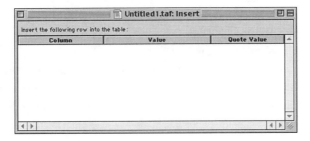

FIGURE 3.4 *An empty Insert action window.*

We must tell the Insert action what columns in the database we want to insert into. To do this in Tango, you use the Data Sources panel of the Workspace window. It lists all the data sources you have told the IDE about.

The data sources are broken up by their types into different folders. Tango supports three types of data sources on both Windows and Macintosh platforms: Pervasive SQL, ODBC, and OCI. On the Macintosh, Tango also supports FileMaker Pro and DAM databases. Pervasive SQL is an SQL database made by Pervasive software, the same company that makes Tango. Tango talks to Pervasive SQL using the ODBC protocol. ODBC stands for Open Database Connectivity, and is an API for talking to relational databases. OCI is a database connectivity standard for talking to Oracle databases. For the purposes of this book, we use Pervasive SQL data sources.

To add a column to the Insert action, we just drag it from the Data Sources panel and drop it in the Insert action window. You can multiple-select a number of columns. If you drag and drop a table from the Data Source panel to an action, it adds all the columns in the table. In this case, we want to add all the columns in the Notify table, so grab it and drag it into the Insert action. After doing so, you will have a window that looks like Figure 3.5.

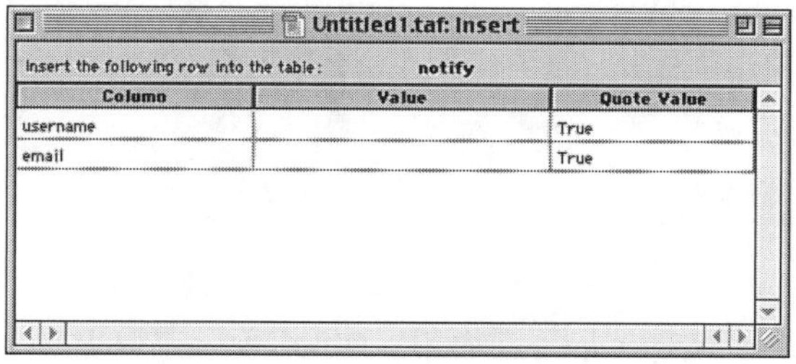

Column	Value	Quote Value
username		True
email		True

FIGURE 3.5   *An Insert action with columns added.*

Now Tango knows that you want to insert something into the notify.username and notify.email columns, but not what that something is. We must tell Tango to put the information passed to us from the form into the database. Remember I said that the values of the form would be passed to the target TAF as arguments? Arguments are given the same name as the form control's name. Their value equals form control's value. For instance, the HTML of our form defines the text field for the user's name like this: `<INPUT NAME="username" TYPE=TEXT SIZE=40 MAXLENGTH=255>`. So, the name of the argument corresponding to the user's name is `username` from the `NAME="username"` part of the HTML. The value of the argument is the text inside the edit field when the user clicks the submit button.

Knowing the values are passed as arguments, just like the arguments in a URL, you've probably already guessed how to specify them here: Use the `<@ARG>` tag. Click in the Value column of the Insert action and enter the appropriate `<@ARG>` tag. It should look like Figure 3.6 when you are done.

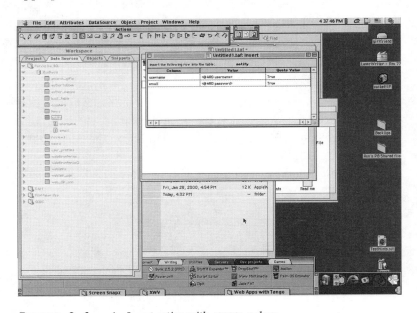

FIGURE 3.6   *An Insert action with `<@ARG>` values.*

Close the action window and save the TAF.

The second thing we must do when the user finishes with the form is to tell him thank you. This is where the second Web page is generated. There are actually two ways you can do this. The simplest way is to drag in another Results action and put your thank you in there. But there is another way, and because you're here to learn, we'll do it that way.

Many actions generate something you want to display to the user. For instance, if you do a search, you probably want to show the results. The Insert action doesn't really generate any data we want to show the user, but we do want to know whether it did the insert without problems. For this purpose, Tango actions can have something called Attributes. Attributes have their own menu and palette, as shown in Figure 3.7.

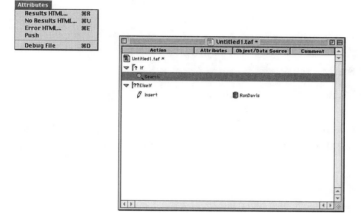

FIGURE 3.7   *The Attributes menu and palette.*

You'll notice in the case of the Insert action there is no No Results HTML attribute. Because an Insert action isn't really getting anything from the database when it works correctly, having no results is the normal case. That leaves us with the Results HTML and Error HTML. I'm leaving the error case to you. But when the Insert works, we want to tell the user thank you, so we must edit the Results HTML attribute.

To edit the Results HTML attribute for the Insert action, select the action and either click the Results button on the Attributes palette or select the menu item Attributes, Results HTML. When you do, you are presented with the window shown in Figure 3.8. It is similar to the window you saw for the Results action, but has tabs for each of the Attribute cases. In the Windows IDE, only those attributes that are available show tabs.

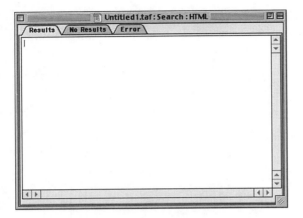

FIGURE 3.8 *The Results HTML attribute window.*

Now you can enter the HTML for the page welcoming users to your site and letting them know that you will notify them when the site is up and ready.

I entered the HTML in Listing 3.3.

Listing 3.3   Successful Insert HTML

```
<!DOCTYPE HTML PUBLIC "-//W3C//DTD HTML 3.2//EN">
<HTML>
<HEAD>
     <TITLE>Thank you.</TITLE>
</HEAD>
<BODY>
You have been added to the notification database for our website. We will send
you an e-mail as soon as we are ready for visitors.
<P>
Thank you.
</BODY>
</HTML>
```

Your TAF is now ready to go. Deploy it to your Web site and point your browser at it. Your browser should display a page that look something like Figure 3.9. Go ahead and add yourself to the notification list and make sure that everything works.

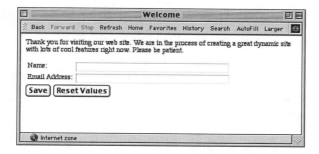

FIGURE 3.9   *The welcome page.*

Everything seems to work if you get the welcome page, but you are probably wondering whether your name was really entered into the database. You could use a database tool to list what's in it, or you could enter a select statement in the SQL Query window in Tango, but we need a Tango solution. That solution is the content of the Admin TAF for this chapter.

Admin TAFs

There are two tasks we want to perform from the Administration point of view. First, we want to list the information we gathered. Second, we want to be able to send a message to everyone on the list. Let's create a TAF to do these two tasks.

Create a TAF named admin.taf and save it in a secure location. Because we don't yet have a TAF-based security system, keep this TAF where only an admin can execute it. Use whatever form of security your Web server provides.

Because we are developing two bits of functionality, let's set up some function branching. The default case for this TAF is to display a list of all the people signed up. First, drag in an If action and add the condition `<@ARG _function>` `Is` `Not` `Empty`. Now drag in an ElseIf action and make its condition `<@ARG _function> = mailForm`. Lastly, drag in an ElseIf action with the condition `<@ARG _function> = sendmail`.

Listing the Users Who Have Signed Up for Notification

We've now got the flow of control for all the admin.taf. Let's start with the default case of listing all the people who signed up. The way you get information out of a data source in Tango is via a Search action. Drag a Search action from the Actions palette in under the default If action. You should get a window that looks like Figure 3.10.

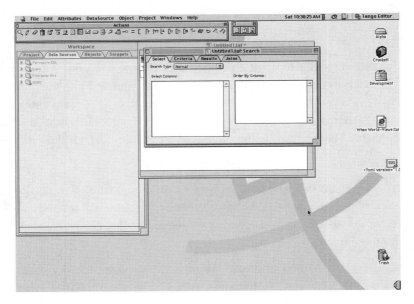

FIGURE 3.10   *An empty Search action.*

There is a lot of functionality in the Search action, but we need only the most minimal part of it, so I won't go into each panel in the action right now. What we want to do is get a list of every record in the Notify table. To do this, we need to tell the Search action which columns we want to see, so drag the Notify table from the Data Sources panel to the Select Columns area of the Search action window. After you do this, the Search action window should look like Figure 3.11.

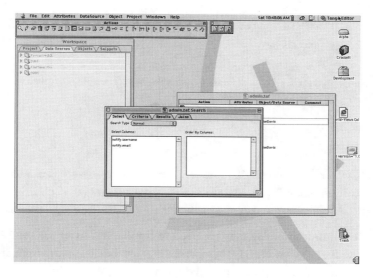

FIGURE 3.11   *The Search action with Notify table columns.*

If we wanted to limit the database rows we got back to a subset of the database, we would set up the Criteria tab; but, in our case, we want all the records, which is what you get if you don't have a criterion. So, we don't need to do anything else in this window.

Because a Search action goes and gets some data, we must tell it how to display that data on our Web page. We do this by editing the Search action's Results HTML attribute. Select the Search action in the TAF window and click the Results HTML attribute on the attribute palette. Add the contents of Listing 3.4 to the Results HTML.

Listing 3.4   Display the Results of Our Search

```
<TABLE BORDER=1>
<TR VALIGN=TOP ALIGN=LEFT>
    <TD>
        <B>Username</B>
    </TD>
    <TD>
        <B>Email</B>
    </TD>
</TR>
<@ROWS>
<TR VALIGN=TOP>
    <TD>
```

continues

Listing 3.4   (Continued)

```
        <@COLUMN "notify.username">
    </TD>
    <TD>
        <A HREF = "mailto:<@COLUMN 'notify.email'>"><@COLUMN "notify.email"></A>
    </TD>
</TR>
</@ROWS>
</TABLE>
```

This HTML creates an HTML table with two columns: username and email address. Then it lists each found record's contents in each row of the table. As an extra, it also makes the email address into a mailto: link.

Some new important meta tags are used in this listing, so let's go over them. The first one you see is the `<@ROWS>` tag. `<@ROWS>` is a paired tag and represents a loop through the found database rows. When Tango does its search, it gets back a set of rows. A `<@ROWS>` loop goes through each row found and does the HTML inside the loop. In this case, it creates a new row in the table.

The next new meta tag you see is `<@COLUMN>`. This tag is replaced by the contents of the specified column in the current database record/row. In our case, the first cell in the row contains the username from the Notify table and the second contains the email address. Notice that I put an `<@COLUMN>` tag inside an HTML `HREF` tag. This is perfectly legal and very useful.

The first part of the admin TAF is now functional; you could deploy the TAF and try it out by hitting the TAF URL with no parameters.

Creating the Form for Sending a Notifying Email

Before we create a form for the admin to enter an email for all the people who sign up for notification, we must add a link to the form page. We should put it at the top of the listing page so that it won't be lost under a long list of names and email address.

What the link needs to do is come back to the same TAF that generates the list page and set the _function parameter to emailForm. If you remember from our other form, the `<@CGI><@APPFILE>` tags are used to refer to the same TAF you are in. Add this `HREF` to the Result action:

```
<A HREF="<@CGI><@APPFILE>?_function=emailForm">Send an email to all the
people on the list.</A>
```

Now there is a link to the Web page we are about to create. All the email
form page really needs to be is a simple HTML form with a large field in
which to enter the text of the message. Enter the HTML in Listing 3.5.

Listing 3.5   Email Form HTML

```
<!DOCTYPE HTML PUBLIC "-//W3C//DTD HTML 3.2//EN">
<HTML>
<HEAD>
    <TITLE>New Email Message for every user.</TITLE>
</HEAD>
<BODY>
Enter a message below to be sent to all of the people on the e-mail list.
<FORM METHOD=POST ACTION="<@CGI><@APPFILE>?_function=sendmail">
<TEXTAREA ROWS=5 COLS=60 WRAP=VIRTUAL NAME="emailmessage"></TEXTAREA>
<P>
<INPUT TYPE=SUBMIT NAME="Submit" VALUE="Submit">
</FORM>

</BODY>
</HTML>
```

From the Form tag, you can see the action will be performed by the calling
TAF in the sendmail block.

Formatting the Email Addresses

Now it's time to create the actions that actually send the emails. The first
thing we need to do is get the list of addresses to which the emails should
be sent. We do this by using a Search action. Drag a new Search action
into the admin.taf under the third If action, the one for sendmail. Now
drag the email column from the Notify table into the Search Columns
area of the Search action window. Once again, we want all the rows in the
table, so we don't specify criteria.

This Search action queries the database and gets back all the email
addresses in the table. But in what format is that list coming back? The
list is an array variable. Arrays are multidimensional variables that contain rows and columns. Tango defines a specific special variable, called
resultSet, for the results of a database query. In most cases, this array has

multiple columns, but because we are searching only on the notify.email column, there is only one column. This somewhat simplifies our next task. We must get the email addresses in a format we can use to send an email. For this module, we want the addresses to be in a list separated by commas.

What we are going to do is create a variable that contains the list of email addresses, and then assign to that variable the contents of the resultSet array in textual form. Tango has an internal array representation, but when you want to see an array in HTML, Tango automatically changes the information to a textual format. Although this textual format is really cool—Tango generates an HTML table—it isn't what we need for out email addresses. But, luckily, Tango is flexible in its approach to textual formatting of tables; it uses attributes for specific parts of the output of the text array. For example, it defines the attribute APrefix as the text going before the entire array and RPrefix as the text going before each row in the array. The following table lists all the attributes and their default values. Unless you specifically define different values, the defaults are used.

Attribute	Location	Default Value
APrefix	Before the array	<TABLE BORDER=1>
ASuffix	After the array	</TABLE>
RPrefix	Before each row	<TR>
RSuffix	After each row	</TR>
CPrefix	Before each column	<TD>
CSuffix	After each column	</TD>

Attribute	Location	Default Value
APrefix	Before the array	<TABLE BORDER=1>
ASuffix	After the array	</TABLE>
RPrefix	Before each row	<TR>
RSuffix	After each row	</TR>
CPrefix	Before each column	<TD>
CSuffix	After each column	</TD>

FIGURE 3.12   *The array textual output attributes.*

In the case of the email addresses, we want the row suffix (RSuffix) to be the comma and all the other attributes to be empty. In order to do that, we have to explicitly set the other attributes to empty when we perform the assign. We're about to use two new Tango meta tags: `<@ASSIGN>` and `<@VAR>`. `<@VAR>` defines or represents a Tango variable. It has a number of attributes that I go into more detail about in later chapters. For now, just be aware that all the array textual attributes are attributes in the `<@VAR>` tag. So, to represent the `resultSet` variable in a `<@VAR>` tag looks like this

```
<@VAR NAME="resultSet">
```

If we want to set all the text output attributes for our case, it looks like this:

```
<@VAR NAME='resultset' TYPE='text' APrefix='' ASuffix='' RPrefix=''
RSuffix=',' CPrefix='' CSuffix=''>
```

Because Tango knows `resultSet` is an array, we must tell it that we want the text version. We do so by setting the TYPE attribute to `text`.

Next, we are going to assign `resultSet`'s textual output to another variable named `"emailAddresses"`. Assigning is accomplished using the `<@ASSIGN>` meta tag. `<@ASSIGN>` will also create a new variable if there isn't one meeting the criteria in it. The simple syntax for `<@ASSIGN>` is

```
<@ASSIGN NAME="emailAddresses" VALUE="">
```

Now what is the value? In our case, the value is the variable `resultSet` in textual form with our custom attributes, or, in other words, the `<@VAR>` tag defined earlier. So, after combining the two statements, you get Figure 3.13. You should put this assignment into the Results HTML attribute of the Search action.

A quick note about quotation marks in Tango meta tags. In Tango, you can use either the single quotation mark or the double quotation marks to delineate an attribute value. In simple cases, you don't even need the quotes. But it is important to remember if you are embedding one meta tag within another, you must use a different quotation mark for each meta tag's attributes. You'll get an example of this in a minute.

```
<@ASSIGN NAME="emailAddresses" TYPE="text" SCOPE="local"
VALUE="<@VAR NAME='resultset' TYPE='TEXT' APrefix=' ' ASuffix=' ' RPrefix='
' RSuffix=',' CPrefix='' CSuffix=''>">
```

FIGURE 3.13   *The assignment for the email addresses.*

Sending the Email

Tango provides an action to send an email, appropriately named the Email action. Drag one of these actions into your TAF under the Search action we just made. You will see an empty window like Figure 3.14.

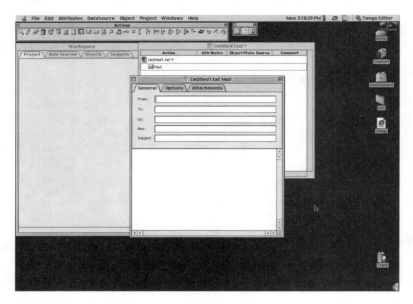

FIGURE 3.14   *An empty Email action.*

You fill in the fields just as you would in a normal email program. First, enter the return address you want on your email. You should also enter the subject of the message. Not only can you enter standard text in these fields, but you can also enter meta tags. This enables us to set the To: address to our list of email addresses. In the To: field, type **<@VAR NAME= "emailAddresses">**. This fills the To: field with our comma-delineated list of email addresses from the database.

We want the contents of the form filled out by the admin to be in the body of the message. Remember how to get the value of a form field? It comes to the TAF as an argument and you use the <@ARG> tag. In the body portion of the window, type **<@ARG emailmessage>**. Now your window should look like Figure 3.15.

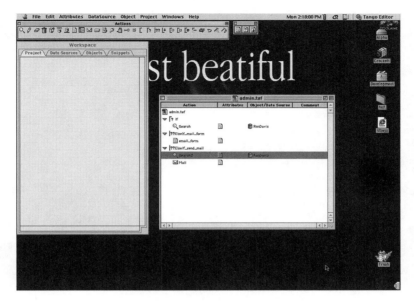

FIGURE 3.15   *Filled-out Email action.*

One last bit of polish to add. Put Listing 3.6 into the Results HTML attribute of the Email action. This is a message that tells us the Email action was successful and shows us the list of email addresses that were used.

Listing 3.6   Acknowledgment of Email Sent

```
<!DOCTYPE HTML PUBLIC "-//W3C//DTD HTML 3.2//EN">
<HTML>
<HEAD>
    <TITLE>Result of sending</TITLE>
</HEAD>
<BODY>
Notification sent to<BR>
<@VAR emailaddresses>
</BODY>
</HTML>
```

That's it. You've now officially written your first Tango Web application.

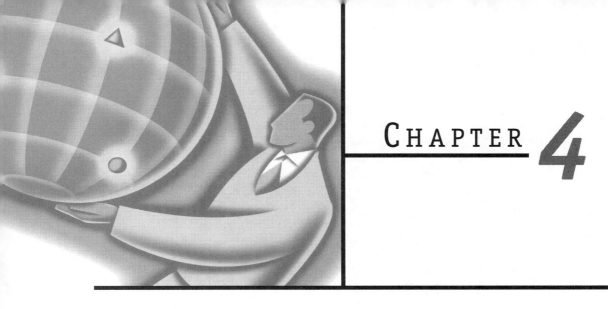

CHAPTER 4

Using Other Tools with Tango

What We'll Learn

- Tango debugging
- Using the debugging.taf file
- SQL Query window

Purpose

Discuss a number of tools associated with Tango you can use to help you in the development process.

Tango Tools

After Chapter 3, "The Coming Soon Page," you have created the first real TAF of your Web site. Before I get into the other parts of the Web site, I want to explain a few features of Tango that will make your development process easier. I'm not going to mention these features other than in passing in the next chapter, but they will come in handy for you while going through the chapters to come.

Debugging

As we go through the various modules of our Web site, I give you a step-by-step process for creating each TAF that you can easily follow. But errors will creep into the process, and sometime you'll run a TAF and it won't work as you expect. Then you are left with the task of figuring out where the bug is and fixing it. Tango provides some basic debugging features.

The Tango Debugger

Because TAFs are executed on a Web server, they present some particular challenges for Tango. Unlike most other development tools, you don't have a debugger running on the same machine as the application. Add to this the facts that a client browser executes TAFs, and the TAFs' output is sent back to that browser, and debugging becomes unique.

What Tango does provide for debugging is a log of events as a given page is executed. You turn on debugging for a given TAF and when you view that URL in your browser, you will get the normal content of the page followed by the debugging output generated by Tango. Figure 4.1 shows the Coming Soon page with debugging turned on.

Figure 4.1 *The Coming Soon page with debugging turned on.*

As you learn more about how Tango executes actions, the debugging output will make more sense. It outputs information about each action executed and how it affected variables. It also shows you the SQL that was generated and sent to the database for each action and the results of that search.

So, how do you turn debugging output off and on? The most common way is to turn it on for a particular TAF while editing that TAF in the IDE. If you have a TAF open, you can select the menu item Attributes, Debug File to turn on debugging for that file. An asterisk appears next to the name of the file on the Mac (a bug icon appears in Windows) to indicate that the TAF is in debugging mode. You can now deploy the TAF and you will get debugging output every time you execute it. In fact, anyone else who executes the TAF will get the debugging output, so you might want to be careful about access to the file.

Another way to turn on debugging is to set the variable debugMode to forceOn. This variable is valid in all the variable scopes, so you have some control over the people for whom you turn it on. Also, changing this variable turns on debugging for every TAF, so you don't have to go through on a TAF-by-TAF basis and turn it on individually. Another advantage is that if you call into Tango class files, you don't have to remember to turn on debugging for each TCF. The common way to use this is to set the user scope debugMode variable, meaning that the variable applies only to the current user. As a matter of fact, you could write a TAF file to turn debugging off and on and have that functionality in your debugging TAF file.

Using the Debugging TAF

On the CD-ROM that comes with this book, you will find a file called debugging.taf. This TAF provides a number of debugging services to help you when you are developing. This is a dangerous file and should be kept secure when it is on your site. After we create a security system, you can add the capability to lock people out of the TAF, but for now put this file under your Web server's security. You will probably want to take the file off the site when you are not actively using it.

I'm not going to tell you how to create this TAF as I do for all the other TAFs in this book. This TAF is a tool you can use, and after you've learned all the things in this book, you can look at the file to see how it works. I am going to tell you what each part of the TAF does. Sometimes this might not make complete sense because a concept hasn't been fully explained in the book yet. Just trust me that, in time, I'll get to all of it.

To deploy the debugging.taf to your server, point your Web browser at it and you should get a page that looks something like Figure 4.2.

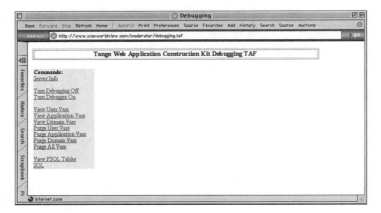

FIGURE 4.2   *The default debugging window.*

On the left side of the window is a list of available commands. When you click one of these commands, its output is displayed on the right side of the window.

Server Info

The first command is Server Info and it displays the version of the Tango Application Server that you are running. This can be helpful if you run into a bug and need to tell tech support what version you are running. Also, if you are using a Tango ISP for hosting, you might need to find out what server you are running to know what features are available.

Turn Debugging Off/On

Selecting one of these commands changes the value of the user variable debugMode. As we discussed earlier, this displays debugging information about all the pages that you view until you turn off debugging. I find it useful to save a bookmark to each of these links, allowing me to turn debugging off and on from wherever I am in the site.

View User/Application/Domain Vars

These next three commands enable you to look at the variables in each of Tango's three scopes. This can be useful when something isn't working right and you know it is being affected by a user variable, but you don't know what that variable's value is.

Clicking one of these links brings up a list of all the variables in that scope. For each variable, you can view or purge. *Purging* a variable makes it cease to exist. *Viewing* enables you to look at the current variable's value. You can also change this value, but that can be a dangerous thing to do because you can put the server in a bad state by changing the variable outside the normal flow.

Purge User/Application/Domain/All Vars

Instead of finding each variable individually and getting rid of it, you can purge all the variables in a scope by clicking one of these commands. This causes all the variables to become undefined. An interesting side effect of purging the user variables is that debugging will turn off if it is on.

View PSQL Tables

The last two commands are for dealing with data sources, which means that you need to modify the TAF to get it to work for your data source. You must open the TAF and select all the actions that have a data source in the Object/Data Source column of the TAF. Then, select Set Data Source from the menu and set the data source to your data source.

The View PSQL Tables command works only for Pervasive.SQL. Clicking it queries the database for the names of each table in your data source. Each table is displayed as a hyperlink in the window. Clicking the hyperlink lists the columns in the table, tells you the number of rows in the table, and gives you a link that displays all the data in the table. Be careful when listing all the data in a table if the table has a large number of rows.

It is likely that other databases have this same capability, you just have to know the hidden table on which to search to get the table names. Consult your database documentation for this information.

SQL

The last command brings up a Web form into which you can enter SQL commands that will be executed on your data source. Again, this can be dangerous to do because if you get it wrong, it messes up your actual data. But it can be very useful when you are having a problem with data in your database.

After the SQL is executed, you are shown the results, if any, and told how many rows were affected by the operation.

SQL Query Window

For large projects, you often have a person dedicated to managing your database for your Web site. But, in smaller projects, you might have to do all the database work yourself. Tango gives you a built-in tool, called the SQL Query window, to help work with databases. The SQL Query window enables you to enter SQL commands, have them executed on a database, and see the results.

Because I used a Tango ASP during the development of most of this book, I used the SQL Query window to create all the tables. This allowed me to work with P.SQL from my Macintosh, even though it was hosted on a Windows machine.

You can open the SQL Query window by going to the Windows menu. This brings up a window like the one in Figure 4.3.

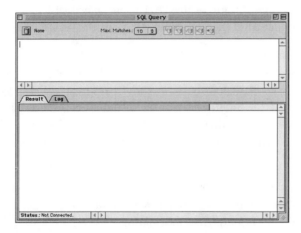

Figure 4.3 *The SQL Query window.*

There are three parts to this window: the toolbar, the SQL pane, and the results pane. Along the top of the window are a number of buttons. The first is the Data Source Selection button. Clicking this button brings up a dialog that enables you to select the Tango data source to be used by the window. After you have selected the data source, its name is displayed in the toolbar.

A popup menu in the toolbar enables you to set the maximum number of results you want to get back from your search. This keeps you from receiving 20,000 records back if you search a big database.

The functionality of the window is done with the five other buttons. They are enabled depending on whether you are connected to a data source. If you aren't connected, you need to click the Connect button. If you are connected and want to disconnect, click the Disconnect button.

After you type something into the SQL pane, the Execute button will be enabled. Clicking this button sends the command to your data source. On a Mac, you can also press the Enter key to make this happen.

If you executed an operation that actually changed the values in the database, you can take back those changes by clicking the Rollback button. Alternatively, you can make the changes permanent by clicking the Commit button. For some databases, this doesn't work. If your database defaults to autocommit, it automatically commits your changes.

If you perform an operation and it generates results, they will be shown in the bottom pane. The results fill a grid based on the data. If there is an error, the Log tab is shown and the error is placed in that panel.

A hidden, but useful, thing that you can do with the SQL Query window is to send the SQL that is generated by an action to the window. This enables you to see how the SQL looks and to test it out. To do this, select an action and right-click it. In the menu, you will find an item called SQL Query. Selecting SQL Query sends the SQL that the action would generate to the SQL Query window.

Use of Projects

A Web project is rarely one TAF file, but rather is usually a group of them. Wouldn't it be great if you could open one file and have all the TAFs you need to use at your fingertips? Well, you can do just that, by using Tango project files. Projects appear in their own tab in the Workspace window. You create a new project from the Project menu. You are immediately asked where to save the project file, and you never have to save that file again because Tango keeps it up to date as you add files.

A new project looks like Figure 4.4. There are five folders in a project. You can add files to the Files folder either from the menu or by dragging them in from the OS.

FIGURE 4.4   *A new project.*

Tango supports an action called the Presentation action, which I talk about more in Chapter 8, "User Management." The Presentation action uses HTML files to help you display information generated by Tango. You can add these HTML files to the Presentation File section of your project for easy access. If you add an HTML page to the Presentation File section of the project, it will show up in the combo box of the Presentation Action window for easy selection.

After files are added to a project, Tango does some analysis on them and fills in the other folders. The Data Source folder shows you all the data sources used in any of the TAFs in the project. The Objects folder does the same thing for objects, such as JavaBeans, TCFs, and COM objects. You will receive a warning if you open a project file that references one of these data sources or objects, and that object or data source is not already in the Workspace window. You are allowed to find the missing dependency and to add it to the Workspace window.

Tango 2000 adds the capability to deploy all the files in a project to a Web site via FTP. You have to define the FTP information in what is called a site. A new site can be created from the menu option Edit, Define Sites.

After a site is defined, you can add it to a project from the Project menu. It will show up in your project and you can tell Tango to deploy all the files in the project to a given site.

All these tools should make using Tango a little easier. If you don't completely understand what they all do right now, don't worry. They will become clearer as you learn more about Tango in the coming chapters. This is the end of the introductory material. Now we start creating our Tango Web site.

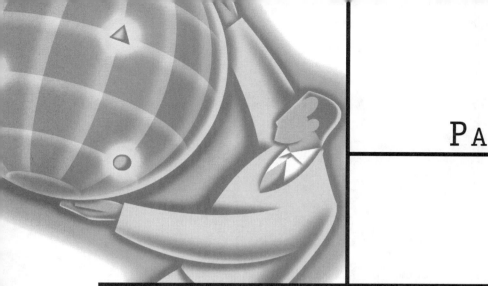

PART II

Getting Started

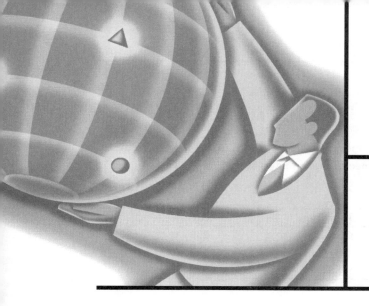

CHAPTER 5

News Services

What We'll Learn

- Search Builder
- New Record Builder

Purpose

In this chapter, we create a module that enables you to have an updated list of news stories. These stories are short messages that are automatically timestamped and displayed to the user in chronological order.

Planning

Feature List

- Create a dynamic listing of short stories that are time stamped and listed in chronological order
- Enable the admin to easily add stories to the list
- Enable the admin to edit or delete stories

Database Schema

The database schema for this module is pretty easy. It's one table with the three bits of information we need for each news story.

Database Table Name: News

Column Name	Data Type	Size
Title	Char	255
DateEntered	Timestamp	
Story	Blob	

```
CREATE TABLE News (
    Title char(255),
    DateEntered  timestamp,
    Story BLOB
)
```

Creating the TAFs

Many sites on the Internet add news stories all day long. When you go to a site, you get a listing of the most recent stories along with the times that they were posted. We're going to create a couple of TAFs that will do this for our Web site. We can also use this as a What's New service for our budding Web site by putting its output on our Coming Soon page.

User TAF

The User TAF for this application is very simple. It lists every news story in the database in our custom format. What we have to do is query the database for all its records and display them.

The Search Action

First, we must query the database and get back all the new stories. To do this, we use a Search action. Create a new TAF called display_news.taf and save it. Do this by choosing the menu item File, New, Tango Application File. From now on I'll assume you know how to create and save a TAF. Now, drag a new Search action into the TAF. Because we are going to display all the fields of the News table, drag the whole table into the Search action. You do this by clicking on the table name item in the Data source panel and dragging into the action.

The Search action enables you to sort the output of the query so that it is displayed in a specific order. We want reverse chronological order, which means the last story entered is at the top of the list. To do this, drag the column news.DateEntered into the Order By Columns panel of the Search action. You can actually drag the column from two different locations, either from the Data Source panel in the workspace window or from the Select Columns panel in the Search action. After you do this, you'll see a little control next to the column name. This is the sort direction control. If it points up, it sorts in ascending order, from smallest to largest. If it points down, it sorts in descending order, from largest to smallest. We want is descending order, so click on the sort direction control and it will change direction. The finished Search action should look like Figure 5.1.

FIGURE 5.1   *The finished Search window.*

We want to find every possible news story in our search, so there are no criteria. But we really should limit the number of stories we show so that the page isn't too crowded. To do this, click the Results tab of the Search action; by default, it looks like Figure 5.2.

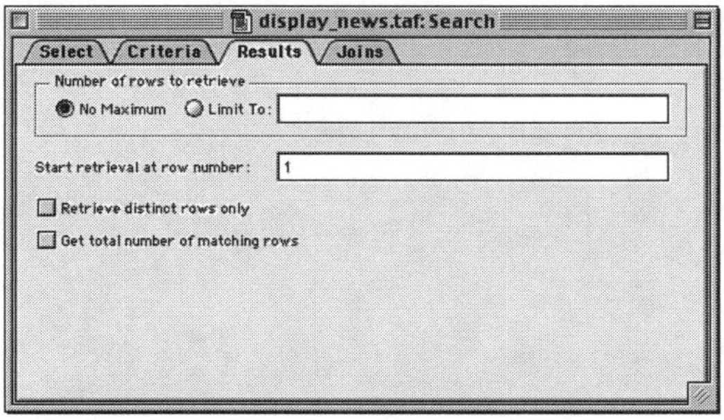

FIGURE 5.2   *The default Results tab.*

We want to limit the number of rows to 5; clicking the Limit To radio button and typing 5 into the field does this. We're still starting our retrieval at the first row, so leave that field alone. Our database doesn't contain duplicate rows, so we don't need to worry about retrieving distinct rows. We don't want to find out how many rows our search found, so leave the two checkboxes alone. Your final window should look like Figure 5.3.

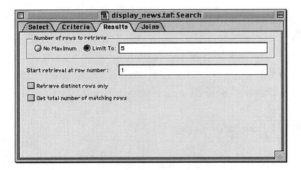

Figure 5.3   *The final Results tab.*

This action gets back all the records in the database. Now, we need to display them. Click open the ResultsHTML attribute for the Search action. Enter the HTML in Listing 5.1.

Listing 5.1   ResultsHTML for Search Action

```
<TABLE Border="0">
<@ROWS>
<TR VALIGN=TOP>
    <TD>
        <B>
            <@COLUMN "News.Title">
        </B>
        <BR>
        <@COLUMN "News.DateEntered">
        <P>
            <@COLUMN "News.Story" encoding="MULTILINEHTML">
        </P>
    </TD>
</TR>
<TR>
<TD>
     
</TD>
</TR>
</@ROWS>
</TABLE>
```

Here, we are creating an HTML table where every other row is a news story and inserting an empty row between each news story. This gives a nice, even spacing to the stories. A lot of this Tango code probably looks familiar—it is almost the same thing we did in the admin TAF in Chapter 3, except this time we don't need the user to be able to edit or delete anything, so there are no links in the table.

That's really all that is needed to display the news. It is in the admin portion of the Web application that life gets exciting.

Admin TAFs

There are two things that an admin needs to be able to do with the news stories: add and edit. An admin must be able to enter a new news story via an HTML form and have it added to the database. The admin might also find that he needs to change or delete a news story. We'll create two different TAFs to do this.

The New Record Builder

To add news stories, you could handcraft a bunch of HTML and create Insert actions to add the stories to the database. But Tango has a way of performing additions that is much easier: the New Record builder. The New Record builder is in the Actions palette and behaves like an action. You drag the New Record builder into your TAF window just like an action and it brings up its own window for editing. The difference between a builder and an action is that a builder generates a series of actions to do a specific task. In the case of the New Record builder, that task is inserting a record into the database.

Create a new TAF and name it add_news.taf. Then drag in a New Record builder from the Actions palette. The editor for the New Record builder opens and looks like Figure 5.4.

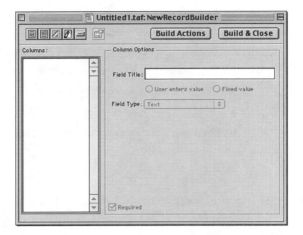

Figure 5.4   *An empty New Record builder.*

On the left is the column panel where you drop the columns into which you want to insert information. Go ahead and drop the entire News table in the column panel. On the right side of the window is an area to configure what you want the builder to do with a given column. Tango is even smart enough to guess much of the information you want over here. For instance, Tango assumes the field title of the column is the column's name.

Select the Title column. On the right side, it says the field title is Title. You can choose whether the user will enter the value of the field, or if you will. For Title, you want the user to enter the value, so leave the User enters value radio button selected. Now you need to tell Tango what kind of field this will be. The default is Text, which generates an HTML text field. That's fine for the news story title, so don't change anything.

Some of the other options are

> Popup Menu—you define all the values of the popup
>
> Selection List—you define a scrolling list of values
>
> Checkbox—you define the initial value
>
> Radio Buttons—you define the list of values

Last, there is a checkbox called Required at the bottom of the panel. If you check this box, the user has to enter a valid value into this field before it will be inserted into the database. In our case, we want to force the admin to enter a title, although we'll be lenient if he doesn't enter an actual story, so check the Required check box. See Figure 5.5 for the finished Title window.

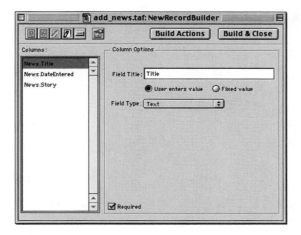

FIGURE 5.5   *The finished Title window.*

The Story column should be handled in a similar way as the Title, except that you don't need to check the Required checkbox. Also, the story could be long, so we need to tell Tango to format the field as a scrolling list that is 80 characters long and 4 rows high. You do this by selecting the Story column and clicking the Field Properties button, which causes a dialog that looks like Figure 5.6 to appear. The Field Properties button is next to the Build Actions button. You will also want to check the Scrolling Field button. Here you can set the width to 80 and the height to 4.

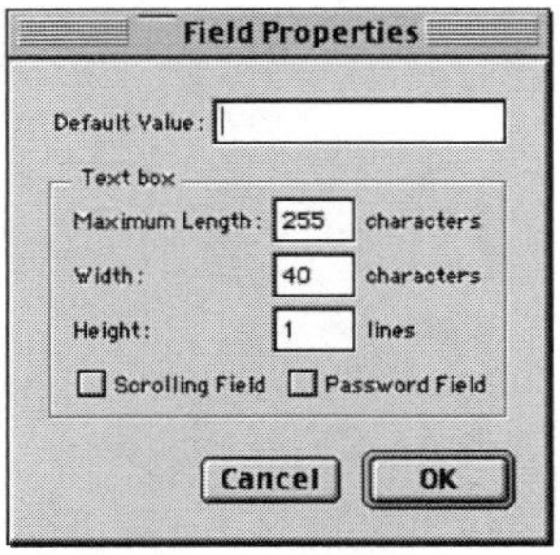

FIGURE 5.6   *The Field Properties dialog.*

The DateEntered field is a little different. We don't want the user to enter the date; we want Tango to do it automatically, so select the Fixed value radio button. When you do this, the panel changes to look like Figure 5.7. Notice there is now a large area for you to enter the value you want to use.

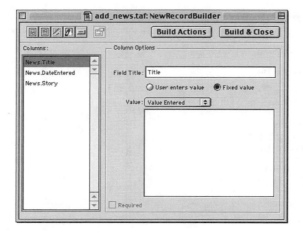

FIGURE 5.7 *The default fixed value builder panel.*

In this field, we want the time that the story was entered. The Value popup contains a bunch of values that you can have the builder insert for you. The default value is Value Entered, which just means exactly what you type in the field under the popup. The value we want is Current Timestamp, so select Current Timestamp from the menu. This automatically enters the time into the database whenever an insert is done.

We've now configured the actual database insert, but we need to do a little work to dress up the pages the builder will build for us. That is what the toolbar at the top of the window does (see Figure 5.8).

FIGURE 5.8 *The New Record builder toolbar.*

The first two buttons are the Header and Footer HTML buttons. The header and footer are the HTML that goes at the top and bottom of all the pages that this builder generates. Click the Header button and a window appears. This window is like the Attributes window for actions, except that the tabs are different. The Header HTML is presented and you will notice the title in the HTML isn't really very descriptive. Change the title so that the HTML looks like Figure 5.9. You can click on the

Footer tab and see the HTML that goes at the bottom of the page. It is pretty boring, but we don't really need anything else.

FIGURE 5.9   *The New News Story HTML.*

When the New Record builder generates your form, it generates a table to hold it. You might want to change the characteristics of the table, and you can do so by clicking the Page Format button. When you do, you will see a window like Figure 5.10. Each of these attributes corresponds to HTML table syntax, and you can easily modify them by changing the values in the popups.

FIGURE 5.10   *The Page Format dialog.*

The next button in the toolbar is the New Record Response button. It enables you to enter some HTML that displays after the insert successfully completes. Like the Thank You page we created in Chapter 1, "Introduction," it's displayed in the same window in which the Header and Footer HTML were displayed. Change the HTML so that it looks like Listing 5.2.

Listing 5.2   New Record Response HTML

```
<!DOCTYPE HTML PUBLIC "-//W3C//DTD HTML 3.2//EN">
<HTML>
<HEAD>
    <TITLE>News Story Added</TITLE>
</HEAD>

<BODY>
<H2>News Story Added</H2>
<P>
    The News Story was added successfully.
</P>
<P>

<A HREF="<@CGI><@APPFILE>?<@UserReferenceArgument>">Add another News Story</A>
</P>
    </BODY>
</HTML>
```

The last button enables you to enter the names for the buttons used in the form. Click it and you will see a window like the one in Figure 5.11.

FIGURE 5.11   *The Button Titles dialog.*

That's it. You now have everything configured and all you need to do is tell Tango to build it. Click the Actions button to build the actions.

> *On the Mac, two buttons are used to perform the build. If you click the Build Actions button, Tango adds the new actions to the TAF, but leaves the Builder window open so that you can keep continue editing. If you click the Build and Close button, Tango builds the actions and closes the window.*

Notice your TAF has changed a lot. It now has a whole bunch of actions in it. With all the actions expanded, your TAF should look like the one in Figure 5.12. You can explore the various actions to see what Tango built for you. The builders are a good way to learn Tango programming because they give you an example of how to write good code.

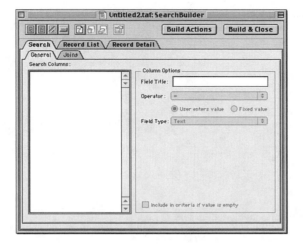

FIGURE 5.12   *The finished Add TAF.*

You can now deploy this TAF on your Web server and add news stories to the database. You can then use the display_news.taf to see the results. Next, we use the Search builder to allow editing of the news stories.

The Search Builder

The Search builder enables you to create a series of pages that search for something in a database, to return a list of found records in a short form, and to click on a link to get a detailed page. In that detailed page, you can edit or delete a record from the database. For example, we are allowing the admin to fill out a form that enables him to search the news titles. Then the found news items are returned as a list of the titles of the articles and their dates. Each title is a hyperlink to a detail page that enables the admin to edit the title or the story. We are also allowing the admin to delete a story from this page.

Create a new TAF and call it edit_news.taf. Now drag a Search builder into the TAF, and a window like Figure 5.13 appears.

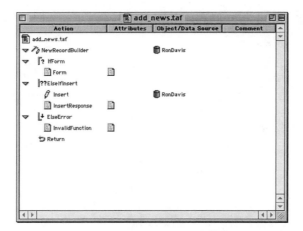

FIGURE 5.13   *An empty Search builder.*

Notice that there are some similarities between the New Record Builder and the Search Builder. For instance, they have similar toolbars. Again we see the Header, Footer, Page Format, Button Title, and Field Properties windows. They all work exactly as they did in the New Record Builder. There are also three new buttons: NoResultsHTML, DeleteResponseHTML, and UpdateResponseHTML.

The Search builder does three main things, so there are three tabs you need to configure. Each of these tabs corresponds to one of the three steps the admin goes through on the Web page. The first step is the Search. The Search tab is a lot like the New Record Builder's window. You drag in the columns you want to search and then configure each column on the right. Make sure that you are in the Search tab, and then drag the News.Title column into the Search Columns panel.

We want to find any news story that contains the entered text. To do this, select the News.Title column, and in the Columns Options area, change the Operator popup to **contains**. The radio buttons and Field Type popup work the same as the New Record builder, and we won't change their default values. The finished Search tab looks like Figure 5.14.

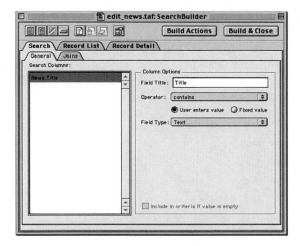

FIGURE 5.14   *The finished Search tab.*

What happens if there no records are found in the search? The No Results HTML is displayed, that's what. To configure this, you use the menu item Attributes, No Results HTML or click the No Results HTML toolbar button in the Search builder.

Now we need to tell Tango what to do with the results. This is done in the Records List tab of the Search builder. First, we want to tell Tango which columns to display—namely, the title and date. Do this by dragging and dropping those columns into the Display Columns panel. Next, drag the Title column into the Order By panel so that the results will be ordered by title.

The default way to display a column is plain text, but we want the title to be a hyperlink. Select the News.Title column and change the Display As popup to Link to Detail. Don't change any other column options for the title. We'll also use the default max number of matches in the bottom panel.

The News.DateEntered column is a date and we want to use the default for display.

The finished Records List tab is shown in Figure 5.15.

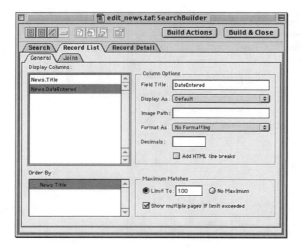

<image>FIGURE 5.15</image>   *The finished Records List tab.*

When the user finally drills all the way down, he sees the details page that we configure in the Record Detail tab. Drag the entire News table into the Display Columns field/panel of the Record Details tab. Before we configure the options for each column, let's activate the Allow delete of record from: checkbox so that the admin can delete a news story. Because this builder uses only one table, there is no reason to change the popup. You'll notice a toolbar button enables when you allowed deleting of the records. This button enables you to edit the text displayed after the delete occurs.

First, let's edit the options of the Title field. Select the Title column. In the Column Options area, click the Allow Update checkbox. This enables the admin to edit this field. When you do this, another toolbar button enables; this button enables you to edit the HTML displayed after the update is finished. You'll also notice the Required checkbox enables. Because we clicked the Required checkbox when we added the news story title, we should also activate it when the admin edits. Click the checkbox on. The Field Type is fine as a text field and all the other options are fine as well.

Select the DateEntered field. First, edit the Field Title so that there is a space between the two words. We aren't allowing the user to edit the date that the story was entered, so just leave everything as it is.

Select the Story field. Click the Allow Update checkbox, but don't click Required. Just as in the New Record Builder, we must configure this field's properties so that we can easily edit it on the Web page. Click the Field Properties button; set the width to 80 and the height to 4, and make it a scrolling field.

You've now configured everything in the Search builder. The Record Detail tab should look like the one in Figure 5.16. Click the Build & Close button to generate the TAF.

FIGURE 5.16   *The finished Record Detail tab.*

The Search builder generates many more actions than the New Record Builder does. Expanded, the TAF looks like Figure 5.17. You can learn a lot about Tango programming by looking at the generated actions.

FIGURE 5.17 *The finished TAF.*

You have now created a complete news system. Remember to put the admin TAFs in a secure place; otherwise, anyone who comes to your site could add news items to the list.

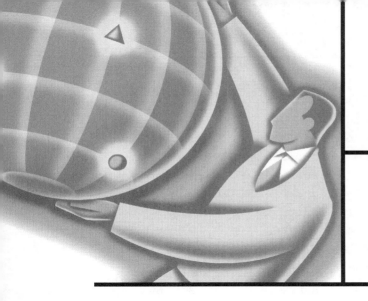

CHAPTER 6

Web Directory

What We'll Learn

- The While action
- The Criteria and Joins tabs of the Search action

Purpose

In this chapter, we create a module that handles a Yahoo-like Web directory.

Planning

Feature List

- Create a hierarchical, Yahoo-like list of Web sites. Web sites are URLs and descriptions of various Web sites.
- Display the path to the current folder as a navigation tool for the user.
- Enable the user to suggest new Web sites and what folder they should go in.
- Enable admins to approve Web sites and add new folders to the hierarchy.
- Enable the user to search the directory, returning folders or Web sites containing the words for which the user searched.

Database Schema

The database for this module is not trivial. Expressing hierarchical data in a relational database isn't easy. Two kinds of data are stored in the Web directory: folders and URLs. Folders have a list of URLs and can also contain other folders, and that's where the directory gets its hierarchy. URLs actually contain more than just the URL. They also contain information about the URL in the form of a description string, and a field that tells whether an admin has approved the URL for display in the Web directory.

We must uniquely identify each folder and URL in the database so that we can associate them with folders. To do this, we assign a unique ID number to each. We also make these ID columns the primary keys of the database. This enables faster searching and enforces the uniqueness of the rows. Given all of this, the two tables that describe URLs and folders are defined in the following ways.

Database Table Name: Weblinks

Column Name	Data Type	Size
url	Char	255
name	Char	30
description	Longvarchar	
weblink_id	Int	Primary Key

```
CREATE TABLE weblinks (
    url    char(255),
    name char(30),
    description longvarchar,
    approved char(7),
    weblink_ID int PRIMARY KEY
)
```

Database Table Name: webdirectories

Column Name	Data Type	Size
name	Char	30
web_dir_ID	Int	Primary Key

```
CREATE TABLE webdirectories (
    name char(30),
    web_dir_ID int PRIMARY KEY
)
```

So, how do we associate a URL or folder with a parent folder? Well, we could just add a parent folder field to each table, but that is a little inflexible and requires searching on the main tables too often. Instead, we are going to put the connections in two separate tables—what I call connector tables—one table for the URLs to folders and one table for folders to folders association.

These two connector tables contain only two columns. Every time you want to create a connection between a folder and URL, you add the URL's weblink_ID and the associated folder's web_dir_ID to the table. Then, if you want to find all the URLs in a given folder, all you have to do is search for the given folder's web_dir_ID. It returns a list of weblink_IDs that you can use to map back to the weblinks table. As a matter of fact, SQL enables us to search on both tables at the same time via a join.

There is one major difference between the two connector tables. In the case of the weblink_con table, we allow many-to-many connections, but for web_dir_con, we allow only one-to-many connections. In other words, we let a Web link exist in more than one folder, but we allow a folder to be in only one folder. We put this restriction on folders because we want to be able to generate a path to the current folder. We do that by searching for the parent folder of the current folder in the web_dir_con. If we allow multiple parents, when we search for the parent, we might not get the folder we came from, which would be confusing and violate the purpose of having a path. We allow a Web link to be in more than one folder because it is not part of the path. This enables us to create an alias or shortcut to a link from another folder.

Here are the database tables for the connector tables.

Database Table Name: weblink_con

Column Name	Data Type	Size
web_dir_ID	int	
weblink_ID	int	

```
CREATE TABLE weblink_con (
    web_dir_ID  int,
    weblink_ID  int
)
```

Database Table Name: web_dir_con

Column Name	Data Type	Size
web_dir_parent_ID	int	
web_dir_ID	int	Primary Key

```
CREATE TABLE web_dir_con (
    web_dir_parent_ID int,
    web_dir_ID int PRIMARY KEY
)
```

There is one other database table you must create, although I'm not going to tell you how it is used now. One of the things we need to do is create unique IDs for the URLs and the folders. There are a number of challenges to this in an environment in which multiple processes may be hitting the database at the same time. One simple way to create unique IDs is available if your database supports an autoincrement or identity column type. P.SQL actually does, so we could define the ID columns to be of identity type. But I want to create these databases in a way that enables you to use them with any SQL database. Luckily, there is a ready-made Tango solution out there. It is in the form of a Tango Class File (TCF) called Utility, and it is included on the CD. TCFs are object wrappers around Tango code. This enables you to have routines that you call, and get results from, anywhere in your code, which is exactly what we need in this case.

I explain how we call object methods during the course of the chapter; right now, let's create the database table we'll use. One of the routines in the Utility TCF is called GetNextID. It returns an ID that is unique. GetNextID keeps a counter in a database table and increments that counter every time it is called. It is actually a little more complicated than that, but I'm asking you to take it on faith that GetNextID works. If you want, you can open the Utility TCF in Tango and look at the code. For now, you need to create the table this function uses to store its counters. Here's the layout of that table.

Database Table Name: counters

Column Name	Data Type	Size
name	char	32
locked	int	
value	int	

```
CREATE TABLE counters (
    name char(32),
    locked int,
    value int
)
```

GetNextID enables you to have multiple counters, each with a unique name.

Creating the TAFs

It is now time to create the code that actually generates the folder listing pages. The first TAF we create displays a page for the user to view a given folder ID. We do this in two different stages. First, we have to create the part of the TAF where it displays the subfolders and URLs for a given folder. Then, we implement phase two, during which we add the path to the folder at the top of the page.

Obviously, creating these TAFs without any data to view makes testing your TAF a little hard. You can either load the finished TAFs for administering from the CD and add a folder structure, or you can not test until you've finished all of the Admin TAF section of this chapter.

User TAF

Phase 1: Listing Folders and URLs

Create a new TAF and name it list_web_directory.taf. The folder ID we want to display is passed in as an argument named directoryID. We don't assume that directoryID exists; instead, we check that the argument exists and assign its value to a local variable named directoryID. If the argument doesn't exist, we assign the ID for the root of the tree, which is zero.

The first thing you must do is drag in an If action. We want to check and make sure that the argument exists, so configure the If action to be like Figure 6.1, checking whether <@ARG directoryID> is not empty.

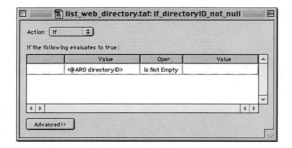

FIGURE 6.1   *An If not null If action.*

Next, drag an Assign action under the If action. When you do, you see a window like Figure 6.2.

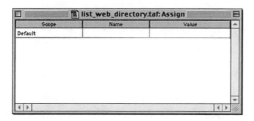

FIGURE 6.2   *An empty Assign action.*

An Assign action works like an <@ASSIGN> meta tag. You must specify the scope of the variable to which you are assigning. You can leave the popup on default if you like, or set it explicitly to Local. It is good programming practice to explicitly set the value so that there is no ambiguity. In this case, default will be local. Next choose a name for the variable and type it in the Name field. Let's call this one directoryID. As with the <@ASSIGN> meta tag, Tango creates a variable if it doesn't exist when you assign a value to it. Last, you need to put the value you want the variable to have in the Value column. We want the value to be <@ARG directoryID>.

FIGURE 6.3   *A finished argument assignment.*

Now we need to handle the case where there is no argument `directoryID`. In that case, we want to assign `0` to our local variable. Drag in an Else action at the same level as the If action, but under the Assign. Else actions have no configuration. Now, drag another Assign action under the Else. Configure the new Assign to look like Figure 6.4.

FIGURE 6.4   *A finished variable assignment.*

From this point on, we are ignoring the argument `directoryID` and only using the variable `directoryID`. There are two ways in Tango to get the value of a variable. One way you already know: the `<@VAR>` tag. The other method is called the short form. The short form has this syntax `@@scope$variableName`. The short form uses two at signs, followed by the scope of the variable, a dollar sign, and the name of the variable. The short form isn't as flexible as the `<@VAR>`. For instance, you can't specify format or encoding, but it is much quicker to type.

Let's get down to displaying the contents of the page. We take the Yahoo approach and first list all the folders by name as links in their own section. Then, we have a section listing all the URLs as hyperlinks followed by their description.

How do we get the listing of all the folders that are a subfolder of the current folder? Well, we search the web_dir_con table, and find all the records that have web_dir_parent_ID equal to the current folder. But how do we display the folders? web_dir_con doesn't have the names of the found folders in it. What we do is a search with a join to the webdirectories table.

Drag in a Search action. Into the Select Columns panel, drag first the entire web_dir_con table. Then drag in the entire webdirectories table. When you do this, Tango displays an alert like the one shown in Figure 6.5, telling you that you need a join for this search and asking whether you want to define one. Choose Define. You are taken to the

Joins tab of the Search action, and a join is added with a column for each table in the Search action. It looks like Figure 6.6.

FIGURE 6.5 *A join warning alert.*

FIGURE 6.6 *The Joins tab.*

A join works by requiring that some column in one table is equal to some key column in another table. A key is a column that has unique values, where no two values are the same. In our case, the key column is webdirectories.web_dir_ID, and the field we want it to be equal to is web_dir_con.web_dir_parent. Tango doesn't figure this one out for us, so we need to change the values of the join. Do this by clicking in the Column fields and selecting the correct columns from the popup. The final result should look like Figure 6.7.

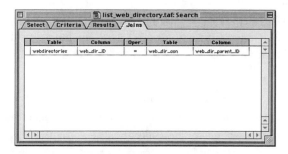

FIGURE 6.7 *A finished Joins tab.*

Our Search action isn't complete. We told it what columns to select and how to match them up across tables, but we haven't limited what rows we want. To do this, we need to set the criteria for the search. Click the Criteria tab. Remember we want to search web_dir_con.web_dir_parent_ID, so drag that column into the Criteria tag. We want only those rows of the table where web_dir_parent_ID is equal to our local variable holding the current folder ID. Click in the Value column of the Criteria view and type the short form of the variable @@local$directoryID. Your final Criteria tab should look like Figure 6.8.

FIGURE 6.8 *A finished Criteria tab for a folder search.*

You've now created a Search action that finds all the records you need, but you still need to display the results. Do this by creating a Results HTML attribute for the Search action. Use Listing 6.1 in ResultsHTML and Listing 6.2 in NoResultsHTML because there might be no subfolders in a given folder.

Listing 6.1 Display Folders ResultsHTML

```
<P>
<H4>
Directories:
</H4>
<UL>
<@ROWS>
    <LI><A HREF="<@CGI><@APPFILE>?directoryID=
<@COLUMN 'webdirectories.web_dir_ID'>">
<@COLUMN 'webdirectories.name'></A>
<BR>
</@ROWS>
</UL>
```

Listing 6.2   Display Directories NoResultsHTML

```
<P>
<H4>
Directories:
</H4>
      There are no sub-directories.
```

Notice what is done in the ResultsHTML to create a hyperlink to the sub-folder. We create a link to the current TAF and we set the directoryID to the web_dir_ID of the row we are displaying. These links cause our TAF to run with a new current folder. You've just created the entire tree of the folder using just this one TAF and routine.

We can finish up this TAF fairly quickly. The next task is to list all the URLs and their descriptions. We need to set up another Search action, this time using the weblink_con table and the weblinks table. Create a new Search action and drag both these tables into the Select Columns area. Configure the Joins tab to look like Figure 6.9, linking the weblink_ID columns in both tables.

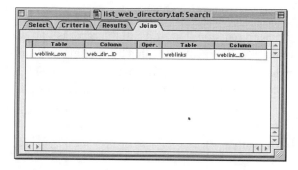

FIGURE 6.9   *A Web link table Joins tab.*

Now the Criteria tab. Drag in the weblink_con.web_dir_ID column. Enter @@local$folderID in the Value column. Close the action. You must display the URLs as you did the folders, but instead of the links coming back to our TAF, we link to the URL provided in the folder. Put Listings 6.3 and 6.4 into the ResultsHTML and NoResultsHTML of the URL search action.

Listing 6.3   URL ResultsHTML

```
<H4>
Links:<A HREF="<@CGI>add_weblink.taf?_function=suggest&directoryID=
@@local$directoryID">
Suggest a new link</A>

</H4>
<UL>
<@ROWS>
    <LI><A HREF="<@COLUMN 'weblinks.url'>"><@COLUMN 'weblinks.name'>
</A> - <@COLUMN 'weblinks.description'>
<BR>
</@ROWS>
</UL>
```

Listing 6.4   URL NoResultsHTML

```
<H4>
URLs:
</H4>
    No URLS were found in this directory.
```

Notice that we also generate a link to an add_weblink.taf file and pass it the current `directoryID`. Later in this chapter, we create this TAF, so just ignore it for now.

You've now created a TAF that lists all the URLs in a folder and enables you to navigate through the folders. That completes phase one of the viewing TAF. Your TAF should look like Figure 6.10. Now we need to do phase two, putting a navigation path at the top of each page.

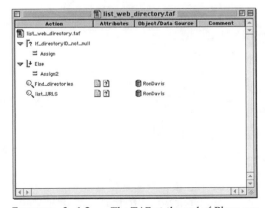

FIGURE 6.10   *The TAF at the end of Phase one.*

Phase 2: The Path

Creating the path seems straightforward, but turns out to be a little tricky. First, you must loop up the folder tree, getting the parent folder of each folder. Then, you must create a string with hyperlinks for each folder in the path. For example, assume you have a folder that is organized like the one in Figure 6.11—the folder ID of each folder is in parenthesis.

```
Root(0)
    Books(3)
        Science Fiction(10)
            Cyberpunk(23)
```

FIGURE 6.11   *A directory structure.*

You are now displaying folder 23. You need to search the web_dir_con. web_dir_ID column for this folder. When you do, you'll find the parent folder ID in the web_dir_com.web_dir_parent_ID column, which in this case is Science Fiction (10). You can search the same table again for the folder ID for Science Fiction (10), and get back Books (3). You keep doing this until you get to the root. That's the ending condition for the loop—when the current folder we are looking for is 0.

How do we do this in Tango? The first thing we need is a variable that holds the current folder we are looking at. Create one by dragging an Assign action between the second Assign and the Find Folder Search actions. Set up the Assign action to assign the value of the @@local$directoryID variable to a variable name curDirID with a local scope. The finished Assign action looks like Figure 6.12. This sets our pointer to the current folder.

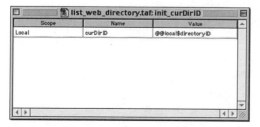

FIGURE 6.12   *Initializing an Assign action.*

Now we are going to create the loop to get each of the folders in our path. This loop is a While action. Drag one into the TAF under the initializing Assign action. While actions take parameters just like an If action. Essentially, an If action is what a While action is doing; it is answering "If this condition is true, keep doing my loop." So, you set up the criteria for a While action just like an If action. In this case, we want the logic to be "while curDirID is not 0, do the loop." Enter **@@local$curDirID** into the Value column and **0** into the Value column. Pop up the Operator column and set it to **!=**. The finished product should look like Figure 6.13.

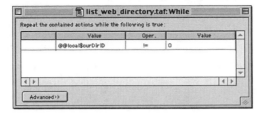

FIGURE 6.13   *Path While action.*

In Tango, a While loop does all the actions below it in the hierarchy. That means everything indented to the right and below the While action. In our loop, we want to search the folder table. So, drag in a Search action under the While action. Then, add the web_dir_con table and webdirectories tables to the Select Columns panel. That should give you a Select panel that looks like Figure 6.14.

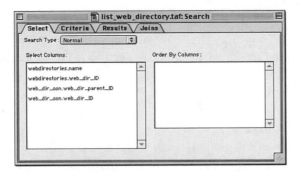

FIGURE 6.14   *Path Select tab.*

When you do this, you are asked to define the joins. Go ahead and define the join on the web_dir_con.web_dir_ID and webdirectories.web_dir_ID columns. Doing so gives you a Joins tab that looks like Figure 6.15.

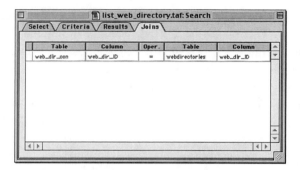

FIGURE 6.15 *Path Joins tab.*

Finally, we set up the Criteria tab. We want the web_dir_con.web_dir_ID column to equal @@local$curDirID. Do this by dragging in the web_dir_con.web_dir_ID column, and setting the Value column to @@local$curDirID. The end result is shown in Figure 6.16.

FIGURE 6.16 *Path Criteria tab.*

We've now defined the search we need to do over and over, but as with any loop, we must make sure that the loop stops. If we don't, the loop will go on forever, an infinite loop. For that to happen, we need @@local$curDirID to reach zero. Right now, it doesn't even change. We also need to build some kind of list of folder names as we move up the tree. We build this list in a slightly unusual way. We create an array called dirPathArray and add a row to it for each new folder name. Then, we can use the special array display syntax we learned in Chapter 3, "The Coming Soon Page," to display the path with links.

We do all of this assigning in the ResultsHTML of the Search action. Enter the code in Listing 6.5 into your ResultsHTML.

Listing 6.5   While Loop ResultsHTML

```
<@ASSIGN NAME='temp' VALUE='<A HREF="<@CGI><@APPFILE>?directoryID=<@COLUMN
'webdirectories.web_dir_ID'>"><@COLUMN 'webdirectories.name'>
</A>' SCOPE='local'>

<@ADDROWS ARRAY="dirPathArray" SCOPE=local VALUE="@@local$temp" POSITION="0">

<@ASSIGN NAME="curDirID" SCOPE="local"


VALUE="<@COLUMN 'web_dir_con.web_dir_parent_ID'>" >
```

The first part of this code is an assignment of the results of the folder search as an HTML link. We assign this generated string to a variable called temp. The value is an HTML HREF tag with a URL that refers to the parent folder we just got and that uses the name of that folder as the link text.

So why do we assign the results to a temp variable? Why not just assign them to the array? Tango has a challenge with quotation marks inside quotation marks. Because there is no way to tell an ending quotation mark from a beginning quotation mark, if you put a quotation mark inside another set of quotation marks, Tango thinks the second quotation mark is the end of the first set. For example, assume that you have the string "something "quotes" something else". You might mean that the inner quotation marks are for the word *quotes* and the outer quotation marks are for the whole sentence. But you could mean the first two quotation marks are for "something" and the second two quotation marks are for "something else". Tango does have a way around this, at least for one set of quotation marks inside another. The single quotation mark (') is also a valid quotation mark character. Therefore, you can use double quotation marks for your outer quotes and single quotation marks for your inner quotes. This approach enables you to use quotation marks one level deep, but after that you are in trouble.

One solution is to assign one string that uses two sets of quotation marks to a temp variable and then use that variable name in another assign. Notice that in this case we used the single quotation mark on the outside.

That is because we are using the double quotation marks for HTML, and HTML wants only double quotes.

Here we assign the entire link syntax to the `temp` variable and then use the `temp` variable in the `<@ADDROWS>` tag to assign it to the array. `<@ADDROWS>` inserts a new row in the specified array, with the values you provide. It also lets you tell it where to insert the row. We are inserting the value of the `temp` variable at the beginning of the array, which is very important in our case; otherwise, our path prints out backwards.

The last thing we do in this ResultsHTML is update our counter variable. We perform an assign with the value of the newly found parent. If this parent is the root, it is zero and that causes the While action to exit. Miss this step and the While action runs forever.

At this point in the TAF, we have all the makings of the path in an array— we just need to display it. Drag in a Results action and add Listing 6.6 to it.

Listing 6.6   Display Path ResultsHTML

```
<@VAR NAME="dirPathArray"
    SCOPE="local"
    APREFIX=""
    ASUFFIX=""
    RPREFIX=""
    RSUFFIX=">"
    CPREFIX=""
    CSUFFIX=""
>
```

Here we're telling Tango to display the array using a > after each row. The > separates each level in the path. This is the same separator that Yahoo uses, but you can use any separator you want.

That's it for our display. Running this TAF should show you the path in the form of a set of hyperlinks separated by colons. You final TAF should look like Figure 6.17.

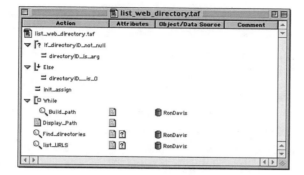

FIGURE 6.17   *The final TAF for list_web_directory.taf.*

The Add URL TAF

You have the means to display a hierarchical directory structure of URLs, but so far you have no way to add folders or URLs. We're going to fix that right now. The next thing we need to do is create the add_weblink.taf file mentioned earlier in the chapter. This TAF enables a user to suggest a new URL to be added to the folder with the ID as an argument to this TAF.

Create a new TAF and name it add_weblink.taf. Save it in the same folder as the list_web_directory.taf. By looking at the previous link we created, you can tell this TAF needs to take a directoryID as an input parameter. It also has a _function of suggest. Let's handle that part first. Drag in an If action and set up its criteria to be _function=suggest. Now drag a Result action in under the If. This Result displays the suggestion form. I used Listing 6.7.

Listing 6.7   Suggest URL Result Action

```
Suggest a URL.<P>
<FORM METHOD=POST ACTION="<@CGI><@APPFILE>?_function=insert">
Name: <INPUT TYPE=TEXT MAXLENGTH=255 SIZE=25 NAME="name" VALUE=""><BR>
URL:<INPUT TYPE=TEXT MAXLENGTH=255 SIZE=25 NAME="url" VALUE="http://">
<BR>
Description:<BR>
<TEXTAREA ROWS=5 COLS=60 WRAP=VIRTUAL NAME="description"></TEXTAREA>

<P>
<INPUT TYPE=HIDDEN NAME="directoryID"   VALUE="<@ARG directoryID>">
<INPUT TYPE=SUBMIT NAME="Submit" VALUE="Submit">
</FORM>
```

This is a standard form, just like the ones we've created before. An important thing to note is it passes its information back to the same TAF, with the _function equal to insert. Also notice it has a hidden field, which passes on the directoryID argument.

Now we know that the TAF must handle this form and that it does so inside the _function=insert. Create a new If action and make its criteria _function=insert. By looking at the weblinks table in the database, you see that some fields map directly to form fields. The two missing fields are approved and weblink_ID. The approved field is easy enough because we know in every case that we don't want it approved, so we can just set it to false when doing the insert into the database. We don't want to use a hidden field because then someone could create a URL with "&approved=true" in it and get his URLs automatically approved.

The real question is how we generate the unique ID that goes into the weblink_ID field? Remember that I told you to create a database table for use with a Tango Class File (TCF) named Utility? This is where we are doing that. We are calling a routine, called GetNextID, inside Utilities that returns to us the next ID for use.

Using Tango Class Files

The first thing we have to do is let the Tango IDE know about the object. We do this in the Objects panel of the workspace window. Click over to the Objects panel and you'll see something like Figure 6.18. If you are using the Windows IDE, there is a folder named COM objects. Each of these folders represents an object handler. Object handlers are code modules added to Tango that allow them to understand different object types, such as Java Beans, COM objects, and TCFs.

FIGURE 6.18   *The Objects panel.*

Objects appear in this panel when they are ready for use. To add an object to the panel, go to the Object menu and select the Add item. A submenu pops out with the available object handlers listed. Selecting one of these submenus brings up a dialog that enables you to select the object you want to add. In the case of TCFs, this is a standard file selection dialog and you tell Tango where the file you want to add is located.

Let's step through the process to add the Utility TCF. Select Object, Add, Tango Class File. A standard file dialog appears. Navigate to where the Utility TCF is located and select it. Now if you look in the Objects panel and twist down the Tango Class File folder, you'll see Utility listed there. Twist it open and you will see all the methods in this file. Now you are ready to use this file.

Using an object in Tango is a two-step process. First, you have to create a new object, and then you have to call methods in that object. You create an object by using the Create Object action. You could drag in one of these actions from the Actions palette and then drag an object from the Object panel to the Create Object action's edit window. Or, you can just drag the desired object right into your TAF and a Create Object action is created for this object. The same process is true of the Call Method action.

Drag the Utility object from the Object panel into your TAF under the If for insert. A window like the one shown in Figure 6.19 will appear.

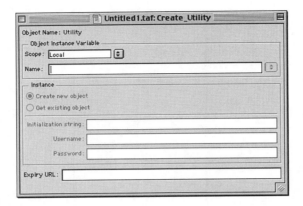

FIGURE 6.19   *A Create Object window.*

All we need to do in this dialog is set a name for the variable with which this object instance is associated. We will use this variable name to associate Call Method actions to the instance of the action in which we are calling the method. In most cases, you only create one instance of a given object in a TAF—and that is true in this case—so give the variable name the same name as the object. In this case, fill in the Name field with Utility.

The only other field we can edit in this window is the Expiry URL, which enables us to set a URL to load when the Object instance expires. It expires when its variable expires. Unless you have changed the variable duration on your server, the variable expires after 30 minutes. Because we're leaving this variable with the scope of local, it goes away after the TAF is finished executing. In any case, we don't want to set an expiry URL.

The next thing to do is actually get a new ID for a given URL. We do this by calling the method `GetNextID` in the Utility TCF. Expand the Utility object and drag the `GetNextID` method in under our Create Object action. You'll get a window like Figure 6.20.

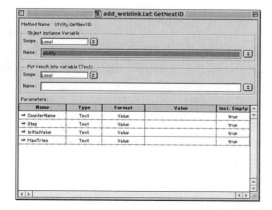

FIGURE 6.20   *An empty Call Method action.*

The first thing you need to set in this window is the name of the object instance variable you are using when calling the method. You'll notice that Tango thoughtfully filled in this field for you. To the right of the field is a popup, which contains all the object instance variables you have defined in this TAF.

Next, you need to define the variable into which the output of this call is going to go. Let's call the variable nextWebID. You can use an existing variable if you want, or Tango creates a variable if it doesn't exist. In the lower part of the window, we have a list of the parameters the method call takes and we must set each one of them.

The first parameter is the name of the counter, CounterName. GetNextID enables you to define any number of counters by name. Here is where you ask for the specific counter. If the counter doesn't exist, it is created the first time you call this routine. Enter the actual value you want to pass into the Value column. For our purposes, let's name this counter weblinkID.

The second parameter is Step, which is how many counts you want between each new ID. For example, if you set Step to 2 and started at 2, you would get numbers such as 2,4,6,8, and 10. We want Step to go up by one, so just enter 1 in the Value field.

The third parameter is InitialValue, which is the starting value for the counter. Set yours to 0.

The fourth and last parameter is MaxTries. The GetNextID method has to take into account the idea that another instance of itself might be trying to get an ID at the same time. In order to handle this, GetNextID locks the counter row in the database while it gets its new value, and then unlocks the counter row when it gets its new value. The process of getting the new value takes very little time, so if the counter finds the field locked, it can try again and the counter will probably be unlocked. MaxTries tells you how long it will try before it gives up. Normally three times is enough, so set the Value column to 3. Now you should have a Call Method action window that looks like Figure 6.21.

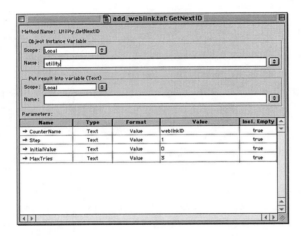

FIGURE 6.21   *A finished Call Method.*

When executing this TAF, we now have a new unique ID for the URL we are getting ready to insert into the database in the local variable nextWeblinkID. Now, we can perform the insert—or I should say *inserts*. We must not only insert into the weblinks table, but we also have to insert into the weblink_con table. You've done a couple of inserts by now, so I'm just going to show you the final version of the Insert actions and you can configure yours to be the same.

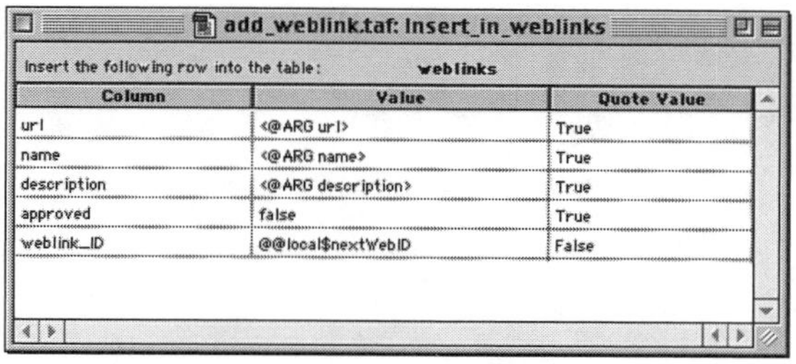

FIGURE 6.22   *The Insert into weblinks action.*

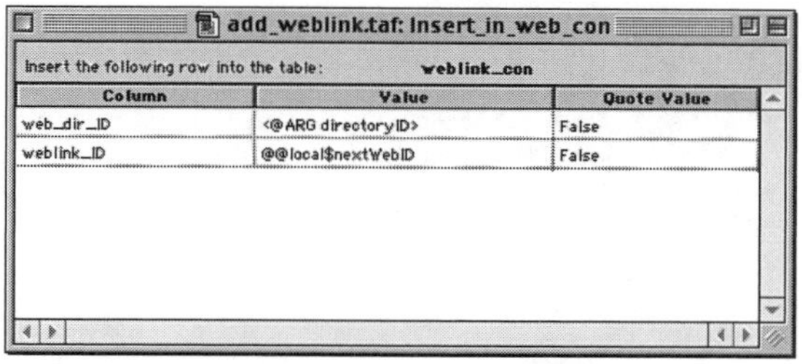

FIGURE 6.23   *The Insert into weblink_con action.*

Notice a couple of things to about these inserts. In the weblinks insert, we explicitly set the approval field to False. All links are unapproved when suggested. For the weblinkID in both inserts, we use the short form of the local variable nextWeblinkID.

We've now created a way for the user of our site to suggest a URL for inclusion in our Web directory. Right now, all of the URLs suggested are not approved. But, right now, our list_web_directory.taf doesn't do anything about unapproved URLs. We need to change it so that unapproved URLs are not shown, which means we must change the search action that lists all the URLs in a folder. So, open list_web_directory.taf and find the list_links Search action. Click to the Criteria tab, drag in the weblinks. approved column, and set the value it needs to True. Your final Search action criteria tab should look like Figure 6.24.

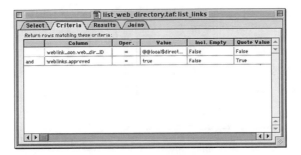

FIGURE 6.24 *The list_links criteria tab.*

After you have done this, listing a folder is always empty because it no longer finds any qualifying, or approved, URLs. We need to develop a way to approve URLs. That is an admin task, so it is now time to start defining the admin TAFs.

Admin TAFs

The URL Approval TAF

Approving a URL should be an easy task. All we want to do is edit the weblinks.approved column from false to true. If we don't want to approve a URL, we should delete it from the database. So, if all I want to do is search for unapproved Web links, list them out, and edit or delete them, what is the easiest way to implement this in Tango? The Search builder.

Create a new TAF named approve_weblinks.taf, drag in a Search builder, and save it. Now we need to step through the configuration of the Search builder. The first thing to do is define the basic search we want to perform. In this case, we just want to search for records in the weblinks table where the Approved column is "false". Do this by dragging the weblinks.approved column into the Search Columns panel of the Search tab. Now, select the column and look at the Column Options part of the tab. We want to use a fixed value and not have the user enter a value. Click the Fixed value radio button. The value column should be Value Entered. Now simply type **false**, no quotes, into the text area. This does our search for us. When you run the TAF, you'll notice that unlike other Search builders, you go right to the record list because the search doesn't require a form page.

Now for the Record List tab. Drag in weblinks.name and weblinks.description. We can use the defaults here, which makes weblinks.name into a link to details.

Last is the Record Detail tab. Drag the entire weblinks table into the Display Columns panel. Move the weblinks.name column up to the top of the list so that the name is listed first.

Select the weblinks.url column, and then go change the Display As popup in the Column Options to Link to URL Stored in Column. This enables us to click on the URL and actually go to that site, which is very useful when deciding to approve a site.

We also want to be able to delete a record in the details page, so check the Allow delete of record from: checkbox.

Select the weblinks.approved column and change the Display As popup to pop-up menu. When you do this, a dialog appears. Click the Add button, and then type **Approve** into the Name field and **true** into the Value field. Click Add again and enter **Disapprove** and **false** into the Name and Value fields, respectively. When you've done this, your window should look like Figure 6.25. Click the OK button to close the window. This creates an HTML popup that shows Approve or Disapprove and sets the field to true or false based on the value.

FIGURE 6.25   *The Approved values dialog.*

Build and close the builder.

You can now load this TAF and approve some of the sites you've added to the folder. After you change the approved/disapproved popup, the URL is approved and you will see it in the folder listing. Clicking the delete button will remove the URL from the weblinks table.

Now you can add URLs to a folder and approve them so that they show up in the listing, but you can't yet add folders. That's the next admin TAF we need to create for this module.

Add Folder TAF

Adding a folder poses a quandary for us. We don't want users to change the directory structure, so we can't add a link from the folder page to the add directory TAF. This gives us the problem of determining where to put the new folder.

We are going to create a simple TAF that has a form for the new folder. One of the fields in that form will be the parent folder ID, and we will fill it in by default with the value of the argument parentDir. In our case, this folder is always empty, but in the future there will be a value for the folder.

To make the whole generation of the form much easier, we are starting with a New Record builder. But there are couple of reasons a standard NRB won't work for us. One reason is that we need to generate a new ID for the new folder on the fly. The other reason is we have to insert records into two tables, webdirectory and web_dir_con. Still, the New Record builder gets us started, and that is a perfectly valid way to use the builder.

Create a new TAF and name it add_directory.taf. Now drag in a New Record builder. Then drag the webdirectory table into the Columns panel of the builder. We use the default values for the Name column, but we need to set up the web_dir_ID a little differently. Select it and click the Fixed value radio button. Then, in the Value box, enter @@local$newDirID. This is the variable that holds our generated unique ID.

Let's look for a moment at our newly generated actions under the builder. There are three If actions, each corresponding to a value for the _function argument. The first one has the insert form in it. The second If action actually does the insert into the database, and the third handles an error.

We like the form, but it needs another field, and that field must have a default value equal to the `parentDirID` argument. So, open the Result action and change the HTML to look like Listing 6.8.

Listing 6.8   New Directory Form

```
<!DOCTYPE HTML PUBLIC "-//W3C//DTD HTML 3.2//EN">
<HTML>
<HEAD>
    <TITLE>New Directory</TITLE>
</HEAD>
<BODY>
<FORM METHOD="POST" ACTION="<@CGI><@APPFILE>?_function=insert&
<@USERREFERENCEARGUMENT>">
<TABLE>
<TR VALIGN=TOP ALIGN=LEFT>
    <TD>
        Parent Directory ID:
    </TD>

    <TD>
        <INPUT NAME="parentDirID" VALUE="<@ARG parentDirID>" TYPE=TEXT
SIZE=30 MAXLENGTH=30>
    </TD>
</TR>
<TR VALIGN=TOP ALIGN=LEFT>
    <TD>
        Name:
    </TD>

    <TD>
        <INPUT NAME="name" TYPE=TEXT SIZE=30 MAXLENGTH=30>
    </TD>
</TR>
</TABLE>
<INPUT TYPE=SUBMIT VALUE="Save"> <INPUT TYPE=RESET VALUE="Reset Values">
</FORM>
</BODY>
</HTML>
```

The main change we made was to add a new input field with the name of `parentDirID`. While there, we also changed the page title.

Now, when the user presses Save, the insert part of this TAF executes. By looking at the Insert action, we can see it is all set up to insert that local variable for the new ID, but we haven't generated the new ID yet. We're going to generate the ID just like we did for URLs, which means using the Create Object and Call Method actions. You could even drag in those actions from the add_weblink.taf and just change the values, but for now create the two actions right before the Insert action, and make them look like Figures 6.26 and 6.27.

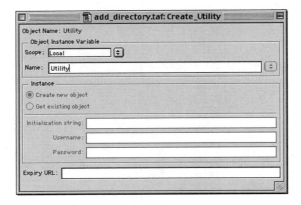

Figure 6.26   *Create_Utility.*

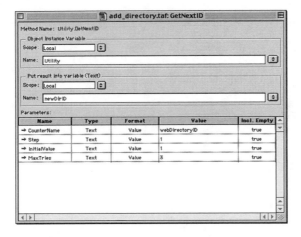

Figure 6.27   *The Call Method action for* newDirID.

Now we need to do our second insert into the web_dir_con table. Drag another Insert action in below the one that is already there. Then, configure it to look like Figure 6.28.

FIGURE 6.28   *The Insert action for web_dir_id.*

That's really it for this TAF, but I need to explain something about builders. Builders are great and one of the best things about them is that you can open them, edit the stuff in them, and rebuild. But what happens if you modify the actions inside the builder outside of the builder? Well, after that you can't change the actions with the builder. If you open the builder whose actions you have changed, and then try to build it again, you are warned that doing so makes you lose your changes. If you go ahead and rebuild, all your changes are lost. In this case, that would mean all our actions for getting a new ID and doing the other insert would be gone. So, I don't want you to reopen the builder; it has outlived its usefulness. What I suggest you do is select all the actions under the New Record builder, and move them out from under it, and then delete the builder. This lowers the chance of a mistake being made in the future.

This was the last TAF we needed in this module. We learned a lot and created a really powerful module in our Web site. We come back to it in future chapters and make a few modifications to enable it to work better with users, but for now it does all the basic stuff you want from a Web directory.

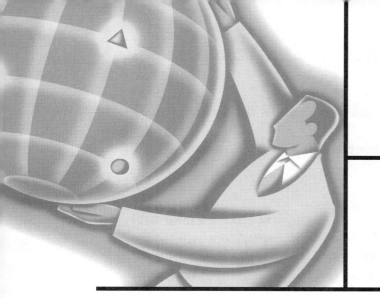

CHAPTER 7

XML Database Backup

What We'll Learn

- Direct DMBS action
- File action
- XML meta tags, <@DOM>, <@DOMINSERT>, <@DOMDELETE>, <@DOMAIN>, <@DOMREPLACE>, <@ELEMENTATTRIBUTE>, <@ELEMENTATTRIBUTES>, <@ELEMENTNAME>, <@ELEMENTVALUE>
- <@COLS> and <@COL> tags
- <@SQ> tag
- <@REPLACE> tag

Purpose

In this chapter, we will create a TAF that saves all the data in a group of database tables as XML, providing a means of backing up your database.

Planning

Feature List

- You must be able to create an XML document holding all the data for all the tables in the database.

- If using P.SQL as your database, table names can be automatically retrieved from the data source.
- If not using P.SQL, you must provide a list of table names.

Database Schema

No new tables are created for this module. Instead, it will use the databases we have already created for our Web site, specifically we'll back up the ones that contain data we don't want to lose, such as user_profiles, users, and so on. We will not back up tables such as events, where we can do without the data.

Creating the TAFs

At this point in the creation of our Web site, we have quite a few database tables that will contain data you don't want to lose. For instance, you don't want to lose all the URLs in your Web directory or the users in your system and their profile information. You can save this information using standard back-up techniques, but what if you are using an ASP and you'd like to keep your own backup of the data? You need a Tango based solution.

You could create a TAF that just listed out each table and each column in the database, separated by commas. But that gets tricky if you want to read it back in. What you need is a standard method of data interchange: something lots of systems recognize, but something you can customize to your needs. The solution is XML. XML stands for Extensible Markup Language. It is a standard developed by the W3 committee, the same people who invented HTML. As a matter of fact, it is a textual tag-based standard and looks similar to HTML. If you aren't familiar with XML, you should check out some of the resources in Appendix B, "Other Tango Resources."

In addition to saving your database in XML, you could transfer or manipulate that data with standard XML tools. This is an advantage over just using a comma-separated ASCII file.

As part of the XML standard, a Document Object Model (DOM) is defined. DOM is a programming interface for accessing data from XML. It is a set of tools you can use to create and read XML. Tango supports this API through a set of meta tags. There are a number of meta tags for accessing and manipulating XML data in Tango, and we'll be using them throughout the chapters. One thing you need to know is how to specify an element in Tango. XML is a hierarchical data store. That means it forms a tree with one root and numerous children. Children can have children and so on: For instance, you could have XML that resembles Listing 7.1.

Listing 7.1   Sample XML Data

```
<?xml version="1.0"?>
<DATABASE>
    <SQL_TABLE NAME="News">
        <SQL_ROW COLNAMES="true">
            <VALUE>
                Title
            </VALUE>
            <VALUE>
                DateEntered
            </VALUE>
            <VALUE>
                Story
            </VALUE>
        </SQL_ROW>
        <SQL_ROW>
            <VALUE>
                Now really online
            </VALUE>
            <VALUE>
                11/12/1999 15:52:12
            </VALUE>
            <VALUE>
                This is a same news message.
            </VALUE>
        </SQL_ROW>
    </SQL_TABLE>
</DATABASE>
```

The root element is the <DATABASE> element. It has one child, an <SQL_TABLE> element that in turn has an <SQL_ROW> element. That element has multiple <VALUE> elements. How would you specify you want the value element that contains Story?

Tango uses a syntax for specifying nodes in the tree called XPointer. XPointer was the leading contender for the standard when Tango 2000 was developed. Unfortunately, it was not the standard for specifying elements chosen by the XML standards board. They chose XPath. Tango 2000 was already written at that point, so you will learn XPointer syntax. XPointer specifies things like this: `"root().child().child()"`. There is only one `root()` element, but it can have multiple children. You can specify exactly which child you want by position, `child(1)`, or with an element syntax that lets you use an attribute of the element. We'll see both of these used in our example. So the element in Listing 7.1 that contains the value `Story` would be `"root().child(1).child(1).child(3)"`. This will be clearer when we start using the Tango XML meta tags.

An *element* is a tag pair in an XML document. In Listing 7.1, `<DATABASE></DATABASE>` is an element.

An *attribute* is a value pair attached to a specific element. In XML syntax, an attribute is the name=value pair inside a tag. In the element `<SQL_ROW COLNAMES="true">` in Listing 7.1, `COLNAMES` is an attribute and the value of that attribute is `true`.

User TAF

The first TAF we need to create is the one that saves out all the tables and rows in our database. This isn't really a user task, but it is read-only on the data; therefore a user couldn't make changes in your database. On the other hand, he could see all your database information, including usernames and passwords. Because of this, you don't really want it to be public.

Defining the XML Schema

When dealing with XML, it is important to know what schema you are going to use for the XML document before you start. In XML, a schema tells you what your XML tags are going to be and in what order will they appear. The XML standard defines a document called DTD, which tells an XML document's schema. The DTD we will be using is in Listing 7.2.

There is a new standard, called XML Schema, from the XML standards board that will replace DTDs. It actually uses XML to define the schema and not the special language of the DTD. XML Schema also specifies things such as type information about a given tag. The XML Schema standard has not been finalized, and Tango 2000 doesn't use it.

Listing 7.2   db.dtd

```
<!ELEMENT DATABASE (SQL_TABLE*)>
<!ELEMENT SQL_TABLE (SQL_ROW*)>
<!ATTLIST SQL_TABLE NAME CDATA #REQUIRED>
<!ELEMENT SQL_ROW (VALUE*)>
<!ATTLIST SQL_ROW COLNAMES CDATA #IMPLIED>
<!ELEMENT VALUE (#PCDATA)>
```

If you are not familiar with DTDs, Listing 7.2 might not mean much to you. You might guess by looking at it that the <!ELEMENT> tag defines a new element or a tag in the XML. An element is a tag, and all the tags we will be using are defined here. The words inside the parenthesis are what items can be subitems of the element, or what kind of value it has. #PCDATA means that there will be textual data inside, which means almost anything. A star after the subelement's name means that there can be as many subelements of this type as you want. The <!ATTLIST> tag defines the attributes of an element. An attribute is a name value pair inside the tag brackets. For instance, an SQL_TABLE tag has a NAME attribute and could look like this: <SQL_TABLE NAME="News">.

Our layout is fairly simple. There is a root item called DATABASE that has no attributes. An asterisk in an !ELEMENT definition in the DTD means that there can be multiple elements of the same type. A DATABASE element can have multiple SQL_TABLE elements, which in turn have multiple SQL_ROW elements, which have multiple VALUE elements. The SQL_TABLE elements have an attribute NAME, which is the name of the table. The SQL_ROW elements have an attribute COLNAMES, which is true if that row contains the names of the columns and false if the table's row contains actual row data.

Creating the XML: db2xml.taf

In order to create the XML, we have to do a few things. First, we have to get a list of the tables we want to back up. Then we go to each of those tables and retrieve all their rows. For each row we then retrieve each column. As we perform each step, we need to insert the proper XML into the DOM.

Let's get started. Create a new TAF to be named db2xml.taf. The first thing we need is a Tango array containing a list of table names to be backed up. The easiest way to do this is to create an `<@ARRAY>` meta tag. Drag a Result action into the TAF and enter the code from Listing 7.3 into it.

Listing 7.3   Creating the Table Array

```
<@ASSIGN NAME='tableTable' VALUE='<@ARRAY NAME="tableTable"
VALUE="News;notify;users" SCOPE="local">'>
<@ASSIGN NAME="numTables" VALUE="<@NUMROWS ARRAY='tableTable'>" SCOPE="local">
```

This creates a new array with the initial values in the VALUE attribute. The semicolon in the VALUE attribute ends a row by default, so we create an array with three rows and one column. You will probably want to include more than these three tables. You need to decide what tables to back up. I'm keeping it to three so that the TAF executes quickly. Backing up all the data in the databases can take a while. After we are done with development, you will want to expand this list of tables to include all tables. You might even want to write a TAF that lets you pick the tables you want, or a TAF that lets you read in an XML file to get the tables to back up.

After we create an array containing all the tables, we also create a variable to hold the number of rows in the table so that we can loop through them and act on each table later. By using the `<@NUMROWS>` tag instead of a explicit value like three, when we add tables to the array, the numTables variable is automatically changed.

Now that we have a list of tables, we need to start creating the XML. In Tango 2000, there is a new kind of variable made specifically for XML; the DOM variable. You can insert elements, or pieces, of XML into a DOM variable at XPointer-specified locations. Then when you ask for the DOM variable to display, you will receive XML. We need to create one of these variables now to hold our back-up database tree. The `<@DOM>` meta tag takes a piece of XML and turns it into a DOM instance. If you use this inside an `<@ASSIGN>` tag ,you will get a new DOM type variable. Add a new Result action to the TAF, and enter the code in Listing 7.4 into it.

Listing 7.4   Creating the DOM Variable

```
<@ASSIGN NAME="sqlDOM" SCOPE="local" VALUE="<@DOM VALUE=
'<DATABASE></DATABASE>'>">
```

The root item of our database XML is the <DATABASE> tag. We put a beginning and ending tag into the DOM to get a valid beginning place. All new items will be subitems of this one tag because there can be only one root element in a XML document.

We need to walk through the tableTable array and insert an element for each table in the list. Create a For loop going through each item in the table. Drag a For loop action into the TAF and configure it as shown in Figure 7.1.

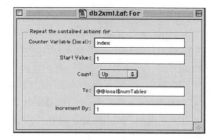

FIGURE 7.1   For *loop for* tableTable *array.*

Now each time you go through this loop, the index variable will point to the current row in our array of tables. After this, we need to create a new DOM element and insert it as a child of the root each time through the For loop. Drag in a new Result action inside the For action, and enter the code from Listing 7.5 into it.

Listing 7.5   Creating the <SQL_TABLE> **Element**

```
<@DOMINSERT OBJECT="sqlDOM" SCOPE="local" ELEMENT="root()" POSITION="append">
<SQL_TABLE NAME="@@tableTable[@@local$index,1]"></SQL_TABLE>
</@DOMINSERT>
```

The <@DOMINSERT> tag inserts all the XML inside it into the specified DOM variable object as a child of the element specified in the ELEMENT attribute. In this case, the new element will be inserted as a child of the root. The POSITION attribute tells where to insert the child, and we want to insert at the end of the list, so we use the "append" keyword. Inside the <@DOMINSERT>, we create a <SQL_TABLE> tag pair. There is no text inside this particular tag, so we put nothing in the middle. But we do want the name of the current row to be in the NAME attribute, so we pull it out of the tableTable array using the For loop's index.

The next step is to get the data for the <SQL_ROW> tag. This tag has no text inside of it, only <VALUE> tags. We do need to set the COLNAMES attribute based on whether those values are the names of the columns. Filling both of these tags could be done easily if we had an array holding the contents of the database table. Asking for every column in a table with no search criteria can easily get this. But there is a problem: in the past, every time we've searched the database, we've used a Search action. To specify what to search for, we've dragged in the columns we want. The problem now is that we want to dynamically select the table we are searching. There is no way to specify the table to search in a Search action using a Tango variable. The solution is the DirectDBMS action, which allows you to send straight SQL commands to the specified data source. You will still have to tell the DirectDBMS action which data source to use, but you don't have to specify which table because that will be done inside the SQL.

Drag a new DirectDBMS action into your TAF inside the For action. When you do this, you will be asked for the data source you want to act on. Select it. The new DirectDBMS action window will resemble Figure 7.2.

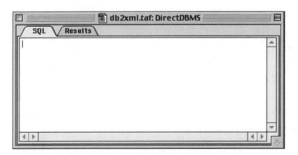

FIGURE 7.2   *Empty DirectDBMS action window.*

Whatever you enter into the SQL panel will be sent directly to the data source you've specified. Our needs are then simple for the search, a simple SELECT * for the current table. Enter Listing 7.6 into the SQL section of the DirectDBMS action.

Listing 7.6   SQL for Searching Current Table

```
SELECT * FROM @@tableTable[@@local$index,1]
```

We use the same variable here that we used for the NAME attribute a minute ago. Meta tags are resolved before the SQL is sent to the database, so we will get the correct table name going to the database. The DirectDBMS action will return all the rows it finds in the resultSet variable, just like the Search action.

Open the Result attribute for the DirectDBMS action, so we can use the resultSet to create our XML. We need to loop through each row in the resultSet and create a new <SQL_ROW> tag and then loop through each column in the row and create new <VALUE> tags. Listing 7.7 does all this, and you should insert it into the Result attribute we just created.

Listing 7.7   Generating Rows and Values Tags

```
<@ROWS start=0>

<@IF EXPR="<@CURROW> = 0">
    <@DOMINSERT OBJECT="sqlDOM" SCOPE="local"
      ELEMENT="root().child(@@local$index)" POSITION="append">
        <SQL_ROW COLNAMES="true"></SQL_ROW>
    </@DOMINSERT>
<@ELSE>
    <@DOMINSERT OBJECT="sqlDOM" SCOPE="local"
      ELEMENT="root().child(@@local$index)" POSITION="append">
        <SQL_ROW COLNAMES="false"></SQL_ROW>
    </@DOMINSERT>
</@IF>

<@COLS>
    <@DOMINSERT OBJECT="sqlDOM" SCOPE="local"
      ELEMENT="root().child(@@local$index).child(<@CALC
      EXPR='<@CURROW>+1'>)" POSITION="append">
    <VALUE>
        <@COL>
    </VALUE>
    </@DOMINSERT>
</@COLS>

</@ROWS>
```

In Listing 7.7, we start off with a <@ROWS> loop like we've used before. We will want to put in the XML a row that contains all the names of the columns in the database. Any time you do a search of the database, the names of each column is in row zero of the table. Most of the time, we don't have anything to do with this row because, by default, a <ROWS> tag starts at row one. This time though, we want the column names, so we make our <ROWS> loop start at row zero.

<SQL_ROW> needs to have its attribute COLNAMES set to the appropriate value of true or false for each row, so we need to check and see if we are in row zero, and if so, set the COLNAMES to true. We use simple IF/ELSE tags to do this. Both the <@DOMINSERT> tags are identical inside the IF and ELSE; only the values inside the tag pair are different. The <@DOMINSERT> is basically the same as the one for tables, except that we specify the position to point to a root's child element. This element is the current <SQL_TABLE> tag and we use the For loop's index to specify which child element.

Next, we need to specify the values of each column in a row. Luckily Tango provides the <@COLS> meta tag to let us walk the columns of the current row just like we walk the rows of the current table. After we've inserted the <SQL_ROW> element into the DOM, we loop through the columns, inserting the <VALUE> elements.

Again the <@DOMINSERT> is the same, except that we specify a different position. The position is the same for the root and its child, but when we get to the child's child, we need to specify which row we are talking about. The difficulty is our <@ROWS> loop is zero based, and the child index is one based. If we attempt to insert at the current row, we'll get an error trying to insert at zero. So we need to insert the child at the current row plus one. We use the <@CALC> tag to do this.

Inside the <@DOMINSERT> tag pair, we generate a <VALUE> pair with the actual value of the current column using the <@COL> tag. This is what gets inserted into the DOM.

The DOM variable now contains all the data from our database. If you'd like to display this XML in your browser, all you need to do is add a Result HTML action and put "@@local$sqlDOM" in it. This will output XML, which will be sent to your browser.

In addition to doing outputting to the browser, we are also going to create a file on the server that contains the XML. Tango provides an action, called the File action, that will create a file for you. Drag one of these actions in at the bottom of the TAF. You should see a window like Figure 7.3. If you don't, switch the pop up at the top of the window to Write, and you will have the same display. You can use this same action to Read, Write, or Delete a file.

FIGURE 7.3 *Empty File write window.*

The first thing you need to specify is the name of the file. We'll call this file db.xml. The File action requires you give a complete path on your actual server for the file, not just a filename. If you are using an ASP and don't know the complete path, you can turn on debugging, run the TAF with just the name in the File action, and look at the first line of the debugging output. It will be the complete path on the server to the TAF being executed.

Before we specify the data we want in the file, let's check the Overwrite radio button in the If File Exists area. We'll leave the other options alone. The data we want to save is the XML in the DOM. There is only one problem with the data. An XML document should start with a header tag saying it is an XML file, but the DOM doesn't automatically put this in. Enter Listing 7.8 into the Data to Write: area, and you will get a complete XML document. Your final window should look something like Figure 7.4.

Listing 7.8 Data to Write for an XML Document

```
<?xml version="1.0"?>
@@local$sqlDOM
```

FIGURE 7.4 *Final File action to write XML.*

You should drag in a Return action for completeness. If you have an XML compliant Web browser like IE5, you can run the TAF and then point your browser to the db.xml file we created and see something like Figure 7.5.

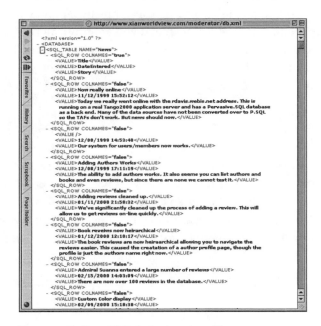

FIGURE 7.5 *XML in browser from file.*

Admin TAFs

One of the most popular uses people make of XML is in business-to-business data transfer. One side will take their data in their own format and convert it to XML, and then transfer the XML file to another company who will read in the XML and output the data in their own format. We have now done the first part of this, we've taken data in our own format—the database tables—and converted it into XML and saved it in a file. Now we are going to do the other part of the transaction. We are going to take the XML and convert it into another data format. In this case, we are going to transform it into SQL Insert statements, which could be used by your database to insert the data into another table with the same structure as our original tables. Of course, you could alter the output from the XML and add the data into a table with a format different from our original.

Create another TAF to be named xml2db.taf. The first thing we are going to do with it is read in the XML file we saved, db.xml, and make a DOM variable from it. Remember the <@DOM> tag takes XML and converts it to DOM, and then you can do an assign to create a new variable of type DOM. Drag in a new Results action and enter Listing 7.9 into it.

Listing 7.9   Create a New DOM Variable

```
<@ASSIGN NAME="sqlDOM" SCOPE="local" VALUE="<@DOM VALUE=
<@INCLUDE FILE='<@APPFILEPATH>DB.XML'>>">
```

This creates a new DOM variable named sqlDOM. For the value of the variable, it uses the output of the <@DOM> tag. The <@DOM> tag gets its XML from the db.xml file in the same directory as the current TAF file.

We need to approach the data in the same way we approached it when creating the XML. First we need to get an array of table names, and a variable with the number of rows in it. Then we'll walk that list and get each row to create the Insert statements.

We're going to use a new XML tag <@ELEMENTATTRIBUTE> to create the table of table names. Remember the name of any given table is in the NAME attribute of the SQL_TABLE tag. <@ELEMENTATTRIBUTE> uses XPointer syntax to specify an element or elements that you want to act on in a given DOM variable, and then it returns the value of a specified attribute. For example, if you said something like `<@ELEMENTATTRIBUTE OBJECT='sqlDOM' SCOPE='local' ATTRIBUTE='NAME' ELEMENT='root().child(1)'>`, it would give you the value of the NAME attribute of the first child element of the root. This is what we want to do; except that we want to return all the child elements of the root, not just one. We'd rather not have to loop through each child element to build our array. Luckily for us XPointer supports getting all the elements at a certain level. Instead of an index number within the parentheses after `child`, insert `all` to specify all the children. Tango handles this by putting the values of these children attributes into a Tango array. To get this into our array, we use the statements in Listing 7.10.

Listing 7.10   Creating the Table Name Array

```
<@ASSIGN NAME="tableTable" VALUE="<@ELEMENTATTRIBUTE OBJECT='sqlDOM'
SCOPE='local' ATTRIBUTE='NAME' ELEMENT='root().child(all)'>" SCOPE="local">

<@ASSIGN NAME="numTables" VALUE="<@NUMROWS array='tableTable'>" SCOPE="local">
```

You can insert this code into the existing Result action or add another one. I added another one because I like to keep pieces of functionality in separate places. Now that we have the table, we need to loop through it and get the columns. Drag a For action into the TAF. Configure it as shown in Figure 7.6.

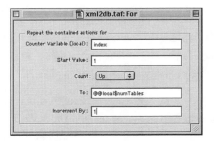

FIGURE 7.6   *Table For action.*

The next thing we are going to do is create an array that contains all the column names for each table. Remember that we set the attribute COLNAMES to true for the rows that contained the names of columns.

This enables us to search for that attribute value to find these rows. When we know what row we want, we can ask for each of the <VALUE> elements to get the actual names. Once again, XPointer helps us do this. Inside the parenthesis, we can specify a great deal about a given element. For instance, instead of using the index of something, we can use an attribute. We could say `root().child(tablename)` to specify a child whose name was tablename. We'll use this ability to specify the table we want to get each row from.

We can also specify an element by name and value. For instance we could say `child(1,#element, COLNAMES, true)` to get the first instance of the child elements in which the COLNAMES attribute is true. So to specify the <SQL_ROW> tag we want for the current table, we use `"root().child (@@local$index).child(1,#element,COLNAMES,true)"`. This points to the <SQL_ROW> tag for the column name, but the values of those columns are in subelements. To specify all those elements, we use `"root().child(@@local$index).child(1,#element,COLNAMES,true).child (all)"` This specifies all the <VALUE> pairs in the column rows. We want the values of these elements; that is, what is in between the tags. To get this, we use the Tango meta tag <@ELEMENTVALUE>. It returns the value of the specified elements; in this case, an array of names. The complete code looks like Listing 7.11, which you should put into a new Result action inside the For loop.

Listing 7.11   Getting the Names of the Columns

```
<@ASSIGN NAME="colNamesElm" VALUE="<@ELEMENTVALUE OBJECT='sqlDOM'
SCOPE='local' ELEMENT=
'root().child(@@local$index).child(1,#element,COLNAMES,true).child(all)'>"
 SCOPE="local">
```

The next piece of information you need is how many rows are in a given table. We find this by retrieving all the children, which returns an array that we can use to retrieve the number of rows. Add Listing 7.12 to your Result action. Notice that we included only those elements in which COLNAMES was false.

Listing 7.12   Getting the Number of Rows

```
<@ASSIGN NAME="dumRows" VALUE="<@ELEMENTNAME OBJECT='sqlDOM' SCOPE='local'
ELEMENT='root().child(@@local$index).child(all,#element,COLNAMES,false)'>"
SCOPE="local">

<@ASSIGN NAME="totalNumRowsInTable" VALUE="<@NUMROWS ARRAY='dumRows'>"

SCOPE="local">
```

Let's loop through the rows and create our Insert statements. Add another For loop configured as shown in Figure 7.7.

FIGURE 7.7   *Row loop For action.*

Add a new Result action under this For. None of the Result actions we've created so far have caused anything to be output. This new Result will be the one that actually outputs the Insert statements. To do this, we have to first create an array that has the values of each <VALUE> pair for the current row. We'll use the same <@ELEMENTVALUE> syntax we used when getting the values of the column names, except we'll check that COLNAMES is false. When we have this array, we can use the <@VAR> attributes for formatting output of array variables as text to create the Insert statements. Basically each row should be prefixed with the beginning of the Insert statement; each row should end with a comma; and each cell should have a single quotation mark around it.

This would almost generate an Insert statement that would work, except that the last value is followed by a comma, which is invalid. What we'll do to fix this is replace the string ,), which ends the invalid Insert, with just). We do this using the <@REPLACE> tag. The <@REPLACE> tag takes a string that is to be searched, the substring to find, and the string to replace it with.

Listing 7.13 puts all of this together, including the simple <@VAR> tag to output the Insert statement we built.

Listing 7.13   Outputting the Insert Statements

```
<@ASSIGN NAME="tempArray" VALUE="<@ELEMENTVALUE OBJECT='sqlDOM' SCOPE='local'
ELEMENT='root().child(@@local$index).child(@@local$rowloop,
#element,COLNAMES,false).child(all)'>" SCOPE="local">

<@ASSIGN NAME="insertCols" TYPE="text" SCOPE="local" VALUE="<@VAR
NAME='tempArray' TYPE='TEXT' APrefix='INSERT INTO
@@local$tableTable[@@local$index,1] VALUES(' ASuffix=')' RPrefix=''
RSuffix=',' CPrefix='<@SQ>' CSuffix='<@SQ>'>">

<@ASSIGN NAME="insertCols" VALUE="<@REPLACE STR='@@local$insertCols'
FINDSTR=',)' REPLACESTR=')'>">

<@VAR NAME='insertCols' ENCODING='NONE'>
```

If you run this TAF, you will get a series of Insert statements that would duplicate all the rows in each table of your database. You could add a File action to output all the Insert statements to a file instead of the browser and pass that file to your database for actual insertion. Hopefully, you have learned how to transfer data from one format to another via XML and Tango.

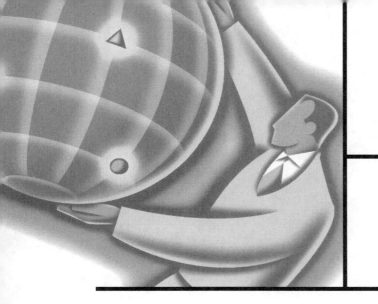

PART III

Users

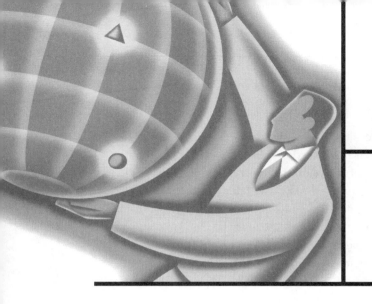

CHAPTER 8

User Management

What We'll Learn

- The Presentation action
- How to validate fields in a form

Purpose

In this chapter, we create a module that is the foundation of everything we do with users in our Web site. It handles the basic user functions, such as logging in and out and adding new users. Other admin functions include adding and deleting users, and editing user levels.

Planning

Feature List

- A user can sign up to become a member of the system. This should check the username for duplicates, add a unique name to the database, and set a default user level.

- Enable the admin to list users, delete users, change user level, and set user information.

Database Schema

Users are a core part of our Web site and a variety of data must be associated with the users in the database. We need to make the addition of new data about the user easy and flexible. We do this by creating one simple basic table for core user information. The basic user table has the username as a primary key. Then, when we need to associate new data with the user, we will create new tables with username foreign keys. We could create some type of user ID number and use it as the key, but the fact is that you won't ever want a username to be used by more than one user—therefore, a username is unique data. It also makes debugging a little easier because you can more easily read a username.

In addition to the unique username, we also want to keep a password and a user level for the user. That is the core information we need. As an aside, I'd like to say I keep a site name associated with a user as well as the username; this enables me to use the same user table for multiple sites.

Database Table Name: users

Column Name	Data Type	Size
username	Char	50
Password	Char	50
Userlevel	Int	

```
CREATE TABLE users (
    username char(30) PRIMARY KEY,
    password char(30),
    userlevel int
)
```

Creating the TAFs

Following our user or admin paradigm, we need to create a TAF that lets a user sign up to be a new user on the system. Once someone is a user they need to be able to log in to the Web site. From the admin point of view we need to be able to edit users and delete them.

User TAFs

New User Taf—Inserts a New User into the Database

The first user TAF is the join now TAF. It inserts a new record into the database for a user. We need to watch for a couple of things. First, each new user must have a unique username. If you attempt to insert a new user into the database with a username that already exists, you will get an error from your database because the username is the primary key. Second, you need to make sure the user correctly enters her password. We'll use a password HTML field in the form, which means the user can't see what she is typing, so we'll make her enter her password in two different password fields. Third, we need to make sure the users actually enter data in the required fields.

While doing all this, we will implement a generalized error-reporting mechanism with the form. If the user makes a mistake and doesn't enter something correctly, we will display an error message at the top of the page and fill in the form with the information the user has entered already so that he doesn't have to enter it again.

Given that there are at least two cases where we are going to be using our form—when the user first enters the data and when an error occurs—wouldn't it be nice if we could share the HTML form and not have to enter it in two places in the TAF? Well, you can do just that by using a Presentation action.

Create a new TAF called new_user.taf. Because we are basically inserting a new record into our users table, we will use the New Record builder as a starting point. Drag in a New Record builder. Now drag all the columns from the users table into the builder. We are allowing the user to enter data in both the username and password fields, but we'll use a fixed value for the user level.

Select the username column. Leave the User enters value radio button unchecked, but click the Required check box.

Select the password column. This column must also be required. In this case, we want the field to be an HTML password field. To set this, use the menu item Attributes, Field Properties. In the Field Properties box, check the Password Field checkbox. The completed dialog should look like the one in Figure 8.1.

Select the userlevel column. This should be a fixed value, so click that radio button. The value should be as entered and you should enter the number 1, which is the lowest level.

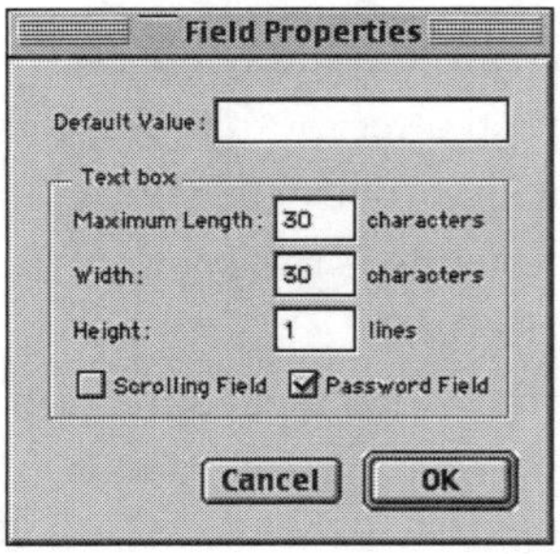

FIGURE 8.1   *Field properties for the password column.*

You can now build and close. This gives us the groundwork for our new user TAF, but we need to change a few things. Because we are departing forever from the builder, we should move the generated actions out from under the NRB and delete it. Select all the actions under the NRB and move them to the root of the TAF. This puts them at the same level as the NRB. Now select the NRB and press Delete and click the OK button to confirm.

Remember that I told you we were going to use a separate file to hold the form for entering? Well, let's do that now. Basically, we are taking the text out of the Result action and putting it into a file. Expand the IfForm action and open the Form Result action under it. Select all and copy. Now, go to the File menu and select New HTML or Text file. When the new text window opens, paste the text into it. While we are here, let's edit the new user form by changing its file title to "New User". Save the file as new_user_form.html in the same directory as your new_user.taf.

What we need to do now is use a Presentation action to display this file instead of the Result action we are currently using. First, delete the Form Result action we used to make our text file. Next drag in a new Presentation action under the IfForm If action. You'll get a window like Figure 8.2.

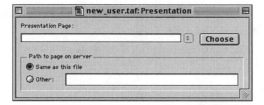

FIGURE 8.2   *An empty Presentation action.*

Now we want to select our saved HTML file for the Presentation action. Do this by clicking the Choose on Macintosh or the Browse button on Windows and finding the new_user_form.html. After you do, the filename appears in the Presentation Page field and the window looks like Figure 8.3.

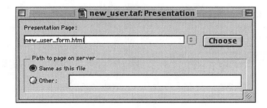

FIGURE 8.3   *A filled-out Presentation action.*

The Presentation action puts the contents of the file you choose into the HTML it is generating. You can either put the file in the same directory as the TAF or in another location on your drive. We're going to put it in the same directory.

If you were to run your TAF now, it would work just as it did before because the content of the Result action is the same as the file. But, if you were to click the submit button on the form it generates without putting anything in the form, you would get an error message saying you didn't have a required field, and asking you to go back and reenter the information. You shouldn't make your users use the Back button if you can avoid it. Why don't you just have the form on the same page as the message? This is where we get to reuse our form.

We need a copy of the Presentation action. There are a number of ways to do this. In Windows, you can actually use the Edit, Copy menu, or Control drag. On the Mac, you can drag the current Presentation action while holding down the Option key. Then, when you drop it, a copy is created. Put the copied Presentation action after the MissingFieldsMessage Result action. Now your TAF will look like the one in Figure 8.4.

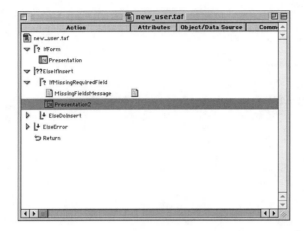

FIGURE 8.4   *The TAF after a copy of the Presentation action is added.*

If you were to run the TAF now and not enter anything, you would get the same message as before, but it would be followed by the same message we had before. To make the error message a little better, replace it with the HTML in Listing 8.1. This changes the error message to red and puts rules before and after it.

Listing 8.1   Required Field Error HTML

```
<!DOCTYPE HTML PUBLIC "-//W3C//DTD HTML3.2//EN">
<HTML>

<HEAD>
    <TITLE>Error: Missing Required Fields</TITLE>
</HEAD>

<BODY>

<HR>
<FONT COLOR=RED>
<H4>Error: Missing Required Fields</H4>

<P>
    The record could not be added because the following
required fields were left empty:
```

```
</P>

<UL TYPE=SQUARE>
<@IFEMPTY <@ARG username>>
    <LI>Username
</@IF>
<@IFEMPTY <@ARG password>>
    <LI>Password
</@IF>
</UL>
</FONT>
<HR>
</BODY>
</HTML>
```

Before you leave this form, you must make another change. I said earlier
that the user needs to enter his password twice to make sure we get the
correct one. We accomplish this by adding a second password field. Open
up new_user_form.html, if it isn't still open. Copy the HTML for the
password field and paste another copy under the first password field.
Change the title text to Confirm password and change the Name attribute
to password2.

We don't want the user to have to reenter all the information in the form
if he forgets one part. So, we want to fill in the form with the former values if there are any. Remember that those values are passed in via the
arguments, so if we put <@ARG username> as the Value attributes of the
form fields, they are prefilled. When you have done all this, you should
have Listing 8.2.

Listing 8.2   Form with Argument Values

```
<!DOCTYPE HTML PUBLIC "-//W3C//DTD HTML 3.2//EN">
<HTML>
<HEAD>
    <TITLE>New User</TITLE>
</HEAD>
<BODY>
<FORM METHOD="POST" ACTION="<@CGI><@APPFILE>?_function=insert&
<@USERREFERENCEARGUMENT>">
<TABLE>
<TR VALIGN=TOP ALIGN=LEFT>
    <TD>
        <B>Username: </B>
```

continues

Listing 8.2   (Continued)

```
    </TD>

    <TD>
        <INPUT NAME="username" VALUE="<@ARG username>" TYPE=TEXT
SIZE=30 MAXLENGTH=30>
    </TD>
</TR>
<TR VALIGN=TOP ALIGN=LEFT>
    <TD>
        <B>Password: </B>
    </TD>

    <TD>
        <INPUT NAME="password" VALUE="<@ARG PASSWORD>" TYPE=PASSWORD
SIZE=30 MAXLENGTH=30>
    </TD>
</TR>
<TR VALIGN=TOP ALIGN=LEFT>
    <TD>
        <B>Confirm Password: </B>
    </TD>

    <TD>
        <INPUT NAME="password2" VALUE="<@ARG PASSWORD2>" TYPE=PASSWORD
SIZE=30 MAXLENGTH=30>
    </TD>
</TR>
</TABLE>
<INPUT TYPE=SUBMIT VALUE="Save"> <INPUT TYPE=RESET VALUE="Reset Values">
</FORM>
</BODY>
</HTML>
```

Now we need to check whether the two passwords the user entered are the same. This is pretty easy to do: All we need is another If action. Drag in an ElseIf right after the IfMissingFields If, make sure it is at the same level and not under it. Configure the ElseIf to check whether the two password fields are not equal. It should look like Figure 8.5.

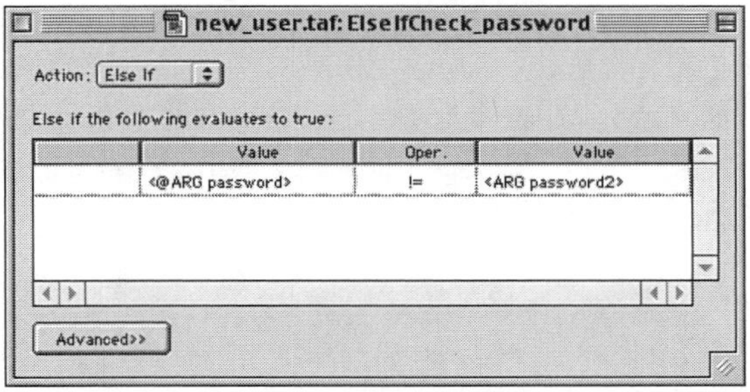

FIGURE 8.5   *Else If passwords not equal.*

If this If evaluates to true, what are we going to do? Pretty much the same thing we did if the user didn't enter one of the required fields, just with a different error message. As a matter of fact, the easiest thing to do is to just copy the two actions under the IfMissingFields action under our new ElseIf. Do that to start and then change the contents of the Result action to match Listing 8.3.

Listing 8.3   Passwords Not Equal Error Message HTML

```
<!DOCTYPE HTML PUBLIC "-//W3C//DTD HTML3.2//EN">
<HTML>

<HEAD>
    <TITLE>Error: Password fields don't match</TITLE>
</HEAD>

<BODY>

<HR>
<FONT COLOR=RED>
<H4>Error: Password fields don't match</H4>

<P>
    The values you entered for password don't match, please re-enter
the password fields.
</P>

</FONT>
<HR>
</BODY>
</HTML>
```

There is one other possible error. The user could enter a username that is already taken, so we must search the database for the username the user entered. As a matter of fact, let's do this check before the rest of the checks.

Drag a Search action in above the IfMissingRequiredFields action. Drag into that Search action the users.username column in the Select Columns panel. Click the Criteria field and drag the users.username column in here. Check whether it is equal to the username argument. The Criteria tab should look like the one in Figure 8.6.

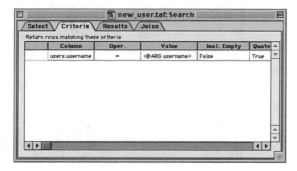

FIGURE 8.6 *Username search criteria.*

Now to check the results. Drag in an If action under the Search action. If the user is not in the database, the number of rows retrieved is 0. If the number of rows is greater than 0, we know the user is already in the database. So, the If must check the <@NUMROWS> meta tag to see whether it is greater than 0. The finished If action should look like Figure 8.7.

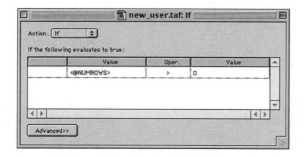

FIGURE 8.7 *Checking whether rows were retrieved.*

To respond to this error, we use the same mechanism we used before. So, copy the Result and Presentation actions from one of the other error cases. Then change the error message to something like Listing 8.4.

Listing 8.4   User Already in Database Error

```
<!DOCTYPE HTML PUBLIC "-//W3C//DTD HTML3.2//EN">
<HTML>

<HEAD>
    <TITLE>Error: User already exists</TITLE>
</HEAD>

<BODY>

<HR>
<FONT COLOR=RED>
<H4>Error:Error: User already exists</H4>

<P>
    The user name, <B><@ARG username> </B>, already exists.
Please enter a different name.
</P>

</FONT>
<HR>
</BODY>
</HTML>
```

The last little bit of cleanup you must do is change the If in the IfMissingRequiredFields into an ElseIf action. You can do this by opening the action and changing the popup.

The insert portion of the TAF should work fine as it is. You might want to change the message displayed when the insert is finished. We now have a TAF that enables you to add users to the database. The next thing we need to do is let the users log in.

Login.taf—Allows Users to Log In, Validating Them

This TAF seems like it should be easy, but it needs a couple things that add at least a little complication. First, it needs to allow a user to log in. This is pretty basic, but it needs to display a message if the login isn't valid. The other thing we need to do here is log out. What does it mean to be logged in? It means that you can move around the Web site, and the site knows who you are and what your user level is until you log out. Also, you should be logged out if you don't come back to the Web site for a while.

The technical details of what it means to be logged in are that Tango understands the concept of a user, and it tracks who a user is as he moves through a site requesting pages. As a matter of fact, you can assign variables that are specific to the user by giving the variables a scope of User. When the user logs in, we are assigning a user variable with her username and user level. In most cases, that means this information is stored in a cookie in the user's browser. When the user logs out, we clear this variable.

Create a new TAF and call it login.taf. The first thing we do is handle the default case, which is logging in. This is really a two-step process; we must first put up the form for logging in and then handle the form. Drag in an If action and configure it to check whether the _function argument is empty or login. It should look like Figure 8.8.

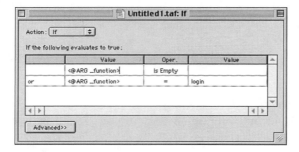

FIGURE 8.8 *The Login If action.*

Now let's create the form by dragging in a Result action and putting the HTML for the form in Listing 8.5.

Listing 8.5   Login Form HTML

```
<form method="POST" action="<@CGI><@APPFILE>?_function=login_w_arg&
<@USERREFERENCEARGUMENT>">
  <table>
    <tr valign=TOP align=LEFT>
      <td> Username:
        <input name="username" type=TEXT size=12 maxlength=32>
      </td>
    </tr>
    <tr valign=TOP align=LEFT>
      <td> Password:
        <input name="password" type=PASSWORD size=12 maxlength=50>
      </td>
    </tr>
```

```
  </table>
  <input type=SUBMIT value="Login" name="SUBMIT">
</form>
<a href="new_user.taf">Join Now!</a>
```

This gives us a form that the user can fill out to log in. When the user is done and clicks the Submit button, our TAF is called again with `_function` equal to login_w_arg. To handle this, we need another If action. Drag one in and make it check for the new `_function` argument.

In order to check the validity of the login, all we have to do is search the user table for the username and password. If any records are found, the login is valid. Drag in a Search action. Add users.username, users.userlevel, and users.password to the Select Columns field in the Select tab, and then drag only username and password to the Criteria tab. In Criteria, check them against the arguments with the same names. The Criteria tab should look like Figure 8.9.

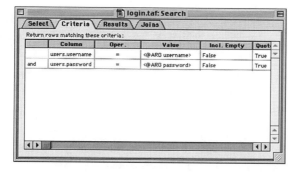

FIGURE 8.9   *Username and password search.*

If there are no results from this search, the user didn't log in correctly and we need to give him an error message. If there is a result, the username and password were found in the same record and the user is valid. Let's handle the valid case first. Close the Search action, select it, and open its ResultsHTML attribute.

What do we need to do to log in someone? We need to set a couple of user variables and then we need to tell the user he is logged in. Do that by entering Listing 8.6 into the ResultsHTML. The first thing this listing does is assign the values of the columns for username and userlevel to user variables with the same names.

Listing 8.6   Log in Response

```
<@ASSIGN NAME="username" VALUE="<@COLUMN 'users.username'>" SCOPE="user">
<@ASSIGN NAME="userlevel" VALUE="<@COLUMN 'users.userlevel'>" SCOPE="user">

<@COLUMN 'users.username'> is now logged in.
<P>
<A HREF="<@CGI><@APPFILE>?_function=logout">Logout</A>
```

Next, let's handle the case where the user logs in incorrectly. Select the Search action and open the NoResultsHTML attribute. Give the user a message saying the login was incorrect and linking him to try again, by entering Listing 8.7.

Listing 8.7   Invalid Login Message

```
<HR>
<FONT Color=Red>
Login incorrect.   The user name or password you supplied was invalid.
</FONT>
<HR>
<P>
<A HREF="<@CGI><@APPFILE>?_function=login">Please try again.</A>
```

Let's handle the logout case. Add another If action for the case where _function is logout. All this case has to do is clear the username and userlevel variables and tell the user she is logged out. We can do the clearing with an Assign action, or we can use the Assign meta tag. We'll use the meta tag so that all our logout code is in one action. Drag in a Result action under the logout If, and then enter Listing 8.8 in it.

Listing 8.8   User Logged Out

```
<@ASSIGN NAME="username" VALUE="" SCOPE="user">
<@ASSIGN NAME="userlevel" VALUE="" SCOPE="user">

You are now logged out.
```

That's all there is to it. Now you can use this TAF to log users in and out of the system. We use the user variables in later chapters to know who a user is and whether he has access to given pages. They are very useful for tracking a user through the Web site as well.

Admin TAFs

user_admin.taf—Allows an Admin to List, Edit, and Delete Users

The list of things an admin needs to do to the user table might look familiar. It is exactly the things the Search builder produces. So, let's use a Search builder to create our user admin TAF. Create a new TAF named user_admin.taf, and then drop in a Search builder.

You really have two choices on how to start the user admin process: You can search for a username or you could just list them all. We use a search paradigm because sometimes you just want to change a single user and a search paradigm is easier for that. If you want to see a list of every user, don't enter anything in the form and its search will bring back a complete list. Drag the column users.username into the Search tab's Search Columns pane. You can go with the default column options.

When the username list is displayed, let's display the userlevel as well. This makes finding a user's level easy. To do this, drag in the users.username and users.userlevel columns. Again, you can go with the default column options.

Last, configure the Details tab by dragging in the whole user table. Because the username is the primary key and we are using it as a foreign key in other tables, we never want to change it. Therefore, don't allow editing of this field. Password should be editable, so click on the Allow Update checkbox.

For the user level, we want to limit the number to a range of numbers. The easiest way to allow selection from a range is if editing of the field uses a popup with the available user levels in the pop-up menu. The builder easily supports this idea. Select the users.userlevel column, click Allow Update on, and then change the Field Type pop-up to Pop-up Menu. When you do, you get a Field Properties dialog. An HTML pop-up tag takes a display name for each item and the value you want sent on for that popup. This dialog enables you to enter each item. Click Add on Mac, New on Windows to add a new item, and then type 1 in the Name field and press the tab key. The value of the Name field will be automatically entered in the Value field. Repeat this process until you have the values 1 through 10 in the dialog. The dialog should end up looking something like Figure 8.10. Click OK to close the window.

FIGURE 8.10 *Pop-up field properties.*

Build and close the builder as well. This should be all we need for user admin. Deploy the TAF and see how it works.

Remember that this is only the beginning of the whole user system. In other chapters in this section, you see how to attach data to a user without modifying the user table, and how to enforce security based on user level.

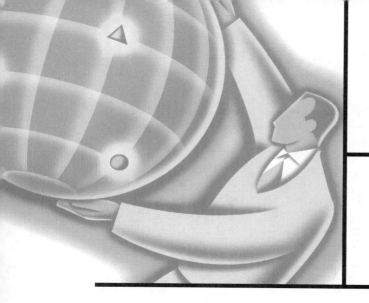

CHAPTER 9

User Profiles

What We'll Learn

- How to associate information to a user
- How to search and insert data into multiple tables from one form
- `<@INCLUDE>` tag for including files in TAFs

Purpose

In this chapter, we expand our user system by associating information in different database tables with a user. This information will be bibliographical information in the form of a profile.

Planning

Feature List

- Create a user profile for a user. A user profile contains information that is used in only one part of the Web site but is specific to a single user.
- The user should be able to edit her profile.
- Other users should be able to view user profiles.

- Some information should be private to a user if he so desires. In this case, the user can choose whether his email address is public. His real name is always private.

Database Schema

One of the purposes of this chapter is to show that we can attach data to a user without having to modify the core user table, so the data itself isn't mission-critical. The only thing that has to be in this table is the foreign key back to the main user table; in our case, that is the username. All the other data is just my personal preference for what I'd like to know about a user, along with some meta data like whether the user wants his email address made available to other members.

Database Table Name: user_profiles

Column Name	Data Type	Size
username	Char	30
realname	Char	30
email_address	Char	50
public_email	Char	10
date_of_membership	Timestamp	
home_city	Char	30
home_state	Char	30
home_country	Char	30
personalURL	Char	255
biography	Char	blob

```
CREATE TABLE user_profiles (
    username char(30) FOREIGN KEY,
    realname char(30),
    email_address char(40),
    public_email char(10),
    date_of_membership  timestamp,
    home_city char(30),
    home_state char(30),
    home_country char(30),
    personalURL char(255),
    biography BLOB
)
```

Creating the TAFs

Why have user profiles? One of the goals of any Web site is to build a community. A community is a web of relationships between people with similar interests. The only way to build those relationships is to have users interact with each other. User profiles are one way to do that. They enable the exchange of information about a user with another user.

I use this table as data for my own Web site, so let me explain what each item is and how it is used. The first thing in the table is the username, which is there mainly to link us back to the core user table.

realname: Back in the day of BBSes, people didn't use their real names on bulletin boards, but instead had handles. I like that idea, but as a Webmaster, I want to know who people really are. So, this field is private to the admins of the site and contains the user's real name.

email_address: This is the user's email address. When the user signs up, he has to give us an email address, and we automatically send him an email. One of the purposes of doing this is to make sure that the user didn't scam us. If the email bounces, we know the user isn't valid and can delete him. This isn't full proof, however. A user could give someone else's email address and it wouldn't bounce, but it wouldn't be the user either. A solution to this is to generate a random password and mail it to the provided email address. This would ensure that the user actually had access to the address he gave.

public_email: This is a flag to tell us whether to make a user's email address public.

date_of_membership: When a user joins, we put the date she did so in this field. It enables users to know how long someone has been on the site.

home_city, home_state, home_country: The Internet is an international forum, and this data tells us where the user is from.

personalURL: Lots of people have Web sites these days, and it is a good way to learn more about them. This URL shows up as a link in the user's profile.

biography: One of the flaws mentioned in Dr. Jakob Nielsen's "The Top Ten *New* Mistakes of Web Design," `http://www.useit.com/alertbox/990530.html`, is a lack of biographies. He says you should always include biographical information about yourself on your Web site. I got to thinking that if people really like this for the owners of the Web site, won't they like it for every member? Look at how popular AOL's member profiles are. So, we are going to allow users to write biographies about themselves for their profiles.

Some of these fields are required, not because we need them for the database, but because we need them for the Web site. We always need a valid email address and a real name. We also need to know whether the user wants his email address made public, but we can just give the user a default value, instead of requiring him to enter something. We default to not making the email address public. The rest of the fields are not required and the user can leave them blank.

User TAF

When a user joins, we want him to enter the information that is required in the user profile. So, it seems we should not make writing the user profile a separate step from providing a username and password for basic user functionality. We will start with the new_user.taf we made for Chapter 8, "User Management," and expand it to include all the information needed in the user profile.

There are two things a user will need to do with his profile: enter it the first time and edit it later. The old new_user.taf enables us to enter it the first time, but not to edit it later. We need to change that.

New Users

Make a copy of your new_user.taf file from Chapter 8 and rename it edit_user.taf. Remember that we reused our form a number of times in the TAF by including it using a Presentation action. The actual form was in a file called new_user_form.html. That form was fairly simple, but as you can guess, our user profile form is considerably more complex. Listing 9.1 contains the new form. Enter it in a text file or get it off the CD, name it new_user_form.html, and put it in the same directory as your new edit_user.taf. Doing this replaces the old form with the new one without changing any of the TAF's actions. This TAF will still work, although it won't put any profile information in the database.

Listing 9.1   New Form for Entering User Profile

```
<HTML>
Becoming a member of Xianworldview is free and easy. Fill out the form
below and we will create a user account for you. You should read our <A
HREF="/articles/articles.taf?_function=emailuse">Privacy Policy</A>
before signing up to be a member of XWV.  By filling out this
form you are consenting to the provisions of the Privacy Policy.<P>

<FORM METHOD="POST" ACTION="<@CGI><@APPFILE>?_function=insert">

Items followed by an asterisk (<FONT COLOR="#FF0000">*</FONT>) are
required. Items followed by a (<FONT COLOR="#00FF00">p</FONT>) are
private and only available to moderators.

 All information except username can be edited in the future.
<TABLE border=1 width="372">
<TR VALIGN=TOP ALIGN=LEFT>
    <TD COLSPAN=2 bgcolor="#CCCCCC">
        User Information:
    </TD>
</TR>

<TR VALIGN=TOP ALIGN=LEFT>
    <TD>
        Username:
    </TD>
    <TD>
        <INPUT NAME="username" TYPE=TEXT SIZE=32 MAXLENGTH=32
VALUE="<@ARG username>"> <FONT COLOR="#FF0000">*</FONT>
    </TD>

</TR>
<TR VALIGN=TOP ALIGN=LEFT>
    <TD>
        Real Name:
    </TD>
    <TD>
        <INPUT NAME="realname" TYPE=TEXT SIZE=32 MAXLENGTH=32
VALUE="<@ARG realname>"> <FONT COLOR="#FF0000">*</FONT>
<FONT COLOR="#00FF00">p</FONT>
    </TD>
</TR>

<TR VALIGN=TOP ALIGN=LEFT>
    <TD>
        Password:
```

continues

Listing 9.1   (Continued)

```
    </TD>
    <TD>
        <INPUT NAME="password" TYPE=PASSWORD SIZE=40 MAXLENGTH=50
VALUE="<@ARG password>"><FONT COLOR="#FF0000">*</FONT>
        <INPUT NAME="sitename" TYPE="HIDDEN" Value="xianworldview.com">
    </TD>
</TR>
<TR VALIGN=TOP ALIGN=LEFT>
    <TD>
        Confirm Password:
    </TD>
    <TD>
        <INPUT NAME="conf_password" TYPE=PASSWORD SIZE=40
MAXLENGTH=50 VALUE="<@ARG conf_password>">
<FONT COLOR="#FF0000">*</FONT>
    </TD>
</TR>

<TR VALIGN=TOP ALIGN=LEFT>
    <TD>
        Email Address:
    </TD>
    <TD>
        <INPUT NAME="email_address" SIZE=40 MAXLENGTH=50
VALUE="<@ARG email_address>" ><FONT COLOR="#FF0000">*</FONT>
    </TD>
</TR>
<TR VALIGN=TOP ALIGN=LEFT>
    <TD>
        <A HREF="/articles/articles.taf?_function=emailuse">Privacy Policy</A>
    </TD>
    <TD>
        <@IFEMPTY VALUE="<@ARG pub_email>">
            <input type=checkbox name=pub_email VALUE="true" >
Allow any XWV visitor to see my e-mail address.
        <@ELSE>
            <input type=checkbox name=pub_email VALUE="true" CHECKED>
Allow any XWV visitor to see my e-mail address.
        </@IF>
    </TD>
</TR>

<TR VALIGN=TOP ALIGN=LEFT>
    <TD COLSPAN=2  bgcolor="#CCCCCC">
        Profile Information:
    </TD>
</TR>
<TR VALIGN=TOP ALIGN=LEFT>
    <TD colspan=2 width="372">
        All of the information in your user profile will be
```

```
publicly available.  You are not required to fill it out,
but we think you will find it fun.
     </TD>
</TR>

<TR VALIGN=TOP ALIGN=LEFT>
     <TD>
          Member Since:
     </TD>
     <TD>
          <@CURRENTDATE>
     </TD>
</TR>
<TR VALIGN=TOP ALIGN=LEFT>
     <TD>
          New Member Rank:
     </TD>
     <TD>
          1
     </TD>
</TR>

<TR VALIGN=TOP ALIGN=LEFT>
     <TD>
          Home Town:
     </TD>
     <TD>
          City: <INPUT NAME="city" SIZE=20 MAXLENGTH=50 VALUE="<@ARG city>">
          State: <INPUT NAME="state" SIZE=3 MAXLENGTH=50
VALUE="<@ARG state>"><BR>
          Country: <INPUT NAME="country" SIZE=20 MAXLENGTH=50
VALUE="<@ARG country>">
     </TD>
</TR>

<TR VALIGN=TOP ALIGN=LEFT>
     <TD>
          Personal Web Site:
     </TD>
     <TD>
          <@IFEMPTY VALUE="<@ARG personalURL>">
               URL: <INPUT NAME="personalURL" SIZE=40 MAXLENGTH=255
Value="http://">
          <@ELSE>
               URL: <INPUT NAME="personalURL" SIZE=40 MAXLENGTH=255
Value="<@ARG personalURL>">
          </@IF>
     </TD>
</TR>

<TR VALIGN=TOP ALIGN=LEFT>
     <TD>
```

continues

Listing 9.1   (Continued)

```
        Biography:
      </TD>
      <TD>
          <textarea rows="10" name="biography" cols="40">
<@ARG biography></textarea>

      </TD>
</TR>


</TABLE>
<INPUT TYPE=SUBMIT VALUE="Sign Up">
</FORM>
</BODY>
</HTML>
```

There is a lot of information in this HTML; let me point out the relevant points.

I'm using the actual text of the new user form from my own personal Web site, Xianworldview.com. The first paragraph on the page thanks the user for joining the site and points him to a privacy policy. It is important to tell users how you will use their personal information, so every site should have a written and available privacy policy, and you should let the users see it before they give you any information. Don't worry about the URL to the privacy policy; just insert your own in the HREF.

Next, we start the form. Any time you require users to fill in certain fields in a long form, you should give them a visual indication of which fields they have to fill out. Some Web sites do this by coloring the title text of the required fields red, but that doesn't help if the reader is colorblind. We are putting a red asterisk after each required field. That way, color-blind people will still see the asterisk. We also want the user to be sure which fields are private, so put a green P next to those fields. Whatever method you choose to tell your users which fields are required, you need to explain it to them above the form.

We also want to let the users know they can edit everything but the user-name in the future, so they don't get panicky about mistakes.

Most of the form is pretty standard and uses the convention of putting the argument tags in the value field that we used in Chapter 8. There are a couple of areas that are a little different.

One is the email address check box. The purpose of this check box is to let users tell us whether they want to make their email addresses public. This translates to the user_profile.public_email column in the database. But what goes in that column? If a user checks the box, we put `true` into the database. If the box isn't checked, we don't put anything in the column—we leave it empty. The challenge is that the HTML for a check box is a little tricky. The value attribute is sent only if the box is checked. If the box isn't checked, nothing is sent. So, we have to check whether the `public_email` argument is empty. If it is, don't check the check box, but still say that its value is `true`. It is the `CHECKED` keyword inside the tag that makes the box show up checked or not.

Another tag that is a little different is the URL box. We set a default value of "http://" so that the users will know they need to enter a complete URL.

Very few changes need to be made to the TAF to make it work. The main change is to add an Insert action so that the user profile information will be added to the database at the same time as the core user information. The second change is that you need to enforce your required field rules. Last, you want to send email after the user is confirmed.

First, let's add the Insert action. Drag a new Insert action into the TAF right next to the existing Insert action. Then drag all the fields from the user_profiles table and configure the values so that the action looks like one in Figure 9.1.

new_user.taf: Insert_profile

Insert the following row into the table: **user_profiles**

Column	Value	Quote Value
username	<@ARG username>	True
realname	<@ARG realname>	True
email_address	<@ARG email_address>	True
public_email	<@ARG pub_email>	True
date_of_membership	<@CURRENTDATE>	True
home_city	<@ARG city>	True
home_state	<@ARG state>	True
home_country	<@ARG country>	True
personalURL	<@ARG personalURL>	True
biography	<@ARG biography>	True

FIGURE 9.1   *An Insert action from the user_profiles table.*

We already check to make sure that the user enters a username and password in the IfMissingRequiredFields action; we just need to add the new fields to this action. Open it and add more criteria until the action looks like the one in Figure 9.2.

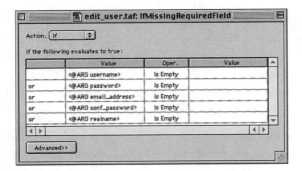

FIGURE 9.2 *The IfMissingRequiredField action.*

Now you need to change the error message in the MissingFieldsMessage Result action to add the check for email address and real name. See Listing 9.2.

Listing 9.2   Missing Fields Error Message

```
<!DOCTYPE HTML PUBLIC "-//W3C//DTD HTML3.2//EN">
<HTML>

<HEAD>
    <TITLE>Error: Missing Required Fields</TITLE>
</HEAD>

<BODY>

<HR>
<FONT COLOR=RED>
<H4>Error: Missing Required Fields</H4>

<P>
    The record could not be added because the following required fields were
    left empty:
</P>

<UL TYPE=SQUARE>
<@IFEMPTY <@ARG username>>
    <LI>Username
</@IF>
<@IFEMPTY <@ARG password>>
```

```
    <LI>Password
</@IF>
<@IFEMPTY <@ARG email_address>>
    <LI>E-mail address.
</@IF>
<@IFEMPTY <@ARG realname>>
    <LI>Real Name.
</@IF>
</UL>
</FONT>
<HR>
</BODY>
</HTML>
```

For our last change, we must add an Email action to send email to the users, using the email addresses they supplied us. Do this by dragging an Email action in under the two Insert actions. Then configure it something like Figure 9.3, but use your own email addresses.

FIGURE 9.3   *The welcome Email action.*

Notice that I used the <@INCLUDE> tag in the email message. This tag works a lot like the Presentation action, putting its argument file in the body of the email message. You could have entered the text of the email message in the body area of the action, but this method makes it easier to change the message in the future without editing the action. The text contained in "welcome_email.txt" is shown in Listing 9.3. Enter it in a text file and put it in the same directory as the TAF.

Listing 9.3   Welcome Email Message

```
Thank you for signing up to be a member of Xianworldview.com.

This e-mail is to assure you gave us a correct e-mail address and let you know
we got your registration.

Name: <@ARG username>
Password: <@ARG password>
Real name: <@ARG realname>
Email: <@ARG email_address>

This is a URL to see what other members see when viewing your profile.

http://www.xianworldview.com/members/profile.taf?_function=find_user&username=
<@ARG username>
```

That handles the entire process for entering a new user.

Editing User Profiles

The user must be able to edit his profile information. We want the user to be able to edit only his user data, not the data of any other users. To ensure this, we provide only an "edit self" interface to the editing. We don't ask the user for a username to edit; instead, we let the user edit only the user they are logged in as. Because there is a lot of overlap between the new user form and the editing, we'll add this functionality to the edit_user.taf.

How do we let a user edit his profile? Let's say that you have a page for handling member functions on your Web site. On that page you might have a link that enables a user to edit his user profile. But if no one is logged in and the user follows this link, he should get an error. Let's add that functionality to our TAF first. Drag a new If action into the edit_user.taf file right before the IfNewUserForm. Configure it to check _function is "edit". You might want to rename the If action to IfEditUser.

Remember that we aren't passing in which user we want to edit; instead, we are depending on the user being logged in. How do we tell whether the user is logged in? We look at the user variable username. We need to handle the case that the user for some reason got into try and edit, but didn't log in. Drag in a new If action under the IfEditUser action. Configure it like the action in Figure 9.4, to see whether the username variable is empty.

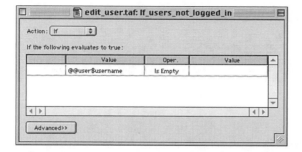

FIGURE 9.4   *Checking to see whether the current user is logged in.*

If the user isn't logged in, you need to put up an error message; use the code in Listing 9.4. You also want to drag a Return action after the Result action so that the TAF won't keep going through the If actions and get the unknown error condition, or execute other code you don't want executed. A Return action stops execution of the TAF at its location.

Listing 9.4   No Logged-In User Error Message

```
<HR>
<FONT Color=Red>
You must be logged in order to edit a user profile.
</FONT>
<HR>
```

The first thing we must do to enable editing of the current user is to get all the information about the user out of the database. We use virtually the same HTML for editing that we used for entering, so we need all the information in both user tables. To get this information, drag in a new Search action at the level under the IfEditUser action, but after the logged-in If. Drag both the users and user_profiles tables into the Search action. Tango will ask you to define a join; make sure that you are using the username column of each table for the join.

The Criteria tab should look like the one shown in Figure 9.5. We are searching for the current user by username. There should only be one record returned because this is the primary key. You could just as easily search on the user_profiles.username column.

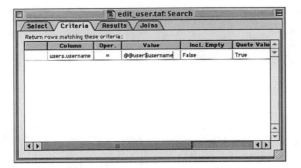

FIGURE 9.5   *Search for user criteria.*

If the current user isn't in the database there will be no result from this
search. Just to be safe, we will handle the no-result case. Open the
NoResult attribute for the search action and enter the code in Listing 9.5.

Listing 9.5   User Not Found Error

```
<HR>
<FONT Color=Red>
Your user record isn't found the database.
</FONT>
<HR>
```

If we find a user, we want to display a form with all the fields already
filled in. The structure of the form is the same as the new user form, but
we won't use arguments as the default values. Instead, we will use the
columns returned by the search. As with the new user form, we want to
keep this form in its own text file. So, create a new text file, name it
edit_user_form.html, and enter the code in Listing 9.6 into it.

Listing 9.6   Edit User Form

```
<HTML>
<FORM METHOD="POST" ACTION="<@CGI>
<@APPFILE>?_function=insert&<@USERREFERENCEARGUMENT>">

Items followed by an asterisk (<FONT COLOR="#FF0000">*</FONT>) are required.
Items followed by a (<FONT COLOR="#00FF00">p</FONT>) are private and only
available to moderators.

All information except username can be edited in the future.
<TABLE border=1 width="372">
```

```
<TR VALIGN=TOP ALIGN=LEFT>
    <TD COLSPAN=2 >
        User Information:
    </TD>
</TR>

<TR VALIGN=TOP ALIGN=LEFT>
    <TD>
        Username:
    </TD>
    <TD>
        @@local$current_user
        <INPUT NAME="username" TYPE="HIDDEN" Value="@@local$current_user">
    </TD>

</TR>
<TR VALIGN=TOP ALIGN=LEFT>
    <TD>
        Real Name:
    </TD>
    <TD>
        <INPUT NAME="realname" TYPE=TEXT SIZE=32 MAXLENGTH=32 VALUE="
<@COLUMN user_profiles.realname>"> <FONT COLOR="#FF0000">*</FONT>
<FONT COLOR="#00FF00">p</FONT>
    </TD>
</TR>

<TR VALIGN=TOP ALIGN=LEFT>
    <TD>
        Password:
    </TD>
    <TD>
        <INPUT NAME="password" TYPE=PASSWORD SIZE=40 MAXLENGTH=50 VALUE=
"<@COLUMN users.password>"><FONT COLOR="#FF0000">*</FONT>
    </TD>
</TR>
<TR VALIGN=TOP ALIGN=LEFT>
    <TD>
        Confirm Password:
    </TD>
    <TD>
        <INPUT NAME="conf_password" TYPE=PASSWORD SIZE=40 MAXLENGTH=50 VALUE=
"<@COLUMN users.password>"><FONT COLOR="#FF0000">*</FONT>
    </TD>
</TR>

<TR VALIGN=TOP ALIGN=LEFT>
    <TD>
        Email Address:
    </TD>
    <TD>
        <INPUT NAME="email_address" SIZE=40 MAXLENGTH=50 VALUE="
```

continues

Listing 9.6   (Continued)

```
<@COLUMN user_profiles.email_address>" ><FONT COLOR="#FF0000">*</FONT>
    </TD>
</TR>
<TR VALIGN=TOP ALIGN=LEFT>
    <TD>
        <A HREF="/articles/articles.taf?_function=emailuse">Privacy Policy</A>
    </TD>
    <TD>
        <@IFEMPTY value="<@COLUMN user_profiles.pub_email>">
            <input type=checkbox name=pub_email VALUE="true">
        <@ELSE>
            <input type=checkbox name=pub_email VALUE="true" CHECKED>
        </@IF>

        Allow any XWV visitor to see my e-mail address.
    </TD>
</TR>

<TR VALIGN=TOP ALIGN=LEFT>
    <TD COLSPAN=2 >
        Profile Information:
    </TD>
</TR>
<TR VALIGN=TOP ALIGN=LEFT>
    <TD colspan=2 width="372">
        All of the information in your user profile will be publicly available.
  You are not required to fill it out, but we think you will find it fun.
    </TD>
</TR>

<TR VALIGN=TOP ALIGN=LEFT>
    <TD>
        Member Since:
    </TD>
    <TD>
        <@IFEMPTY value="<@COLUMN user_profiles.date_of_membership>">
            <@CURRENTDATE>
            <INPUT NAME="date_of_membership" TYPE="HIDDEN" Value="
            <@CURRENTDATE>">
        <@ELSE>
            <@COLUMN user_profiles.date_of_membership>
            <INPUT NAME="date_of_membership" TYPE="HIDDEN" Value="<@COLUMN
            user_profiles.date_of_membership>">
        </@IF>
    </TD>
</TR>
<TR VALIGN=TOP ALIGN=LEFT>
```

```
        <TD>
            New Member Rank:
        </TD>
        <TD>
            <@VAR NAME="rank_name_array[1,<@COLUMN users.userlevel>]">
        </TD>
</TR>

<TR VALIGN=TOP ALIGN=LEFT>
        <TD>
            Home Town:
        </TD>
        <TD>
            City: <INPUT NAME="home_city" SIZE=20 MAXLENGTH=50 VALUE="
                 <@COLUMN user_profiles.home_city>">
            State: <INPUT NAME="home_state" SIZE=3 MAXLENGTH=50 VALUE="<@COLUMN
                 user_profiles.home_state>"><BR>
            Country: <INPUT NAME="home_country" SIZE=20 MAXLENGTH=50 VALUE="
                 <@COLUMN user_profiles.home_country>">
        </TD>
</TR>

<TR VALIGN=TOP ALIGN=LEFT>
        <TD>
            Personal Web Site:
        </TD>
        <TD>
            <@IFEMPTY VALUE="<@COLUMN user_profiles.email>">
                URL: <INPUT NAME="personalURL" SIZE=40 MAXLENGTH=255 Value="http://">
            <@ELSE>
                URL: <INPUT NAME="personalURL" SIZE=40 MAXLENGTH=255 Value=
                     "<@COLUMN user_profiles.personalURL>">
            </@IF>
        </TD>
</TR>

<TR VALIGN=TOP ALIGN=LEFT>
        <TD>
            Biography:
        </TD>
        <TD>
            <textarea rows="10" name="biography" cols="40">
            <@COLUMN user_profiles.biography></textarea>

        </TD>
</TR>


</TABLE>
<INPUT TYPE=SUBMIT VALUE="Submit">
```

continues

Listing 9.6   (Continued)

```
</FORM>
</BODY>
</HTML>
```

After you create this file, open the Results attribute for the Search action and add this statement to include the file:

```
<@INCLUDE FILE="<@APPFILEPATH>edit_user_form.html">
```

Also, drag in a Return action after the Search action.

There isn't much that is different from the new user form except for the replacement of the `<@ARG>` tags with `<@COLUMN>` tags. You'll notice even the URL for posting the data is the same as the new user form. But doesn't that mean we are doing an insert for the data passed in? As a matter of fact, it does; so, we need to change that. But it also means that after the user clicks Submit on this form, we use the new user form for any future edits. If the user enters invalid data, it is passed back to the new user form as arguments.

Let's handle the case where the user changes something and clicks Submit. Now the insert portion of our TAF is called, and we must make sure that we don't try to insert the user again. We already check whether the user exists, so let's just add a check here for whether there is a logged in user. If there is a logged-in user, we are editing, not creating a new user.

Drag a new If action inside the If_username_found action. Have that action check whether `@@user$username` is empty. If it is empty, we want to do the same thing we have been doing in this case. After the If is created, drag the two actions that were already there under the If.

Now handle the opposite case, where there is a logged-in user. Drag an Else action under the If action. This Else action is where we perform the update of the database. You need to drag in two Update actions and configure them like the actions in Figures 9.6 and 9.7. One update handles the user table, and the other action handles the user_profiles table.

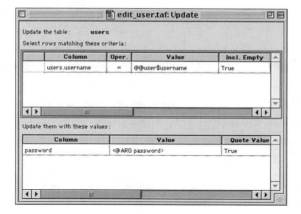

FIGURE **9.6**   *Update the users table.*

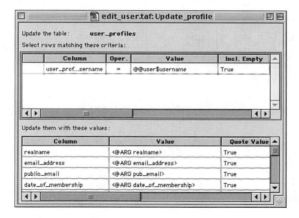

FIGURE **9.7**   *Update the user_profiles table.*

After these actions are executed, the user's profile information will have been updated. You want to give the user a message telling him so. Drag a Result action under the Updates, and enter something like Listing 9.7 into it. You also want to drag in a Return action to stop the TAF at this point.

Listing 9.7   Update Done Message

```
You user profile has been updated.
```

There are a couple of housekeeping chores we need to perform. First, we need to make sure that the user filled in the required fields before we update the database. There are already actions to do this in the TAF, but we need to move them where they will affect the update as well as the new user. Instead of the If/IfElse/Else logic we used for the new user, we will check each field individually and put in Return actions to end the program flow after an error. Select the IfMissingRequiredField action and the ElseIfCheck_password action and drag them over the find_user_name Search action. Now, we first check to make sure that the user filled in all the fields. Add a Return to the end of this If so that the TAF won't continue to execute after it puts up the error and the page again.

Next, open the ElseIfCheck_Password action and change it to a simple If action. You might want to change the name of the action for completeness. Expand this action and add a Return action to the end.

The TAF checks whether there is a username and handles both cases here. But if this is the new user case, we want the TAF to perform the Insert if the If_username_found isn't true, so we can leave the Else Do Insert where it is. The final TAF should look like the one shown in Figure 9.8.

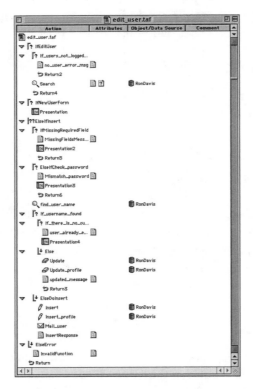

FIGURE 9.8   *The final user TAF.*

Showing the Profile

The last TAF we need for the user is the one that displays the user profile without allowing it to be edited. This is what other users see and shows only the public data.

It is a fairly simple TAF. It requires that you pass in the username to be displayed. We pass it in the username argument. It uses this argument to do a search on the database and displays the profile.

Create a new TAF called profile.taf. Drag a Search action into the TAF. Add the users and user_profile tables to the Search action. Set the Criteria to look for the argument username in the username column of the users table.

Open the ResultHTML attribute. We are going to store the display information for the profile in a file called display_profile.html. Add an include statement, and list the following to the ResultHTML:

```
<@INCLUDE FILE="<@APPFILEPATH>display_profile.html">
```

Create a new text file, enter Listing 9.8 into it, and save it as display_profile.html in the same folder as the TAF. This will display the user's profile information.

Listing 9.8   User Profile HTML

```
<TABLE border=1 width="372">

<TR VALIGN=TOP ALIGN=LEFT>
    <TD COLSPAN=2>
        <@COLUMN 'user_profiles.username'>
    </TD>

</TR>

<@IFEQUAL VALUE1="true" VALUE2="<@COLUMN 'user_profiles.public_email'>">
<TR VALIGN=TOP ALIGN=LEFT>
    <TD>
        Email Address:
    </TD>
    <TD>
        <A HREF="mailto:<@COLUMN 'user_profiles.email_address'>"><@COLUMN
'user_profiles.email_address'></A>
    </TD>
</TR>
```

continues

Listing 9.8   (Continued)

```
</@IF>

<TR VALIGN=TOP ALIGN=LEFT>
    <TD>
        Member Since:
    </TD>
    <TD>
        <@COLUMN 'user_profiles.date_of_membership'>
    </TD>
</TR>
<TR VALIGN=TOP ALIGN=LEFT>
    <TD>
        Rank:
    </TD>
    <TD>
     <@VAR NAME="rank_name_array[1,<@COLUMN 'users.userlevel'> ]" SCOPE=DOMAIN>

    </TD>
</TR>

<TR VALIGN=TOP ALIGN=LEFT>
    <TD>
        Home Town:
    </TD>
    <TD>
        <@COLUMN 'user_profiles.home_city'>, <@COLUMN
'user_profiles.home_state'>, <@COLUMN 'user_profiles.home_country'>
    </TD>
</TR>

<TR VALIGN=TOP ALIGN=LEFT>
    <TD>
        Personal Web Site:
    </TD>
    <TD>
        <A HREF="<@COLUMN 'user_profiles.personalURL'>"><@COLUMN
         'user_profiles.personalURL'></A>
    </TD>
</TR>

<TR VALIGN=TOP ALIGN=LEFT>
    <TD>
        Biography:
    </TD>
    <TD>
        <@COLUMN 'user_profiles.biography' ENCODING=multilinehtml>

    </TD>
```

```
</TR>
```

```
</TABLE>
```

There are a number of ways to get the `username` argument filled for calling
the Profile.taf. One of the easiest ways is to create a page that lists all the
users of the site and their usernames in a link to this TAF. I leave that as
an exercise for the user.

Admin TAFs

There are two main things an admin will want do to users: edit and
delete. We already have the ability to delete a user in the user_admin.taf
from Chapter 8. All we need to do is add a delete in the new user_profile
table. What we'll do here is add all our functionality to the current
user_admin.taf.

Open user_admin.taf. Expand the ElseIfDelete action. Under this is a single Delete action that deletes the selected user from the users table. It uses
the `<@ARG users_uid1>` to specify the user. If you go back up to the
ElseIfDetails action and open the ResultHTML attribute of the Search
action, you can find out what users_uid1 is. It is the column users.user-
name, which is the primary key of the table.

To do the delete from the user_profiles table, we need another Delete
action. Drag one in under the existing Delete action. Then set it up to look
like the one in Figure 9.9.

Column	Oper.	Value	Incl. Empty	Quote Value
user_profiles.username	=	<@ARG users_uid1>	True	True

FIGURE 9.9   *Delete from the user_profiles table.*

To do an edit, we must piggyback on the Details view of the previous
user_admin.taf. There is only one Search action in this action. We need to
modify the search to include the user_profiles table. Drag all the fields
from the table into the action and define the join like all the others.

We need to display the information for editing in a way that lets us change all the fields. I took the edit_user_form.html file and added a couple of the parts of the ResultHTML attribute of the existing Search action. We can now change the userlevel and delete the user from this new set of source file. Create a new text file and put Listing 9.9 in it; save it with the name admin_user_form.html.

Listing 9.9   Editing Form for the Admin

```
<HTML>
<FORM METHOD="POST" ACTION="<@CGI><@APPFILE>?_function=update&">

Items followed by an asterisk (<FONT COLOR="#FF0000">*</FONT>)
are required. Items followed by a
(<FONT COLOR="#00FF00">p</FONT>) are private and only
available to moderators.

All information except username can be edited in the future.
<TABLE border=1 width="372">
<TR VALIGN=TOP ALIGN=LEFT>
    <TD COLSPAN=2 >
        User Information:
    </TD>
</TR>

<TR VALIGN=TOP ALIGN=LEFT>
    <TD>
        Username:
    </TD>
    <TD>
        <@COLUMN "users.username">
        <INPUT NAME="users_uid1" TYPE="HIDDEN"
Value="<@COLUMN "users.username">">
    </TD>

</TR>
<TR VALIGN=TOP ALIGN=LEFT>
    <TD>
        Real Name:
    </TD>
    <TD>
        <INPUT NAME="realname" TYPE=TEXT SIZE=32
MAXLENGTH=32 VALUE="<@COLUMN user_profiles.realname>">
<FONT COLOR="#FF0000">*</FONT><FONT COLOR="#00FF00">p</FONT>
    </TD>
</TR>
<TR VALIGN=TOP ALIGN=LEFT>
    <TD>
        Userlevel:
    </TD>
```

```
    <TD>
        <SELECT NAME="userlevel" SIZE=1>
    <OPTION VALUE="1" <@IFEQUAL <@COLUMN "users.userlevel"> "1">
SELECTED</@IF>>1
    <OPTION VALUE="2" <@IFEQUAL <@COLUMN "users.userlevel"> "2">
SELECTED</@IF>2
    <OPTION VALUE="3" <@IFEQUAL <@COLUMN "users.userlevel"> "3">
SELECTED</@IF>>3
    <OPTION VALUE="4" <@IFEQUAL <@COLUMN "users.userlevel"> "4">
SELECTED</@IF>>4
    <OPTION VALUE="5" <@IFEQUAL <@COLUMN "users.userlevel"> "5">
SELECTED</@IF>5
    <OPTION VALUE="6" <@IFEQUAL <@COLUMN "users.userlevel"> "6">
SELECTED</@IF>6
    <OPTION VALUE="7" <@IFEQUAL <@COLUMN "users.userlevel"> "7">
SELECTED</@IF>>7
    <OPTION VALUE="8" <@IFEQUAL <@COLUMN "users.userlevel"> "8">
SELECTED</@IF>>8
    <OPTION VALUE="9" <@IFEQUAL <@COLUMN "users.userlevel"> "9">
SELECTED</@IF>>9
    <OPTION VALUE="10" <@IFEQUAL <@COLUMN "users.userlevel"> "10">
SELECTED</@IF>>10</SELECT>
    </TD>
</TR>

<TR VALIGN=TOP ALIGN=LEFT>
    <TD>
        Password:
    </TD>
    <TD>
        <INPUT NAME="password" TYPE=PASSWORD SIZE=40 MAXLENGTH=50
VALUE="<@COLUMN users.password>">
<FONT COLOR="#FF0000">*</FONT>
    </TD>
</TR>
<TR VALIGN=TOP ALIGN=LEFT>
    <TD>
        Confirm Password:
    </TD>
    <TD>
        <INPUT NAME="conf_password" TYPE=PASSWORD SIZE=40
MAXLENGTH=50 VALUE="<@COLUMN users.password>">
<FONT COLOR="#FF0000">*</FONT>
    </TD>
</TR>

<TR VALIGN=TOP ALIGN=LEFT>
    <TD>
        Email Address:
    </TD>
    <TD>
        <INPUT NAME="email_address" SIZE=40 MAXLENGTH=50
```

continues

Listing 9.9   (Continued)

```
VALUE="<@COLUMN user_profiles.email_address>" >
<FONT COLOR="#FF0000">*</FONT>
    </TD>
</TR>
<TR VALIGN=TOP ALIGN=LEFT>
    <TD>
        <A HREF="/articles/articles.taf?_function=emailuse">
Privacy Policy</A>
    </TD>
    <TD>
        <@IFEMPTY value="<@COLUMN user_profiles.pub_email>">
            <input type=checkbox name=pub_email VALUE="true">
        <@ELSE>
            <input type=checkbox name=pub_email VALUE="true" CHECKED>
        </@IF>

        Allow any XWV visitor to see my e-mail address.
    </TD>
</TR>

<TR VALIGN=TOP ALIGN=LEFT>
    <TD COLSPAN=2 >
        Profile Information:
    </TD>
</TR>
<TR VALIGN=TOP ALIGN=LEFT>
    <TD colspan=2 width="372">
        All of the information in your user profile
will be publicly available.  You are not required to
fill it out, but we think you will find it fun.
    </TD>
</TR>

<TR VALIGN=TOP ALIGN=LEFT>
    <TD>
        Member Since:
    </TD>
    <TD>
        <@IFEMPTY value="<@COLUMN user_profiles.date_of_
membership>">
            <@CURRENTDATE>
            <INPUT NAME="date_of_membership" TYPE="HIDDEN"
Value="<@CURRENTDATE>">
        <@ELSE>
            <@COLUMN user_profiles.date_of_membership>
            <INPUT NAME="date_of_membership" TYPE="HIDDEN"
Value="<@COLUMN user_profiles.date_of_membership>">
        </@IF>
    </TD>
</TR>
<TR VALIGN=TOP ALIGN=LEFT>
```

```
      <TD>
            New Member Rank:
      </TD>
      <TD>
            <@VAR NAME="rank_name_array[1,<@COLUMN users.userlevel>]">
      </TD>
</TR>

<TR VALIGN=TOP ALIGN=LEFT>
      <TD>
            Home Town:
      </TD>
      <TD>
            City: <INPUT NAME="home_city" SIZE=20 MAXLENGTH=50
VALUE="<@COLUMN user_profiles.home_city>">
            State: <INPUT NAME="home_state" SIZE=3 MAXLENGTH=50
VALUE="<@COLUMN user_profiles.home_state>"><BR>
            Country: <INPUT NAME="home_country" SIZE=20 MAXLENGTH=50
VALUE="<@COLUMN user_profiles.home_country>">
      </TD>
</TR>

<TR VALIGN=TOP ALIGN=LEFT>
      <TD>
            Personal Web Site:
      </TD>
      <TD>
            <@IFEMPTY VALUE="<@COLUMN user_profiles.email>">
                  URL: <INPUT NAME="personalURL" SIZE=40 MAXLENGTH=255
Value="http://">
            <@ELSE>
                  URL: <INPUT NAME="personalURL" SIZE=40 MAXLENGTH=255
Value="<@COLUMN user_profiles.personalURL>">
            </@IF>
      </TD>
</TR>

<TR VALIGN=TOP ALIGN=LEFT>
      <TD>
            Biography:
      </TD>
      <TD>
            <textarea rows="10" name="biography" cols="40"><@COLUMN
user_profiles.biography></textarea>

      </TD>
</TR>


</TABLE>
<INPUT TYPE=SUBMIT VALUE="Submit">
```

continues

Listing 9.9   (Continued)

```
</FORM>

<FORM METHOD=GET ACTION="<@CGI><@APPFILE>">
<INPUT TYPE=HIDDEN NAME="_function" VALUE="delete">
<INPUT TYPE=HIDDEN NAME="users_uid1" VALUE="<@COLUMN "users.username">">
<INPUT TYPE=HIDDEN NAME="_userReference" VALUE="<@UserReference>">
<INPUT TYPE=SUBMIT VALUE="Delete">
</FORM>

</BODY>
</HTML>
```

For this form to be used, you must change the ResultHTML attribute for the Search action to include the file. Here's the include line:

```
<@INCLUDE FILE="<@APPFILEPATH>admin_user_form.html">
```

Now your user_admin.taf file will handle editing both tables, but the new information won't go into the database until you make a change to ElseIfUpdate. Just as we had to do a delete for both tables, we must also do an update for each table. Drag in a new Update action right under the one that is already there. Configure the Update action to handle the user_profiles table. It should look like the one in Figure 9.10.

FIGURE 9.10   *Update the user_profiles table.*

Now you have a complete user management system. If you need to add any other data that had to do with a user, you know how. It might be a little tedious to add deletes and updates for each new user element, but in the end it is much easier than trying to modify your database any time you have to add data.

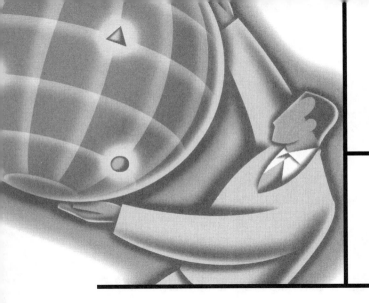

CHAPTER 10

User Security

What We'll Learn

- How to create a Tango Class File (TCF)

Purpose

We will create a TCF that contains various functions for users, including a means of getting a user's level and using that information to lock people out of a given page based on user level.

Planning

Feature List

- Create a TCF method to get the current user's username and another TCF method to get the current user's level

- Create a TCF method for displaying a userbar, which is HTML that contains the current user's name and level or an alternative message if there is no current user

- Create a TCF method that can be used to validate a user's login and log him in

Database Schema

This chapter doesn't create any new database tables, but uses the tables created in the other chapters.

Creating the TAFs

This chapter doesn't build a specific page for the user, but rather creates a toolbox of routines for use on any page. We create a routine for checking a user's level, and I explain how to use this routine to keep users out of pages they shouldn't be in.

User Security TCFs

In Tango, an *object* is a self-contained collection of code. This code is broken up into methods, each of which performs a specific function. Tango supports three types of objects: JavaBeans, Tango Class Files, and COM objects (on Windows).

A *method* is a piece of code inside an object that performs a specific piece of functionality. Methods can have parameters, or values, passed into them. Methods can also return values to the calling application.

A TCF is a Tango Class File, which is an object that contains Tango actions. TCFs are created in the Tango IDE, similar to the way we create TAFs. In this chapter, we will create a TCF that contains methods to perform various user security functions. These functions provide admin-like functionality, but are generally used in TAFs to enforce security.

From the File menu, select New, and then select Tango Class File from the submenu. You will get a window like the one shown in Figure 10.1. Name this TCF user_sec.tcf.

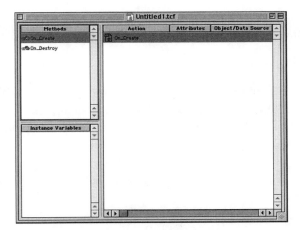

FIGURE 10.1   *An empty TCF window.*

There are three subpanes in this window. At the top left is the Methods subpane, which lists all the methods inside this TCF. If you click a given method name, it is highlighted and the right-side panel shows you the Tango actions that make up that method. The right-side pane is almost identical to the TAF window you are used to. It contains a series of Tango actions that are executed just as actions are executed in a TAF.

On the bottom left is the Instance Variables subpane. TCFs introduce two new variable scopes: method and instance. A *method variable scope* allows the variable to exist only during the current call to this method. All method parameters are method scopes. *Instance variable scope* means that the variable exists for as long as the current object exists. Remember when we used the Utility TCF that there was a two-step process: First, you created the object by using the Create Object action, and then you called a method by using a Call Method action. You could call multiple methods from the single Create Object action call because the Create Object call actually created a variable for that object. An instance variable stays around as long as the object variable in your TAF does. A method variable exists only from the time you call with the Call Method action until that action returns some result.

Two methods are already there when you create a new TCF: On_Create and On_Destroy. On_Create is called when the object is created, enabling you to do setup before any methods are called. On_Destroy is called just before the object is destroyed to enable you to do any clean up you might need.

For this TCF, we will create four new methods to fulfill our requirements: GetCurrentUserName, GetCurrentUserLevel, GetUserBar, ValidateLogin.

GetCurrentUserName

To create a new method, in the Method subpane, pop up the contextual menu by Control-clicking (on the Macintosh) or right-clicking (on Windows). Select New Method from the context menu. A new method will appear in the Methods pane, and you can rename it GetCurrentUser Name. Notice the right-side panel also changes when this method is selected. The TCF window should look like the one in Figure 10.2.

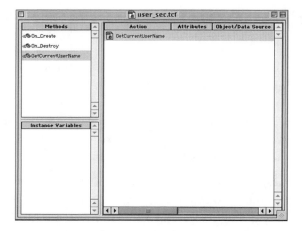

FIGURE 10.2   *A TCF window with a new method.*

The user system keeps the current user's name in a user scope variable, so all we need to do to get the username is to return this variable. You might ask, "Why do we even need this method? Why not just use the variable directly?" Suppose that you change the way you keep track of the current user? You would have to go through every TAF you used the variable in, and change it to this new method. If you have a method to make the change, all you have to do is change the method.

We need to do some configuration of the method before we implement it. Double-click the method name, and a window like the one in Figure 10.3 will appear.

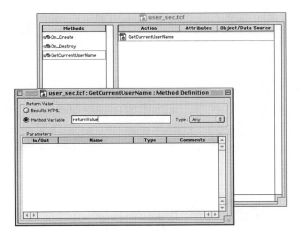

FIGURE 10.3   *A method configuration window.*

This method returns a simple value: the username. We can choose one of two ways to specify this return value—either return whatever is in the ResultsHTML or return a particular method variable. It is a good practice to be as explicit as possible about what you are returning, and, depending on the ResultsHTML, is a little murky in my opinion. Also, in this case, all we need to do is a simple assign, so we should just assign to our return variable. Stay with the default value of Method Variable and leave the name returnValue. There are no parameters for this method, so don't do anything in the bottom part of the window.

Now we need to write the code for this method. It is really simple, consisting of an assign statement. Drag an Assign action into the right-side panel of the TCF window. Configure it as shown in Figure 10.4. This assigns the value of the user variable username to our returnValue variable.

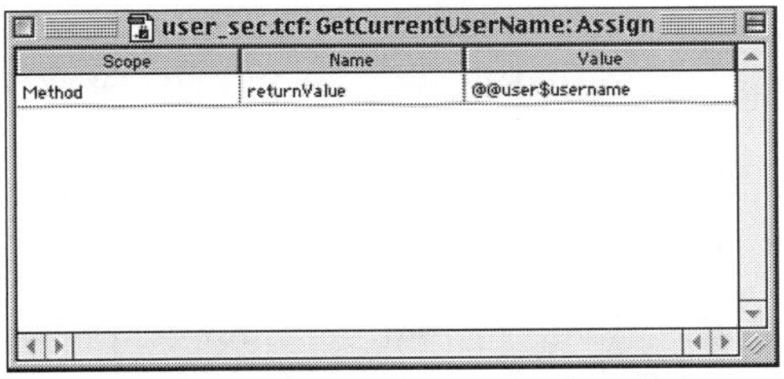

FIGURE 10.4   *An Assign action for the username.*

Drag a Return action into the bottom of the method for completeness. You've now written your first TCF method. We'll talk about how to use this method after we define the other methods.

GetCurrentUserLevel

This routine is almost identical to GetCurrentUserName. The only difference is what gets assigned. Repeat the steps to create the method you used to create GetCurrentUserName, but configure the Assign action as shown in Figure 10.5 instead.

Scope	Name	Value
Method	returnValue	@@user$userlevel

FIGURE 10.5   *An Assign action for user level.*

GetUserBar

I have found that with a user system, it is common to want to display either the name and level of a user or an opportunity to log in on many Web pages in a site. I use this functionality on xianworldview, in a sidebar that appears on every Web page and is part of every TAF I create. Therefore, if it changes, I don't want to have to change this in every TAF, and I don't want to have to put all this code in every TAF. The solution is to put this functionality in a TCF method and then just call the method. The method returns a chunk of HTML that is displayed in the TAF from which it is called.

Create a new method called GetUserBar. Again, this routine has no parameters, so leave the bottom half of the window alone. We will generate HTML over a number of actions, so we want to return the entire ResultsHTML for this routine. Click the ResultsHTML radio button.

The user bar displays two kinds of information, depending on whether there is a logged-in user. So, we need to start with an If/Else block. Drag in an If action and then add an Else action under it. The If needs to check whether the current user's user variable is empty. We could just check @@user$loggedInUser, but didn't I just tell you not to do that? Instead, we want to call this object's method for getting the username. You can do this via a Call Method action. Save this TCF and then add it to your Object panel via the Object, Add, TangoClassFile menu options, just as we did back in Chapter 6, "Web Directory." After you have it in the object panel, you can drag the method GetCurrentUserName from the object panel to the TCF, right above the If statement.

Did you notice what we did differently with this call than what we did when using it in a TAF? We didn't first create an object. You're calling one method from inside an instance of the object, so you can use a special instance variable called this. When you drag in the method and the Call Method action window comes up, this is already filled in the Object Instance Variable name field. Set the result variable to username. The finished window should look like Figure 10.6.

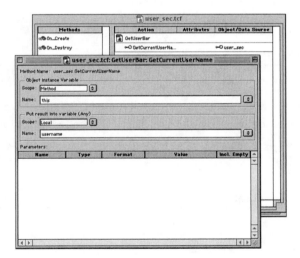

FIGURE 10.6   *The Call Method action for* username.

We want the user level for display later in the method, so add another Call Method action for the method GetCurrentUserLevel. Make the result variable userlevel.

We now have local variables that either contain the values we want or are empty. Configure your If action to look like the one in Figure 10.7.

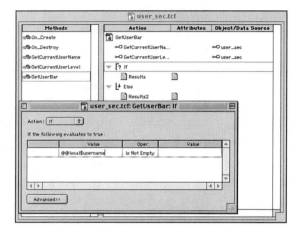

FIGURE 10.7   *An If action to check for the username.*

If there is a username, we want to display the user's name and his user level. Drag a Result action in under the If. Put Listing 10.1 into the Result action. This displays the user's username and his user level in parentheses.

Listing 10.1   User Bar with User

```
<@VAR name=username> ( <@VAR name=userlevel> )
```

If there is no logged-in user, we need to display some HTML that gives the user the options to log in or join the site. There will be two links to the appropriate TAFs. Drag in another Result action under the Else. Fill in the Result action with Listing 10.2.

Listing 10.2   User Bar with No User

```
<A HREF="<@APPFILEPATH>login.taf?_function=login">Login</A>
<BR>
<a href="<@APPFILEPATH>newuser.taf">Join Now!</a>
```

ValidateLogin

The last method we will create for this TCF is one to validate the username and password from a login. This method actually completes the login process, and enables us to hook in at this point if we need to do anything more at the point of login. In the next chapter, we'll do some more things for user tracking at login.

Create a new method named ValidateLogin. This routine needs parameters—namely the username and password to validate. It will return the text `"valid user"` if the login worked and will return an error message if the login didn't work.

In the method definition window, leave the Method Variable radio button active and the returnValue name. Now, we need to add some parameters. Click in the Parameters panel and pop up the context menu there. Select Insert. You can also select the menu item Edit, Insert. After you do this, a new row will appear. Click in the Name column, and enter **username**, and change the type to Text. Create a second parameter, and name it **password** with a type of Text. When you are finished, it should look like Figure 10.8.

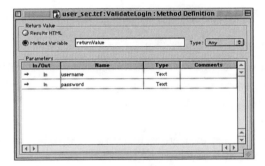

FIGURE 10.8   *The method configuration window for ValidateLogin.*

A *parameter* is a value passed from the calling code to a method. There can be multiple parameters for a single method and they are defined in the Method Definition window. All method parameters are turned into method variables inside the method.

The first thing this method needs to do is check its parameters. If the username parameter is empty we need to return an error. Drag in an If action and configure it to check whether @@method$username is empty. We don't check the password because we might want to allow empty passwords to be valid.

If this method is called and fails for any reason, I clear the user variables for logging in. This causes a logged-in user to be logged out if there is a problem. I think this is a proper course of action, but you might not. If you don't want to do it this way, ignore any reference to setting the user variables to empty.

Now drag in an Assign action to handle the case where there is no username. The first variable we want to set is the returnValue. We will put an error message into it. Next, we want to assign nothing to the @@user$username and @@user$userlevel variables. The final window should look like the one in Figure 10.9. Drag in a Return action under the Assign action.

FIGURE 10.9   *Invalid parameter if window.*

Next, we need to validate the login. We do this by searching the database for the username and password. Create a new Search action outside the If and under it. Drag all three columns from the users table into the select panel. Then configure the Criteria tab to check the username and password columns against the passed in username and password. It should look like the tab in Figure 10.10.

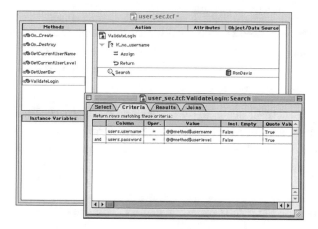

FIGURE 10.10   *The username and password criteria tab.*

This search should never return more than one row because the username field is unique. The search will return no rows if there is no user with the passed-in name or if that user's password column isn't the same as the one passed in. So, now we need to check whether the login was valid and handle both cases. Remember that if a result was found, the ResultsHTML for the Search action will be invoked. This would mean we got a valid user, so this would be a good place to handle the login actions.

Open the ResultsHTML attribute and add the code in Listing 10.3 to it. This sets the return value to "valid user" and sets the user variables to the found user.

Listing 10.3   Logging in a User

```
<@ASSIGN NAME="returnValue" VALUE="valid user" SCOPE="method">

<@ASSIGN NAME="userlevel" VALUE="<@COLUMN Name='users.userlevel'>" SCOPE="USER">

<@ASSIGN NAME="username" VALUE="<@COLUMN Name='users.username'>" SCOPE="USER">
```

If no records were found in the search, the NoResultsHTML attribute will be invoked. We can use this attribute to return the error message and clear out the user variables. Use Listing 10.4 to do this.

Listing 10.4   Invalid User Login

```
<@ASSIGN NAME="returnValue" VALUE="Invalid log in" SCOPE="method">

<@ASSIGN NAME="loggedInUserLevel" VALUE="" SCOPE="USER">

<@ASSIGN NAME="loggedInUser" VALUE="" SCOPE="USER">
```

Drag in a Return action to complete the method. You've now created a TCF that can be used in a variety of places. Let's modify some existing TAFs to use these various methods.

User TAF

We will modify the login.taf file we created earlier to use the new TCF. This will show you how to use the various parts of the TCF. Create a copy of the Login.taf from Chapter 8, "User Management."

First, let's pretty up the page a little and use the user bar part of the TCF. We will create a two-column page, with a sidebar on the left and the login information on the right. Because we are going to display the user bar, we need to get that user bar before we display the left sidebar.

Drag the user_sec object in at the top of the TAF. Name its variable user_sec in the Create Object Instance action window. Now call the user bar and assign the results to a local variable named userbar. Drag in the GetUserBar method from the object panel under the Create Object action. Configure it to look like the window in Figure 10.11.

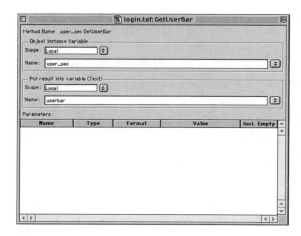

Figure 10.11   *Call GetUserBar method.*

We are ready to create the HTML that will make the left sidebar. Drag a Result action into the TAF right after the Call Method action. Insert the Listing 10.5 into the Result action. This HTML creates a table with two columns. The first column contains some static text and then the user bar. Then the HTML ends the column and starts the next one. This next column will contain all the HTML generated from the rest of the TAF.

Listing 10.5   Left Column HTML

```
<!DOCTYPE HTML PUBLIC "-//W3C//DTD HTML 3.2//EN">
<HTML>
<HEAD>
    <TITLE>Column testing</TITLE>
</HEAD>
```

```
<BODY>

<table width="535" border="0">
    <tr>
        <td width="132" valign="top">

Left column.
<P>
<@VAR name=userbar encoding=none>
<P>

<! end of left column !>
                     </p>
                 </td>
<! begin of main right column !>
                 <td width="372" valign="top" align="left">
```

Drag in another Result action at the end of the entire TAF. Put the code in Listing 10.6 into it to close up the table and the page.

Listing 10.6   Finish Page

```
            </td>
        </tr>
    </table>
</BODY>
</HTML>
```

If you run the TAF just as it is, you'll see the new column on each page, and the user bar will show up in the left column. If you log in, it will show your username and level.

Leave the If_login part of the TAF alone; it works as the login form.

The login_w_arg part of the TAF needs to be changed to use the TCF. Delete the Search action that is currently there. Drag in the user_sec method ValidateLogin. Configure the Call Method action to match Figure 10.12.

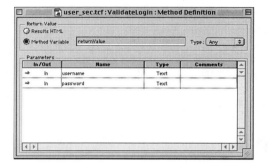

FIGURE 10.12 *Validate user Call Method action.*

Close the window and drag an If action under the Call Method action. We need to see whether we got the valid login message. Configure the If action to check whether @@local$validateResponse is equal to "valid user". If it is, we have a valid user and we should tell the user that he is now logged in. Drag in a Result action under the If and put some spiffy text in it, such as "You are now logged in."

To handle the case where the user isn't logged in, we need an Else action. Drag a Result action under the Else. Remember that the ValidateLogin method returns an error message, so we need to display that message. You can do that by putting the code in Listing 10.7 in the Result action.

Listing 10.7   User Error Message

```
<HR>
<FONT Color=Red>
<@VAR name=validateResponse encoding=none>
</FONT>
<HR>
```

Now our login.taf uses the TCF we create for validating the user.

Admin TAFs

Way back at the beginning of this journey, I promised to show you how to lock users out of your admin pages using your own security system. The means we'll use will work for any TAF you want to lock people out of, but we'll just do it for the user_admin.taf from Chapter 8.

Copy and open the user_admin.taf. Drag in the user_sec object from the object panel to the top of the TAF. Name the local variable for this object user_sec for clarity. Now drag in the GetCurrentUserLevel method under the Create Object action. Set the result variable to userlevel. We now have the user level of the current user. All we need to do is check it.

Drag in an If action under the Call Method action. Configure the If to check whether the user level is over what you want. If you want to lock out anyone who doesn't have a user level greater than or equal to eight, the If would look like the one shown in Figure 10.13.

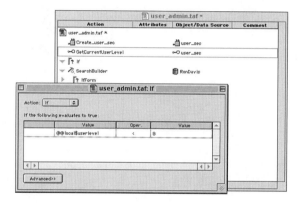

FIGURE 10.13   *A lockout If action.*

If this action fails, we need to tell the user and end execution of the TAF. Drag in a Result action. Put a message in the Result action, such as "You hacker scum, you don't belong here!" or just "You don't have sufficient user level to access this area." Then drag in a Return action. This locks out the user from this page. It is as simple as that.

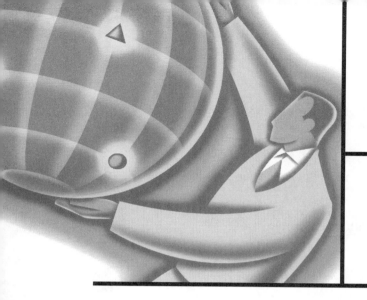

CHAPTER 11

User Tracking

What We'll Learn

- `<@CGIPARAM>` meta tag
- `<@CREATEOBJECT>` meta tag
- `<@CALLMETHOD>` meta tag

Purpose

In this chapter, we create a module that enables an admin to track users through the site. We can add tags to different TAFs that will add a notation of a user view to a database. Later, the admin can view a user's history.

Planning

Feature List

- Develop a means of recording events on a given TAF. Events are any action the TAF programmer wants to remember.

- When an event is recorded, get information from the Web server. The URL of the current page, with arguments, the referring URL, the IP address from which the page is being viewed, and the logged-in user if there is one.

- Create a report available to moderators that shows all the events that occurred on the entire site.

- Create a report available to moderators that shows a given user, and all the events associated with that user.

Database Schema

There is one new table for this chapter, the events table. We will track events in the database and later generate reports on the data gathered as part of these events. The data is the key to this whole section. We want a snapshot of everything that occurs at a given event point.

Database Table Name: events

Column Name	Data Type	Size
event	char	20
timestamp	timestamp	
URL	char	255
username	char	30
user_ref	char	36
client_add	char	30
client_IP	char	15
referrer	char	255
browser	char	255

```
CREATE TABLE events (
    event          char(20),
    timestamp         timestamp,
    URL            char(255),
    username       char(30),
    user_ref         char(36),
    client_add     char(30),
    client_ip         char(15),
    referrer         char(255),
    browser        char(255)
);
```

Creating the TAFs

Pervasive provides a tool that performs user tracking, the Tango Web Analyzer (TWA), which comes with the Windows version of the Tango Application Server. TWA is an excellent tool for tracking users, so you might wonder why I included this chapter.

First, TWA runs only on Windows. If you use a non-Windows server, you can still use TWA, but the TWA server has to run on Windows. For instance, you can use a Mac server that sends data to the TWA server, which is running on another machine running Windows.

Second, TWA does a lot of stuff. It isn't limited to just tracking users in TAFs; it doesn't even need a Tango Application Server. TWA watches raw HTTP and tracks from the user from that. This chapter creates a mini-TWA, with only a subset of TWA's functionality.

Third, this version is more customizable in what it records. TWA tracks every HTTP request. Our tracking system tracks user-defined events, and those events can be anything.

As in TWA, our user-tracking system collects a set of data for each thing we are tracking and then uses Tango's database ability to create reports that are completely customizable.

We need a system that is flexible and easy to implement, but expandable in the future. What we will do is develop a means of tracking events. An *event* is a named entity that has a group of information associated with it. For instance, you might want to track whenever a page is hit. So, we define a pageHit event and we add code to a page to enable it to tell our Tango app about the event. Tango grabs a bunch of information about the current Web page and saves it in the database with the name of our event. We can then search for all the pageHit events and display them.

The type of information we save with each event is always the same. Looking back at the database table, you can see the information we want to save. Here's a description of each item in the table and how we will get it.

- Event—The actual name of the event we are recording. The calling TAF provides this.

- Timestamp—The time the event occurred. This is provided by the `<@CURRENTTIMESTAMP>` meta tag.

- URL—The URL of the current page, including the arguments in the URL. This is provided by concatenating various <@CGIPARAM> attributes.

- Username—This is the name of the currently logged-in user, if there is one. This is provided by calling the User TCF method GetCurrentUser.

- User_ref—The Tango user reference for the current user. Tango distinguishes users by giving them a unique reference number, which is a number available from the meta tag <@USERREFERENCE>. This enables us to track visitors, even if they don't log in. Tango generates a user reference number based on a number of criteria. It is possible to define your own means of generating the user reference. If you do this, it might make the key larger than 36 digits, and you must change the size of the database column accordingly.

- Client_add—The fully qualified domain name (for instance, www.altavista.com) of the connected client, if available. This is a <@CGIPARAM> attribute.

- Client_IP—The IP address of the connected client. It is always provided, so we use it as a backup to the client_add. It, too, is a <@CGIPARAM> attribute.

- Referrer—This is the URL that referred the user to this URL. If the user clicked a link to get to this page, there should be a referring URL and it should show up in this field. This is another <@CGIPARAM> attribute.

- Browser—The USER_AGENT attribute provided by the client browser. It should tell you what browser was used and what platform. This is also another <@CGIPARAM> attribute.

This is all the information we want to gather for each event. We need to centralize the gathering of this information so that it can be called from anywhere in any TAF. We do this by using a TCF method call.

Tracking TCF

We could add the new tracking method to the User TCF we created in the last chapter, but I want to keep it in its own TCF, to allow for future expansions. So, create a new TCF called tracking.tcf. Now, create a new method named RecordEvent, with one parameter event. The finished configure method window should look like Figure 11.1.

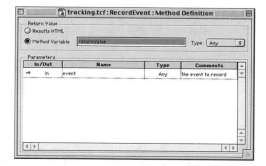

FIGURE 11.1   *The RecordEvent window.*

The functionality of this method, mainly doing an insert of a bunch of data, is trivial. It could almost be one Insert action. But there is a slight complication that causes us to need two actions. There is no way to get the URL of the current page from inside Tango, but we can get all the parts and generate the URL. So, we need to create this URL before doing the insert. We'll use meta tags to generate the URL and assign it to the variable URLtags. We can generate most of the URL in one assign, but we need to handle arguments in a special way.

The `<@CGIPARAM HTTP_SEARCH_ARGS>` tag gives us a list of the arguments. It gives us every thing that comes after the ? in the URL, but it doesn't give us the ?. That means we have to check whether there are arguments and add a ? if arguments exist, but don't add a ? if there are no arguments. We end up with the contents of Listing 11.1. You need to add a Result action to your TCF and put Listing 11.1 in it.

Listing 11.1   Generating the URL

```
<@IFEMPTY VALUE="<@CGIPARAM HTTP_SEARCH_ARGS>">
    <@ASSIGN NAME="args" VALUE="" SCOPE="method">
<@ELSE>
    <@ASSIGN NAME="args" VALUE="?<@CGIPARAM HTTP_SEARCH_ARGS>" SCOPE="method">
</@IF>

<@ASSIGN NAME="URLtags" VALUE="http<@IF EXPR='<@CGIPARAM SERVER_PORT>
 = 443' TRUE='s'>://<@CGIPARAM SERVER_NAME><@CGI><@APPFILE>
@@local$args" SCOPE="method">
```

We first check whether there are any HTTP search arguments and then generate an args variable. If the URL has no arguments, our variable contains nothing. If there are arguments, our variable contains a ? and the arguments.

Next, we generate the URL in an assignment tag. We put the http prefix on the string, and then check whether the user is connecting on the secure port. If it is the secure port, we add an s to the string, and then we finish the prefix by adding the ://. We get our server's name, which is our domain. The path is the path to the current file, and finally we add our arguments. This gives you a complete URL.

Another piece of data we need before we can do the insert is the currently logged-in user's name. We get this by calling the user_sec TCF. Drag in the user_sec object under the Result action. Name its variable user_sec. Then drag in the GetCurrentUserName method and name its return value username. We set the scope of the object and the return value of the method call to the method scope. Method scope lasts only as long as the method is executing.

Now we are ready to do an insert. Drag in an Insert action and configure it by adding the whole events table to it. Make the values look like those in Figure 11.2.

Column	Value	Quote Value
event	@@method$event	True
timestamp	<@CURRENTTIMESTAMP>	True
URL	@@local$URLtags	True
username	@@local$username	True
user_ref	<@USERREFERENCE>	True
client_add	<@CGIPARAM CLIENT_ADDRESS>	True
referrer	<@CGIPARAM REFERER>	True
browser	<@CGIPARAM USER_AGENT>	True
client_ip	<@CGIPARAM CLIENT_IP>	True

Insert the following row into the table: events

FIGURE 11.2 *The Events Insert action.*

Drag in a Return action for completeness. That is all you need to do to record an event. Later, you can expand this routine by adding new data to save, or by filtering events with some other criteria, such as the URL on which the event acts.

User TAF

Now we need to use the TCF we created. I show you only one event, but you should learn the principle sufficiently to use it for any event you want to define. The event we will define is pageHit. That means, well, you hit the page. If you want to be able to track a user through every area of your Web site, you will need to know anytime he loads a page.

There are two ways to add the call to create an event to a TAF. One way is to call it using the Create Object and Call Method actions. This way works well and you already know how to do it.

Another way is to use the meta tag equivalent of these two actions. This is useful if you want to put the call inside a Result action or inside a file included via a Presentation action. For xianworldview.com, I included a page header file that creates the masthead on every page. I could go through every TAF in my site and add the Create Object and Call Method actions, but I already include this one header file in every TAF, so why not add it there? I added the content of Listing 11.2 to the masthead HTML file and—boom—my site had tracking throughout.

Listing 11.2   Meta Tags for Recording an Event

```
<@ASSIGN NAME="app" SCOPE="method" VALUE=
<@CREATEOBJECT OBJECTID="tracking.tcf" TYPE="TCF">>
<@CALLMETHOD OBJECT="app" SCOPE="method"
METHOD="RecordEvent('pagehit')" METHODTYPE="invoke">
```

The code is pretty straightforward. You use the <@CREATEOBJECT> tag to create an object, telling it the name of the TCF file and the fact that it is a TCF. Then you assign the object to a local variable. After that, you use the new object variable in a <@CALLMETHOD> tag. This tag takes the name of the method with its parameters and tells Tango to invoke the method. The RecordEvent method doesn't have a return value, so we don't have to worry about doing an assign.

After you have added these calls throughout your Web site, you can begin collecting data on how users move around your site. Next, we need to develop reports on that data.

Admin TAFs

All Site Events

The first report we will create is one that lists all the events in the database. It would be a little cumbersome to get a list of all the events in the database on one page. Instead, we'll create a page that lists each kind of event in the database as a link to a more detailed list of events.

We'll put all our reports into one TAF, so create a new TAF named view_events.taf. This is an admin TAF, so we want to limit access to people with a user level higher than 8. Set up the user level check at the top of the TAF, as we did in Chapter 10, "User Security." For the rest of the book, I assume that you do this for all admin TAFs and I don't mention it. You might want to create a template file with this code in it already and use that template to create new TAFs.

On the Mac, you can use a stationary file, by creating the file the way you want it, selecting Get Info on the file, and then checking the Stationary File checkbox.

We are ready to start creating the actions for the summaries. Because we are using the same TAF for all the pages, we need to create an IF/ELSE structure for each page. Drag in an IF action and configure it to check whether <@ARG _function> is listEvents or empty.

The first report page will be a list of the distinct events in the database. For instance, there will be many pageHit events in the database, but only one instance of pageHit will appear on this page. To do this, we must search the events table. Drag in a Search action and then drag the column events.event into the Select panel. We want only unique rows, so click the Results tab and click the Retrieve Distinct Rows Only checkbox. This Search action will generate the data from the database for us, but we must display that data.

In the Search action's ResultsHTML attribute, enter Listing 11.3.

Listing 11.3   Showing Events

```
<!DOCTYPE HTML PUBLIC "-//W3C//DTD HTML 3.2//EN">
<HTML>
<HEAD>
```

```
    <TITLE>View All Events</TITLE>
</HEAD>
<BODY>

<TABLE BORDER=1>
<TR ALIGN=LEFT VALIGN=TOP>
<TD>Event</TD>
</TR>

<@ROWS>
<TR ALIGN=LEFT VALIGN=TOP>
<TD>
    <A HREF="<@CGI><@APPFILE>?_function=eventDetails&event=
<@COLUMN 'events.event'>"><@COLUMN 'events.event'></A>
</TD>

</TR>
</@ROWS>
</TABLE>
</BODY>
</HTML>
```

This code loops through the results of the search and creates a link on the name of the event. This link refers back into this TAF and asks for the eventDetails for the event. Drag in a Return action for completeness.

Because we refer to an eventDetails function, we need to define it next. Drag a new ElseIf action into the TAF. Configure it to check whether `<@ARG _function>` is equal to eventDetails.

Again, we search the database. This time, we limit our output to the requested event. Drag in a Search action under the ElseIf. You can create a report that shows anything about each event you want. I find that if I use too many columns, it gets very hard to pick out individual items. So, for this case, I display only some of the data. Drag in events.event, events.timestamp, events.URL, events.username, and events.user_ref. This enables us to know what happens, when it happens, where it happens, and by whom. We need to drag events.timestamp into the Order By panel so that we can view things in chronological order.

Set up the Search action's Criteria tab to match the tab in Figure 11.3.

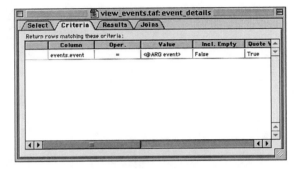

FIGURE 11.3 *The event Criteria tab.*

Now we need to display the results of this search. Listing 11.4 shows how to do it. We list things in chronological order, so display the time first. Then display the actual URL hit as a hyperlink so that you could go to it if you choose. Then display the logged-in user, if there is one. For the sake of display, we end a table row and start a new one, skip the first column, and display the user reference number in its own cell. The user reference number is a link to the user page we will create in a minute.

Listing 11.4   Event Details

```
<!DOCTYPE HTML PUBLIC "-//W3C//DTD HTML 3.2//EN">
<HTML>
<HEAD>
    <TITLE>View All <@ARG event> Events</TITLE>
</HEAD>
<BODY>

<H1>View All <@ARG event> Events</h1>
<P>

<TABLE BORDER=1>
<TR ALIGN=LEFT VALIGN=TOP>
<TD>Time</TD>
<TD>URL</TD>
<TD>Logged In<BR> user</TD>
</TR>

<@ROWS>
<TR ALIGN=LEFT VALIGN=TOP>
<TD><@COLUMN 'events.timestamp'></TD>
<TD><A HREF="<@COLUMN 'events.URL'>"><@COLUMN 'events.URL'></A></TD>
<TD><@COLUMN 'events.username'></TD>
</TR>
<TR>
```

```
<TD></TD>
<TD>
    <A HREF="<@CGI><@APPFILE>?_function=userDetails&
userref=<@COLUMN 'events.user_ref'>"><@COLUMN 'events.user_ref'></A>
</TD>
</TR>
</@ROWS>
</TABLE>
</BODY>
</HTML>
```

We now have a report for events. It is useful for tracking specific events you've created. But what we'd really like to do is see how specific users use the site. We want to follow users around. We can do this if we have added pageHit events to every page.

List and Show Users

The other report we need to create is one that shows a list of all the users who have hit the site. Remember that every user who comes to your site can be tracked, even if he doesn't become a member and log in. Tango associates a user reference with each user. So, to list all the users of your Web site, you need to list all the user references stored in your database. We will create a page that lists each distinct user reference and a username, if there is one. We'll make the user reference a link to a details page, which will list in chronological order all the events associated with that user.

Continuing in our view_events.taf, add another IfElse action, this time checking whether <@ARG _function> is listUsers. This page turns out to be almost exactly the same as the one for listing the events. Again, add a Search action and drag in the columns events.username and events.user_ref. Next, turn on the distinct row checkbox in the Results tab. To display this list, use the code in Listing 11.5.

Listing 11.5   User List

```
<!DOCTYPE HTML PUBLIC "-//W3C//DTD HTML 3.2//EN">
<HTML>
<HEAD>
    <TITLE>View All Events</TITLE>
</HEAD>
```

continues

Listing 11.5   (Continued)

```
<BODY>

<TABLE BORDER=1>
<TR ALIGN=LEFT VALIGN=TOP>
<TD>User Ref</TD>
<TD>Logged in user</TD>
</TR>

<@ROWS>
<TR ALIGN=LEFT VALIGN=TOP>
<TD>
    <A HREF="<@CGI><@APPFILE>?_function=userDetails&
userref=<@COLUMN 'events.user_ref'>"><@COLUMN 'events.user_ref'></A>
</TD>
<TD><@COLUMN 'events.username'></TD>

</TR>
</@ROWS>
</TABLE>
</BODY>
</HTML>
```

This will display the list of user references as links to the details page for the user. We display the username next, but you'll find there are many more users who aren't logged in.

The last thing we need to create is a way to display the user details. This is the core report for user tracking. It's the one that enables us to look over the user's shoulder as he goes through the Web site. Drag in another ElseIf and configure it to check whether <@ARG _function> is equal to userDetails. Next, drag in a Search action and add the columns events.event, events.timestamp, events.URL, events.username, events.user_ref, and events.referrer. Make events.timestamp the Order By column. The Critiera is events.user_ref equal to <@ARG userref>. For display, use the code in Listing 11.6.

Listing 11.6   User Details

```
<!DOCTYPE HTML PUBLIC "-//W3C//DTD HTML 3.2//EN">
<HTML>
<HEAD>
    <TITLE>View All <@ARG usseref> Events</TITLE>
</HEAD>
```

```
<BODY>

<H1>View All <@ARG userref> Events</h1>
<P>

<TABLE BORDER=1>
<TR ALIGN=LEFT VALIGN=TOP>
<TD>Time</TD>
<TD>URL</TD>
</TR>

<@ROWS>
<TR ALIGN=LEFT VALIGN=TOP>
<TD><@COLUMN 'events.timestamp'></TD>
<TD WIDTH=300><A HREF="<@COLUMN 'events.URL'>">
<@COLUMN 'events.URL'></A></TD>
</TR><TR><TD></TD>
<TD>Reffer:<A HREF="<@COLUMN 'events.referrer'>">
<@COLUMN 'events.referrer'></A></TD>
</TR>
</@ROWS>
</TABLE>
</BODY>
</HTML>
```

You can run this TAF and see what URLs a particular user went to and see those URLS in chronological order. Because we include the arguments in the URL, you can often get a very good feel for what particular items a user looked at. I think you will find it fascinating to see what a user did on your site. Maybe lots of users went to a certain page, and had to navigate through a number of pages to get there, when there was an easier way. That information would tell you that the easier way isn't obvious to your users.

Did you notice that all our reports were really easy to create and use very similar structures? You performed a search and displayed the results. You've probably already got an idea or two for new reports. The data we've gathered is the key. You can mine it using Tango and create all kinds of reports. Do you want to know what the most popular browser is for your site? Create a report that shows this or counts the browsers.

Pervasive's Tango Web Analyzer works in a similar way, in that it saves all the data it collects in a SQL database. You can create your own reports from that data, too.

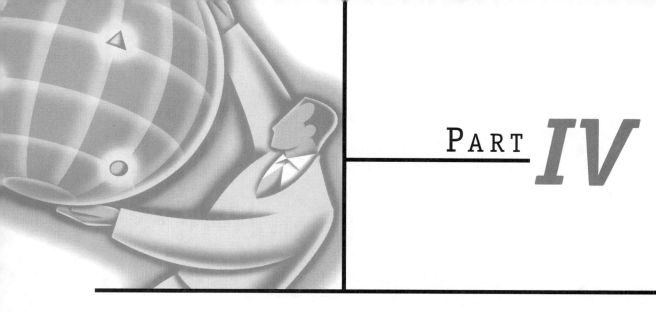

PART *IV*

E-commerce

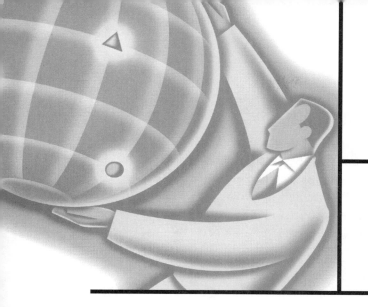

CHAPTER 12

Loyalty Points System

What We'll Learn

- Using the <@CALLMETHOD> tag when the method has a return value

Purpose

In this chapter, we create a module that tracks loyalty points for users of our Web site. Loyalty points are rewards for doing different things on a Web site. For example, you might earn a loyalty point for posting to a forum or buying a particular product.

Planning

Feature List

- Have an easy means of adding loyalty points to a user
- Have an easy means of adding an arbitrary number of points to the current user
- Be able to display a user's current number of points
- Give the admin the ability to change a user's points

Database Schema

We will use the same method we used for user profiles to associate a user's point total with his username. The points table will contain the username as primary key, which will provide a foreign key from the user table. The second column in the points table will be the total number of points a user has. We won't be keeping track of how each point was earned. If you really want to do that, you could create an event for user tracking when you add points.

Last, we will add a column that tells whether a given user's points are locked. This will mainly be used by the increment method to keep multiple pages from stepping on each other if they access the table at the same time, but it could be used to keep a user from gaining any more points. For instance, you might have a maximum number of points a user can get, and when the user reaches that number, you could lock the row.

Database Table Name: points

Column Name	Data Type	Size
username	Char	50
points	int	
locked	in	

```
CREATE TABLE points (
    username    char(30) PRIMARY KEY,
    points   int,
    locked    int
)
```

Creating the TAFs

One of the constant frustrations of Webmasters is getting people to be active on their Web sites—to get people to do something. The Web is a very passive medium; even the verb we use to describe Web viewing—*surfing*—implies skimming the surface. This chapter attempts to give you a tool to combat that. Everyone wants to be rewarded. They want to gain something for work they do, and the same is true on the Web and on your Web site. Loyalty points are a means of rewarding people for doing something. The height of doing this is the Web site http://www.iwon.com/, which gives users points for doing just about everything on the site, from clicking on banners to following links. If you click the copyright notice, you get a point! Each point is a chance to win a drawing for thousands of dollars.

You might not want to go to such extremes; you might just want to get people to post to your forums or add a URL to your Web directory. You can still use loyalty points to accomplish these goals. You might use loyalty points to sell more products by giving one Web buck for each dollar spent on your site, and later allowing the user to redeem the Web bucks for product. Loyalty points are just a name that I've chosen for an arbitrary reward system; you can call them whatever you want.

How do we implement this system? As with user tracking, we will use loyalty points all over our Web site and, therefore, we want to centralize management of the points in a TCF, with methods that can be called from anywhere.

TCFs

Add_points Method

The first method we want to add is the capability to add points to a user's total. It should be a simple method that takes a username and the number of points to add as parameters. Internally, the method will look for a row with the passed-in username, and if it finds that username, it will add the values to the user's current total. If there is no row in the table for the user, we will insert one.

We might guard against the possibility that two pages might attempt to change the row at the same time. Suppose that you have a Web page that gives a user five points for suggesting a URL for your Web directory, and another page that gives a point for people replying to their posts in the forums. The user currently has 50 points in the database. Then, at the same time that the user suggests a URL, someone else replies to one of the user's posts in the forums. The URL request is a microsecond faster, and searches the database for the username and gets back that he has 50 points. Then the forum post searches and finds that the user has 50 points as well. In its next action, the URL request changes the database to 55 points. Then the forum comes back and changes the database to 51. The five points from the URL are eaten in the process because of the lag between the reading of the current value and the writing of the new one.

The solution to this problem is developing a means of locking a user's record before you attempt to change it. Let's look at the same scenario if we have locking. The same two events happen, but this time the URL request first locks the row. Then the forum request comes in and finds the row locked, so it doesn't do anything and waits to try again. The URL request comes back and gets the current value. The forum request checks again, but the record is still locked. The URL request changes the value of the points and unlocks the row. The forum request checks again, finds the record unlocked, locks it, and goes through the same process that the URL request did. We must keep trying if the record is locked, but we really don't want to try forever, so we'll limit the number of retries. This is the same method that the GetNextID method of the Utility.tcf uses, which we've used in previous chapters.

Create a new TCF named, points.tcf. We need to create a new method, so select New Method (either from the Edit menu or the context menu of the method area of the TCF window), and name the new method Add_points. Open the method and configure it as shown in Figure 12.1.

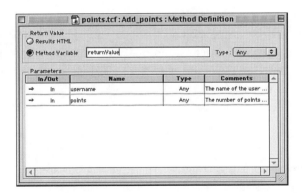

FIGURE 12.1   *The Add_points method definition.*

This method has two parameters, username, which is the name of the user you want to add the points to, and points, which is the number of points to add to the user's totals. There really isn't any return value for this method, so we just leave the return value as a method variable and we never set it.

Close the configuration window and select the method in the TCF window. The first thing we need to do in this method is decide how many times we will try to read a locked user, and set a variable to that value. Call the new variable maxTries, and then set the value to 5 by using an Assign action at the top of the method. Set the scope to Method so that the variable goes away when the method ends.

The next thing to do is try to get the user we are looking for. We do this by querying the database using a Search action. Create a new Search action under the Assign action you just added. Drag all the columns of the points table into the Select panel. In the Criteria tab, we want to check whether the username column is equal to the passed-in username. All passed-in values and all parameters, are method scope variables, so we are searching for @@method$username. Your finished Criteria tab should look like Figure 12.2.

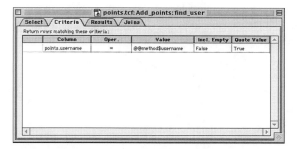

FIGURE 12.2   *The Criteria tab for searching for a user to add loyalty points to.*

There are two possible outcomes of this first search: We find the user or the user is not yet in the loyalty points table. We could have made it a requirement that the user already exists in the table, and it would probably work out in most cases because you could always add the user when a new user was created, but that would mean changing other parts of the site.

Instead, we will handle the case in which the user isn't in the table. Let's handle that case first. Open the NoResults attribute of the Search action. All we need to do in this attribute is set a flag variable signifying that we didn't find anything. This is done with a simple <@ASSIGN> tag like this:

```
<@ASSIGN NAME="founduser" VALUE="false" SCOPE="local">.
```

To handle the case where we do get a user back from the table we will again set the founduser variable, but we'll also save the data returned by the search. Enter Listing 12.1 into the ResultsHTML.

Listing 12.1   Save the Returned Data About the Points

```
<@ASSIGN NAME="curPoints" VALUE="<@COLUMN 'points.points'>" SCOPE="method">
<@ASSIGN NAME="locked" VALUE="<@COLUMN 'points.locked'>" SCOPE="method">
<@ASSIGN NAME="founduser" VALUE="true" SCOPE="method">
```

We now know whether there is a user, so let's put in an If action to check the value of founduser. We'll handle the case where we didn't find the user first, so make the If action check for false. If there isn't a user, our job is easy. We don't have to get any data from the table or worry about other users hitting it at the same time. Instead, all we have to do is insert the user in the table with the number of points we are currently being asked to add. We do this with an Insert action. Drag in a new Insert action under the If action and configure it as shown in Figure 12.3. After the Insert action, drag in a Return action to stop execution of the TAF.

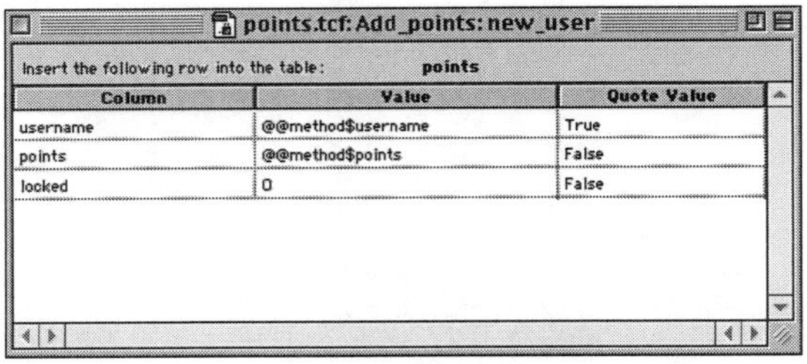

FIGURE 12.3   *Inserting a new user into the points table.*

Now we are ready to do the main task of updating a user who already exists. Remember that we will try to lock the record before we change it, so we must set up a loop and create the locking code inside it. The loop is a For action with the counter variable set to try and the start value set to the maxTries variable. We'll count down by one and end at zero.

The first thing we do inside the loop is check whether the row is unlocked. We got the locked state during our first search and put it in the variable locked. Drag in an If action and configure it to check whether @@local$locked is equal to zero.

If the row is not locked, we'll do what is inside this If action. Drag in an Update action and configure it as shown in Figure 12.4, which will cause the locked flag to be set for the row.

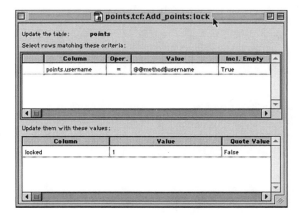

FIGURE 12.4   *An Update action to lock the user's record in the points table.*

Now that we have the row locked, we need to get its contents again. We do this because the contents could have changed since we last checked it because the row was unlocked. The easiest way to handle the check is to copy the other Search action under the Update action. All the handling of the results will come with the copy and we don't have to change anything.

We have the current point value and we need to calculate the new value based on totaling the number of points to be added and the current number of points. Do this by dragging in an Assign action under the Search action and configuring it as in Figure 12.5. Notice that you can enter meta tags inside an Assign action, just as with an Assign meta tag.

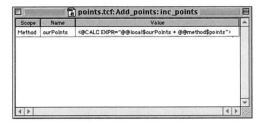

FIGURE 12.5   *Adding the passed-in loyalty points to the current total.*

The local variable curPoints now contains the new point value for the user and we need to update the database with that value. Drag in an Update action and configure it as in Figure 12.6.

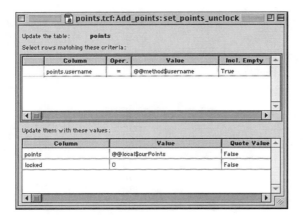

FIGURE 12.6   *Updating the user's point total in the database.*

Notice we also unlock the row as we perform the update. Because we don't use the row anymore, we don't need to keep it locked and we can easily do it inside this same action. We're finished at this point, so drag in a Return action to end the method.

All that is left is handling the case in which the row was locked at the beginning of the loop. Drag in an Else action to be parallel with the If action. If the row was locked last time we checked, we must check again at this point. Drag another copy of the Search action we used before into the If action. We have now retrieved the current values for the row, including an updated value for the row if it was locked. We can safely let the For loop check the values of our local variable for locked state at the start of the loop.

If the For loop tries its maximum number of times, it will exit at the end of the method, causing no change to the database. It is good practice to add a Return action to the end of things here, even though it isn't needed.

Get_user_points Method

We need another method that will return a user's current point total. Insert another method into the TCF and name it Get_user_points. The Get_user_points method has one parameter, the username whose loyalty points you want to get. Configure the method as shown in Figure 12.7.

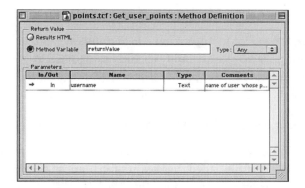

FIGURE 12.7   *The parameter configuration of the Get_user_points method.*

This routine doesn't have to do anything complicated. It simply searches the points table for the passed-in username and returns the number of points the user has. If the user isn't in the table, the routine just returns zero because that is, in fact, how many points the user has. We could go through the process of adding the user to the table, but we get a valid result of zero without the user being in the database and we might not ever add points to their total, so why add the user to the table? If you wanted to always give users a default number of points, you could have this method check to see whether there is a user, and if not, call Add_points, with the default number of points.

Drag in a Search action and configure it just as you did the Search actions in the Add_points method. You don't have to include the points.locked column in the search if you don't want to. All we do in the ResultsHTML attribute is assign the value of the points.points column to @@method$returnValue, using an <@ASSIGN> tag as in Listing 12.2.

Listing 12.2   Assign Statement to Return a User's Points

```
<@ASSIGN NAME="returnValue" VALUE="<@COLUMN 'points.points'>" SCOPE="method">
```

In the NoResultsHTML, add the same line, except the value should just be zero. Add a Return action to end the method.

These two methods are the core of the loyalty points systems. They handle tracking the points for a given user and they can be used from any part of your site.

User TAF

Now that we have the toolkit to implement a user points system, let's apply it to something we've already built. The first thing we'll do is display a user's point total in his user profile. The second thing we'll do is give a user five points for suggesting a URL for our Web directory.

Showing a User's Points in His Profile

The file we need to modify is from Chapter 9, "User Profiles." We put all the display HTML in a text file called display_profile.html, so to add something new, all we need to do is change this file. We would have to make changes to the profile TAFs if we needed to edit this value, but for the user, their total number of points is read only. Make a copy and open the display_profile.html file and open it for editing. Change it as shown in Listing 12.3. All this change does is display the user's total number of points immediately after the rank display in the profile.

Listing 12.3 The HTML to Display the User's Profile with His Number of User Points

```
<TABLE border=1 width="372">

<TR VALIGN=TOP ALIGN=LEFT>
    <TD COLSPAN=2>
        <@COLUMN 'user_profiles.username'>
    </TD>

</TR>

<@IFEQUAL VALUE1="true" VALUE2="<@COLUMN 'user_profiles.public_email'>">
<TR VALIGN=TOP ALIGN=LEFT>
    <TD>
        Email Address:
    </TD>
    <TD>
        <A HREF="mailto:<@COLUMN 'user_profiles.email_address'>">
<@COLUMN 'user_profiles.email_address'></A>
    </TD>
</TR>
</@IF>

<TR VALIGN=TOP ALIGN=LEFT>
    <TD>
        Member Since:
    </TD>
    <TD>
```

```
                <@COLUMN 'user_profiles.date_of_membership'>
        </TD>
</TR>
<TR VALIGN=TOP ALIGN=LEFT>
        <TD>
                Rank:
        </TD>
        <TD>
                <@COLUMN 'users.userlevel'>

        </TD>
</TR>

<TR VALIGN=TOP ALIGN=LEFT>
        <TD>
                User Points:
        </TD>
        <TD>
                <@ASSIGN NAME="points" SCOPE="local" VALUE=<@CREATEOBJECT
OBJECTID="points.tcf" TYPE="TCF">>
                <@ASSIGN NAME='userpoints' SCOPE='local'
VALUE=<@CALLMETHOD OBJECT="points" SCOPE="local"
METHOD="Get_user_points(<@COLUMN 'user_profiles.username'>)"
 METHODTYPE="invoke"> >
                <@VAR userpoints>

        </TD>
</TR>

<TR VALIGN=TOP ALIGN=LEFT>
        <TD>
                Home Town:
        </TD>
        <TD>
                <@COLUMN 'user_profiles.home_city'>, <@COLUMN
 'user_profiles.home_state'>, <@COLUMN 'user_profiles.home_country'>
        </TD>
</TR>

<TR VALIGN=TOP ALIGN=LEFT>
        <TD>
                Personal Web Site:
        </TD>
        <TD>
                <A HREF="<@COLUMN 'user_profiles.personalURL'>">
<@COLUMN 'user_profiles.personalURL'></A>
        </TD>
</TR>

<TR VALIGN=TOP ALIGN=LEFT>
        <TD>
                Biography:
```

continues

Listing 12.3   (Continued)

```
    </TD>
    <TD>
        <@COLUMN 'user_profiles.biography' ENCODING=multilinehtml>

    </TD>
</TR>


</TABLE>
```

As with the code we used to insert our user-tracking calls in Chapter 11, "User Tracking," we are using the meta tag syntax here to call the Get_ user_points method of our TCF. The big difference is that in this case, we do have a return value, so the `<@CALLMETHOD>` tag has to be inside an `<@ASSIGN>` tag to get the return value into a local variable called userpoints. The `<@VAR>` tag is there to display the actual value of userpoints. It is possible to do this without the assign because the `<@CALLMETHOD>` tag displays the return value in the HTML by default.

Giving a User Points When a Suggested URL Is Approved

We want to give users points for doing various things on the Web site. In this section, we'll give a user points for suggesting URLs for the Web directory we created in Chapter 6, "Web Directory." The means of doing this are generalized by calling the Add_points method in our TCF. We just need to figure out where to hook in to make this call. All the functionality that adds URLs to the database happens in the add_weblink.taf file. In this file, we find the specific location where the insert of the URL into the database happens under the If_Insert If action.

After we know where to call Add_points, we need to know the current user's name to add points to his total. We can get this information from about anywhere in the Web site simply by calling our User TCF. We also need to know how many points to give the user. We'll just decide that suggesting a URL is worth five points.

Open add_weblinks.taf for editing. We'll add our code immediately after we insert the record into the database. First, we need to get the current user, so drag in the userlogin object and configure it as shown in Figure 12.8. If you haven't added the userlogin TCF to the Objects panel, do so now.

FIGURE 12.8   *Configuration of the object to get the user.*

Next, we need to get the current user from this object and put it in a local variable. Drag in the Current_User method and configure it as shown in Figure 12.9. This puts the currently logged-in user's name in the local variable curUser.

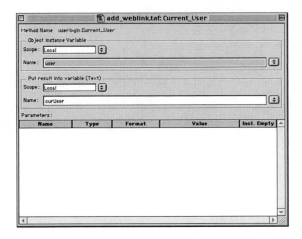

FIGURE 12.9   *Configuration of the method to get the current user.*

In some cases, you will need to check here to make sure there is a current user, but in this case we don't because you can suggest a URL only if you are logged in. We can now call our Add_points method. Drag in the points object, and configure it as shown in Figure 12.10.

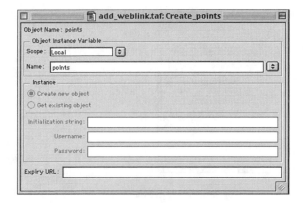

FIGURE 12.10 *Configuring the creation of the points object.*

Follow this up by dragging in an Add_points method and configuring it as shown in Figure 12.11.

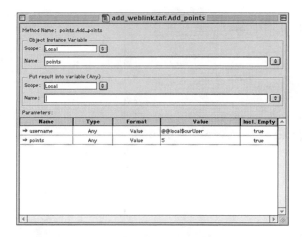

FIGURE 12.11 *Calling the Add_points method.*

We pass in the local variable with the current user's username in it as the username parameter, and we pass in the value of five for the number of points to add. That's all it takes for you to give a user five points for suggesting a URL.

Admin TAFs

Two things need to be done from an administration point of view: You need to delete the user from the points table when you delete the user from the users table, and you need to be able to edit the points a user has.

Deleting a User's Points

When you delete a user from the users table, you also need to delete him from the points table. This is a fairly simple thing to do. We need to find where the user is deleted from the users table and perform another delete on the points table. Also some databases will automatically do this for you.

Open the file user_admin.taf created in Chapter 8, "User Management." This file was created by the Search builder, and we are now going to change the output of the Search builder to delete from the points table as well. Expand the If action called ElseIfDelete. Under it, you will find a Delete action. Drag another Delete action into the TAF right under the existing one. Configure this Delete action as shown in Figure 12.12.

FIGURE 12.12   *Deleting the user from the points table.*

Editing a User's Points

We'll use the Search builder to create a TAF that enables us to edit a user's points. Create a new TAF named points_admin.taf. Drag a Search builder into the TAF. In the Search tab, drag in the column points.username, and leave all the settings on the default. In the Record List tab, drag in points.username again because we want a list of usernames as links. In the Record Detail tab, drag in points.username and points.points. We want to be able to edit the user's points, so select that column and check the Allow Update checkbox. We also might want to delete a user, so check the Allow Delete of Record from: checkbox. Now you have a means of editing the number of points a user has. If someone abuses the system you can delete him or take points away from him.

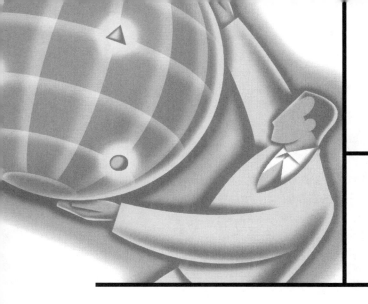

CHAPTER 13

Forums

What We'll Learn

- Group action

Purpose

In this chapter, we create a module that handles discussion groups or forums.

Planning

Feature List

- Be able to create and display individual messages that include a title, the username of the person who posted them, the time and date posted, and the message body.

- Be able to associate multiple messages with a thread. A *thread* is a group of related messages. Each thread can have a title and description of its own.

- Be able to group threads into folders. Threads for a similar topic can be grouped into a single folder.

- Be able to display various levels of the forum tree. First, display a list of folders. Clicking a folder gives you a list of threads in that folder, and clicking a thread gives you a list of message titles in that folder. Clicking a message title gives you the actual message.
- Be able to post replies to messages in a thread.
- Be able to set a minimum user level necessary to add subfolders or messages to a folder or thread.
- Be able to delete folders, threads, or messages.

Database Schema

The database tables for the forums are fairly easy. We will keep the individual messages all in one table, and all the folders and threads in another table. A folder and thread have the same basic content, so we will treat them as the same, and just add a column that tells whether a folder is an actual folder or a thread.

Every folder will have a parent, the ID of which will be kept in a column in the folder table. The root level will be folder zero. A similar scheme is used in the message table to associate a message with a thread.

Database Table Name: forum_folder

Column Name	Data Type	Size
folderID	int	
parentID	int	
isThread	int	
secLevelToAdd	int	
name	char	50
description	char	255

```
CREATE TABLE forum_folder (
    folderID    int PRIMARY KEY,
parentID    int,
isThread    int,
secLevelToAdd    int,
name        char(50),
description    char(255)
)
```

A value of 1 in the isThread column means the folder is a thread, a zero means it is a folder. The minimum user level needed to add a new sub-folder or thread is kept in the secLevelToAdd column.

The message data is pretty straightforward and self-explanatory. The repliedID is an optional piece of data. If a user clicks the reply button next to an existing message, that message's ID will be put in the repliedID field of the new message. This enables us to connect replies to one another.

Database Table Name: forum_message

Column Name	Data Type	Size
messageID	char	
title	char	50
poster	char	50
date	timestamp	
repliedID	int	
message	longvarchar	

```
CREATE TABLE forum_message (
    messageID    int PRIMARY KEY,
    parentID    int,
    title        char(50),
    poster    char(30),
    date        timestamp,
    repliedID    int,
    message    longvarchar
)
```

Creating the TAFs

Forums are great community-building tools. People can discuss topics that are of interest to them and relate to your Web site's subject. Forums give people a reason to come back to your site and enable your site to grow in content without you doing anything.

There are lots of different ways people do forums on the Net. Basically, all forums have messages and a way to group messages together. Most also have a means of grouping these groups of messages together. Different people have different names for these parts, so let's take a second and define some terms. For our purposes, a message will be called a *message*. A group of messages will be called a *thread*, and a group of threads will be called a *folder*. In our case, a folder can contain subfolders as well as threads.

TCF

There are two functions that we will find ourselves doing over and over from a couple of different places, so we want to implement those functions in a TCF to make them easily accessible and available from anywhere. The two things we need to do are get the name of a folder from a folder ID, and get the user level needed to be able to add to a folder or thread. Create a new TCF called forum.tcf.

Folder_name_from_ID Method

Insert a new method called folder_name_from_ID. This method will have one parameter, called `folderID`, which is the ID of the folder whose name we want. Its configuration should look like Figure 13.1.

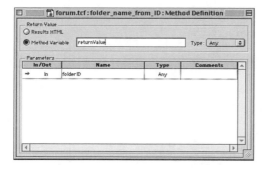

F IGURE 13.1 *Configuration of the method to get a folder's name from its ID.*

The implementation of this method is also easy. We just need to search the table of forum folders looking for the ID passed in. Because the folderID column of forum_folder is the primary key, we will never get back more than one row. Drag a new Search action into the folder_name_from_ID method then add the folderID and name columns of the forum_folder to the Select tab. For the Criteria tab, we want to check forum_folder.folderID against the method variable `folderID`, as shown in Figure 13.2.

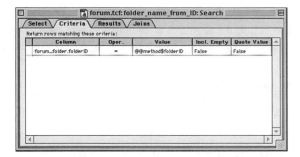

FIGURE 13.2   *Checking for the passed-in* `folderID` *in the forum_folder table.*

After the search is done, we need to handle the results. If a value is found, we must assign the value of the forum_folder.name column to the `returnValue` method variable. Put the Assign meta tag shown in Listing 13.1 into the ResultsHTML attribute of the Search action.

Listing 13.1   Assigning the Found Folder Name into Our Return Value

```
<@ASSIGN NAME="returnValue" VALUE="<@COLUMN 'forum_folder.name'>"
 SCOPE="method">
```

The only other possible result of the search is to find nothing. If nothing is found, this generally means you are at the root level of the forums because `folderID` zero isn't in the database. Put the Assign meta tag shown in Listing 13.2 into the NoResultsHTML attribute of the Search action.

Listing 13.2   Assigning the Default Name into Our Return Value

```
<@ASSIGN NAME="returnValue" VALUE="Root" SCOPE="method">
```

Add a Return action to end the method.

secLvl_from_ID Method

This method will return the minimum user level needed to change the folder with the passed-in ID. It works almost identically to the Folder_name_from_ID method, except for what it returns. Its configuration is exactly the same as the previous method, so create a new method and configure it as you did Folder_name_from_ID.

Drag in another Search action and this time add the columns forum_folder.folderID and forum_folder.secLevelToAdd. The criterion is the same as shown in Figure 13.2. We handle the return of the retrieved value by assigning the value of the found forum_folder.secLevelToAdd to returnValue. Use the code in Listing 13.3 for the ResultsHTML attribute.

Listing 13.3   Returning the Found Minimum User Level

```
<@ASSIGN NAME="returnValue" VALUE="<@COLUMN 'forum_folder.secLevelToAdd'>"
 SCOPE="method">
```

If the folder isn't in the database, it is probably the root folder, and we need to return some default value. I choose to return a minimum level of 8 to add folders to the root level of the forums. Use Listing 13.4 to accomplish this.

Listing 13.4   Returning the Minimum Level of 8 for the Root

```
<@ASSIGN NAME="returnValue" VALUE="8" SCOPE="method">
```

Drag in a Return action to end the method.

These two methods will be used later in the user TAFs to determine what options are displayed for a given user.

User TAF

We will implement the display of the forum in two TAFs: one to display folders and their contents, and one to display a thread and its messages. We will try to separate our business logic from our presentation logic as much as possible. That means we'll be doing a lot of data-gathering in actions of the TAFs, and that the display logic will be in a separate HTML file that will be included at the end.

Forum_folder.taf

When you refer a user to your forums section, the first thing you want him to see is the list of folders at the root of your forum tree. Create a new TAF called forum_folder.taf.

This same TAF will handle displaying any forum folder, not just the root folder. We need it to be flexible and to take a passed-in folder ID and list all the subfolders and threads in that folder. The challenge is that it needs to handle the root case, where we are passed no folderID. So, the first thing we need to do in this TAF is check whether there is a `folderID` argument. If there is, we will assign it to a local variable; and if there isn't, we'll assign the local variable the value of zero, for the root folder.

Using If and Else actions should be easy for you now; so, I'll let you set them up. Add an If action that checks to see whether `<@ARG folderID>` is empty. Under it, put an Assign action that assigns zero to the local variable `folderID`. Inside the Else action, assign the value of `<@ARG folderID>` to the local variable `folderID`. For the rest of the TAF, we'll ignore the argument `folderID` and only use the variable `folderID`.

We need to do four things in this TAF: display a form for adding a new thread, display a form for adding a new folder, insert the values of those forms into the forum_folder table, and display a list of folders. We want the default to display a list, and we want to display a list after a new item is inserted in the database, so the listing actions will not require a special case. We'll handle each of the other tasks by using the _function argument. The first task we'll handle is displaying the form for a new thread.

Drag in a new If action and configure it to check whether `<@ARG_function>` is equal to `add_thread`. All we need to do here is display a form, so drag in a new Result action and enter the HTML in Listing 13.5 into it.

Listing 13.5   The HTML for the New Thread Form

```
<!DOCTYPE HTML PUBLIC "-//W3C//DTD HTML 3.2//EN">
<HTML>
<HEAD>
    <TITLE>Forums:New Thread</TITLE>
</HEAD>
<BODY>

<FORM METHOD=POST ACTION="<@CGI><@APPFILE>?_function=insertFolder">

<TABLE border=1 width="372">
<TR VALIGN=TOP ALIGN=LEFT>
    <TD>
        Parent Folder:
    </TD>
    <TD>
<@ASSIGN NAME="forum" SCOPE="local" VALUE=<@CREATEOBJECT
OBJECTID="forum.tcf" TYPE="TCF">>
<@ASSIGN NAME="folderName" SCOPE="local" VALUE=
<@CALLMETHOD OBJECT="forum" SCOPE="local"
```

continues

Listing 13.5   (Continued)

```
METHOD="folder_name_from_ID(@@local$folderID)" METHODTYPE="invoke">>
        @@local$folderName
<INPUT TYPE=HIDDEN NAME="parentID"  VALUE="@@local$folderID">
    </TD>
</TR>

<TR VALIGN=TOP ALIGN=LEFT>
    <TD>
        Thread Name:
    </TD>
    <TD>
        <INPUT TYPE=TEXT MAXLENGTH=255 SIZE=25 NAME="folder_name" VALUE="">
    </TD>
</TR>

<TR VALIGN=TOP ALIGN=LEFT>
    <TD>
        Thread Description:
    </TD>
    <TD>
        <TEXTAREA ROWS=4 COLS=60 WRAP=VIRTUAL
NAME="folder_description"></TEXTAREA>
    </TD>
</TR>

<TR VALIGN=TOP ALIGN=LEFT>
    <TD>
        Min Security Level to add to folder:
    </TD>
    <TD>
        <INPUT TYPE=TEXT MAXLENGTH=255 SIZE=5 NAME="minSecLevel" VALUE="1">
    </TD>
</TR>

<TR VALIGN=TOP ALIGN=LEFT>
    <TD>
        <INPUT TYPE=HIDDEN NAME="isThread"  VALUE="true">
    </TD>
    <TD>
        <INPUT TYPE=SUBMIT NAME="Submit" VALUE="Submit">
    </TD>
</TR>

</FORM>

</BODY>
</HTML>
```

Let's look at the salient points of this HTML. First, the form itself will pass its data back to this TAF with the `<@ARG_function>` argument equal to `insertFolder`. That is the section we will define for handling the insert.

Next, we come to the part of the table that displays the parent folder's name. We get into this section by clicking a link in a page displaying a folder. Part of that link is the ID of the displayed folder, to which we want to add a thread. That's the `parentID` of the new folder. So, the first thing we do is use the parentID to look up the folder name of the parent folder and display it. Then we set up a hidden form field to pass it on along with the other data about the new folder.

We enable the user to set the minimum level needed to modify a thread in this form as well. You may choose to set that value yourself, either as a hidden field or by hardcoding it into the Insert action later. Here, we set a default value of 1.

The form for entering a new folder and the one for entering a new thread are almost identical, but the thread form sets the `isThread` argument to true and the folder form sets it to false.

After the form is displayed, we don't want anything else to happen— especially not listing of the current folders—so add a Return action after the Result action.

The next case to handle is the form for a new folder. Drag in an ElseIf action and configure it to check whether `<@ARG _function>` is `add_folder`. All it does is display a form for adding a new folder as well, so drag in another Result action and a Return action. Then put Listing 13.6 into the Result action.

Listing 13.6   Form for Entering New Folder

```
<!DOCTYPE HTML PUBLIC "-//W3C//DTD HTML 3.2//EN">
<HTML>
<HEAD>
    <TITLE>Forums</TITLE>
</HEAD>
<BODY>

<FORM METHOD=POST ACTION="<@CGI><@APPFILE>?_function=insertFolder">

<TABLE border=1 width="372">
```

continues

Listing 13.6   (Continued)

```
<TR VALIGN=TOP ALIGN=LEFT>
    <TD>
        Parent Folder:
    </TD>
    <TD>
<@ASSIGN NAME="forum" SCOPE="local" VALUE=<@CREATEOBJECT
OBJECTID="forum.tcf" TYPE="TCF">>
<@ASSIGN NAME="folderName" SCOPE="local" VALUE=<@CALLMETHOD
OBJECT="forum" SCOPE="local" METHOD=
"folder_name_from_ID(@@local$folderID)" METHODTYPE="invoke">>
        @@local$folderName
    </TD>
</TR>

<TR VALIGN=TOP ALIGN=LEFT>
    <TD>
        Folder Name:
    </TD>
    <TD>
        <INPUT TYPE=TEXT MAXLENGTH=255 SIZE=25 NAME="folder_name" VALUE="">
    </TD>
</TR>

<TR VALIGN=TOP ALIGN=LEFT>
    <TD>
        Min Security Level to add to folder:
    </TD>
    <TD>
        <INPUT TYPE=TEXT MAXLENGTH=255 SIZE=5 NAME="minSecLevel" VALUE="1">
    </TD>
</TR>

<TR VALIGN=TOP ALIGN=LEFT>
    <TD>
        Folder Description:
    </TD>
    <TD>
        <TEXTAREA ROWS=4 COLS=60 WRAP=VIRTUAL
NAME="folder_description"></TEXTAREA>
<INPUT TYPE=HIDDEN NAME="parentID"  VALUE="@@local$folderID">
    </TD>
</TR>
<TR VALIGN=TOP ALIGN=LEFT>
    <TD>
        <INPUT TYPE=HIDDEN NAME="isThread"  VALUE="false">
    </TD>
    <TD>
<INPUT TYPE=SUBMIT NAME="Submit" VALUE="Submit">
    </TD>
</TR>
```

```
</FORM>

</BODY>
</HTML>
```

As I said earlier, this form is almost identical to the new thread form. The only difference is the value of isThread, which is false in this case.

We already have handled two of the three values of <@ARG_function>. The third value is the insertFolder case referenced by our two forms. Drag in another ElseIf action and configure it to check <@ARG _function>.

The first thing we will do is check our parameters. I find that while doing development, I often do an insert looking at the results in my browser. Then I decide to change something, and I want to see the results, so I click the Refresh button. The problem is that none of the form parameters are passed in with the refresh, and I insert an empty record into the database. We will avoid this by checking the parameters at the start of the code. Drag in a new If action and configure it as shown in Figure 13.3.

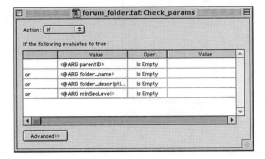

FIGURE 13.3   *Checking all the parameters to the insert.*

This checks each parameter to make sure none is empty. If all the parameters have values, we will execute the rest of the routine. If any of them is empty, we will display an error message and return. Drag in a Result action under the If action. Put Listing 13.7 in it. Drag a Return action under it to keep the rest of the TAF from being executed.

Listing 13.7   Invalid Parameter Error HTML

```
<HR>
<FONT Color=Red>
Missing parameters
</FONT>
<HR>
```

If this If action does not evaluate to true, we have valid data for the database table, but we don't have a new folder ID for this thread or folder. We get a new ID by calling our Utility TCF's method, GetNextID. Drag in a new Utility Create Object and then drag in a Call Method action to call GetNextID. You need to configure this call as shown in Figure 13.4.

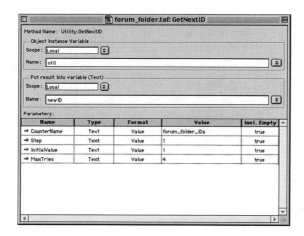

FIGURE 13.4   *Calling GetNextID to get a new unique ID for the new folder.*

Next, we need to determine what the value for the isThread column is going to be. We have an isThread argument, but it is text and we need an integer value. We need another If/Else action set with assigns. Drag in a new If action and check to see whether <@ARG isThread> is true. If it is, use an Assign action to set the local variable isThread to zero. Under the Else action, the Assign action can set the variable isThread to one.

Now we are finally ready to do the insert. Drag in a new Insert action and configure it as shown in Figure 13.5.

Column	Value	Quote Value
folderID	@@local$newID	False
parentID	<@ARG parentID>	False
name	<@ARG folder_name>	True
description	<@ARG folder_description>	True
isThread	@@local$isThread	False
secLevelToAdd	<@ARG minSecLevel>	False

Insert the following row into the table: forum_folder

FIGURE 13.5 *Inserting all the values for a new folder.*

The last thing we want this TAF to do is display a list of folders in the current folder. We will do this by adding a Search action at the end of the TAF, and we want to let the insertFolder If action fall through to the listing Search action. This means that immediately after you click Submit to add a new folder, you will see the page of the folder you just added to, with the new folder. There is one problem: In the case of insertFolder, the value of the argument folderID is empty. If we let it go on to execute the next action, we'll get strange results because @@local$folderID will be undefined. The solution to this problem is easy. Assign the value of the argument parentID to the local variable folderID. Add an Assign action to do this after the insert.

At the end of this TAF, we need to do the search that will give us the list of folders and threads for the current folder. Drag in a Search action at the bottom of the TAF, making sure that it isn't placed under the insert If action. Drag all the columns from the forum_folder into the Select tab. Order them by the name column. Configure your Criteria tab to look like the one in Figure 13.6.

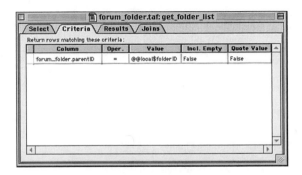

Return rows matching these criteria:

Column	Oper.	Value	Incl. Empty	Quote Value
forum_folder.parentID	=	@@local$folderID	False	False

FIGURE 13.6 *Criteria to get only those folders that are in the current folder.*

In the Results tab, you need to get the total number of matching rows, so check that box.

To keep our presentation logic separate, we will put the HTML to display the page into a separate file called folders_disp.html. Open the ResultsHTML attribute of the Search action and put the code in Listing 13.8 in it.

Listing 13.8   Include Statement to Use HTML File for Showing List

```
<@INCLUDE FILE="<@CGI><@APPFILEPATH>folders_disp.html">
```

We will handle the case in which there are no folders found in the same file, so put Listing 13.8 into the NoResults attribute as well.

The work of the folder display is done in the HTML of Listing 13.9.

Listing 13.9   HTML for the Display of a List of Folders and Threads

```
<@ASSIGN NAME="forum" SCOPE="local" VALUE=
<@CREATEOBJECT OBJECTID="forum.tcf" TYPE="TCF">>
<@ASSIGN NAME="folderName" SCOPE="local" VALUE=
<@CALLMETHOD OBJECT="forum" SCOPE="local"
METHOD="folder_name_from_ID(@@local$folderID)" METHODTYPE="invoke">>
<@ASSIGN NAME="folderSecLevel" SCOPE="local" VALUE=
<@CALLMETHOD OBJECT="forum" SCOPE="local"
METHOD="secLvl_from_ID(@@local$folderID)" METHODTYPE="invoke">>

<@ASSIGN NAME="user" SCOPE="local" VALUE=
<@CREATEOBJECT OBJECTID="user_sec.tcf" TYPE="TCF">>
<@ASSIGN NAME="currentUserLevel" SCOPE="local"
VALUE=<@CALLMETHOD OBJECT="user" SCOPE="local"
METHOD="GetCurrentUserLevel()" METHODTYPE="invoke"> >
<@ASSIGN NAME="currentUser" SCOPE="local"
VALUE=<@CALLMETHOD OBJECT="user" SCOPE="local"
METHOD="GetCurrentUserName()" METHODTYPE="invoke"> >

<HTML>
  <HEAD>
    <TITLE>
      Forums: @@local$folderName
    </title>
  </head>
  <BODY bgcolor="#ffffff" text="#000000"
link="#0000ff" alink="#ff0000" vlink="#000088" topmargin=0>
    <HR>
    <FONT SIZE="+1" face="Verdana, Arial, Helvetica, sans-serif">
      <B>
```

```
      Folder:   @@local$folderName
   </B>
</FONT>
<HR>
<table border=0 width=95%>
   <TR>
     <td>
       <FONT SIZE="1" FACE="Verdana, Arial, Helvetica, sans-serif">
         <@IF EXPR="<@VAR currentUserLevel> >=
         <@VAR folderSecLevel>" >
           Welcome <B>@@local$currentUser</B>,
           you are level @@local$currentUserLevel.
           Level @@local$folderSecLevel
           is required to add folders or threads.<BR>
           <B>
             <A HREF="<@CGI><@APPFILE>?_function=
             add_folder&folderID=@@local$folderID">New Folders</A>:
           </B>
           All registered users may add new folder to this folder.
           <BR>
           <B>
             <A HREF="<@CGI><@APPFILE>?_function=
             add_thread&folderID=@@local$folderID">New Thread</A>:
           </B>
           All registered users may add a new discussion thread to this folder.
         <@ELSEIF EXPR="<@VAR currentUserLevel> > 0">
           Welcome <B>@@local$currentUser</B>,
           you are level @@local$currentUserLevel. Level
           @@local$folderSecLevel is required to post.<BR>
         <@ELSE>
           You must be logged in to post to this thread.
         </@IF>
       </font>
     </td>
   </tr>
</table>

<table border=0 cellpadding=0 cellspacing=0 width="95%">
   <TR>
     <td bgcolor="#ffffff">
       <table border=0 cellpadding=4 border=0 cellspacing=1 width=100%>
         <tr bgcolor="#777777">
           <td width=40>
              
           </td>
           <td width=200>
             <FONT SIZE="1" FACE="Verdana, Arial, Helvetica,
             sans-serif" color="#ffffff">
               <B>
                 Topic
```

continues

Listing 13.9 (Continued)

```
                </B>
              </FONT>
            </td>
            <td>
              <FONT SIZE="1" FACE="Verdana,
              Arial, Helvetica, sans-serif" color="#ffffff">
                <B>
                  Description
                </B>
              </FONT>
            </td>
            <td width=40>
              <FONT SIZE="1" FACE="Verdana,
              Arial, Helvetica, sans-serif" color="#ffffff">
                <B>
                  Replies
                </B>
              </FONT>
            </td>
          </tr>

<@ROWS>
          <TR>
            <TD >
              <@IF EXPR="<@COLUMN
              'forum_folder.isThread'> = 0">
                <IMG SRC="folder.gif"
                ALIGN=LEFT ALT="folder">
              <@ELSE>
                Thread
              </@IF>
            </td>
            <td >
              <FONT SIZE="2" FACE="Verdana, Arial,
              Helvetica, sans-serif">
                <@IF EXPR="<@COLUMN
                'forum_folder.isThread'> = 0">
                  <A HREF="<@CGI><@APPFILE>?
                  _function=listFolder&folderID=<@COLUMN
                  'forum_folder.folderID'>">
                  <@COLUMN 'forum_folder.name'></A>
                <@ELSE>
                  <A HREF="<@CGI><@APPFILEPATH>
                  forum_message.taf?_function=listThread&
                  folderID=<@COLUMN 'forum_folder.folderID'>"><@COLUMN
                  'forum_folder.name'></A>
                </@IF>
              </FONT>
            </td>
```

```
                      <td NOWRAP >
                        <FONT SIZE="2" FACE="Verdana,
                      Arial, Helvetica, sans-serif">
                          <@COLUMN
                          'forum_folder.description'>
                        </FONT>
                      </td>
                   </tr>
</@ROWS>

<@IF EXPR="<@NUMROWS>=0">
                 <TR>
                    <TD >
                    </td>
                    <td >
                      <FONT SIZE="2" FACE="Verdana, Arial,
                      Helvetica, sans-serif">
                        <A HREF="<@CGI><@APPFILE>?_function=
                        add_folder&folderID=@@local$folderID">
                        New Folder</A><BR>
                        <A HREF="<@CGI><@APPFILE>?_function=
                        add_thread&folderID=@@local$folderID">
                        New Thread</A>
                      </FONT>
                    </td>
                    <td NOWRAP >
                      <FONT SIZE="2" FACE="Verdana, Arial,
                      Helvetica, sans-serif">
                        There are no folders or threads
                      </FONT>
                    </td>
                 </tr>

</@IF>

            </table>
          </td>
        </tr>
      </table>
      <br>


      <table border=0 width=95%>
        <TR>
          <TD align=right>
            <FONT SIZE="2" FACE="Verdana, Arial, Helvetica, sans-serif">
            <@nextpages maxrows="<@MAXROWS>" totalrows="<@TOTALROWS>">
            </font>
          </td>
```

continues

Listing 13.9   (Continued)

```
        </tr>
      </table>
      <BR>
  </font>
  </body>
  </html>
```

This HTML starts by calling some objects to get some data. First, it calls the forums TCF and saves the folder name and minimum user level in local variables. Then it calls the user_sec TCF we created in Chapter 10, "User Security," and saves the current user's name and user level in local variables.

We use these local variables for display in a couple of places. We put the folder's name in the title of the window and display it as a heading across the top of the page.

The commands you can use on the page are displayed before the table containing the folders. But we don't want to display the options to add things if the user doesn't have the required user level. We check this and display only the new folder and new thread commands if the logged-in user's level is high enough. If there is no logged-in user, the @@local$currentUser should contain zero. So, use the @ELSEIF check to see whether it is greater than zero. That would mean that someone is logged in, but his level is not high enough to enable him to add to the forum. We display a message telling him his current level and the level needed to post. The last possibility is that there is no logged-in user, and we tell him he has to be logged in.

The values of the search are displayed in a table and the next section of HTML displays the table's header. Then we go into a <@ROWS> loop for each row in the table. The first column in the table is displayed by checking the value of the isThread column. If it is zero, we display a graphic of a folder; if it is one, we display the word "Thread".

Because we want to do something different if we click the title of a folder than we do if we click the title of a thread, the next column also has to display different things based on the isThread column. If the folder is a thread, we want to link to the forum_message.taf file to handle the listing, but if it is just a folder, we want to link back to the same TAF. Notice that when we link back to this TAF, we say we want <@ARG_function> listFolder, which doesn't exist. By setting its value, we make sure that we don't hit any other <@ARG_function> case and we will fall through to this Search action.

The next column simply displays the description of the folder and is the same for both threads and folders.

What would happen in this loop if there were no folders in the current one? Nothing. The header for the table would be generated, but there would be no rows under it. What we would like to see is a message saying that there are no folders and a link to add some. We accomplish this in the next <@IF>. It checks to see whether <@NUMROWS> was zero; if so, it inserts a row with a set of links and a message saying there were no folders or threads.

This TAF displays our folder and enables us to insert new subfolders. Now, we need to set up the message portion of our forums.

forum_message.taf

In the HTML for the folder listing, we created links to a different file for threads than we did for folders. It is now time to create this TAF, called forum_message.taf.

Unlike the folder listing TAF, forum_message.taf should be called only if the folderID we want to display is known, so we don't have to convert that argument to a variable. This TAF is going to have a number of <@ARG_function> parts. The first is listThread, which is also the empty case and will list all the titles of the messages in a thread. The second is listAllMsg, which lists all the messages in a thread, showing all their data. The third is post, which displays the form for entering a new message into a folder. The fourth is InsertMessage, which handles actually putting the message in the database. The final part is showMessage, which displays one message.

The first case we want to deal with is the default case, which lists all the messages in a thread, showing just their titles as links to the message. We'll do this by first dragging in an If action and configuring it to check whether <@ARG_function> is empty or equal to listThread. Under that If, drag in a Search action. Configure the Select tab like the one in Figure 13.7.

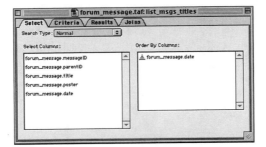

F I G U R E 1 3 . 7   *A column from the forum_message table selected for the title list.*

To display a thread, we have to get all the items in the same folder. To do this, we look at the parentID column for each message. Set your Criteria tab so that forum_message.parentID equals `<@ARG folderID>`. Again, you'll need the total number of rows, so check that box in the Results tab.

This Search action gives us a list of the messages in the passed-in folder. Now we need to display those messages. Keeping with the idea of putting our presentation logic in a separate file, put the code in Listing 13.10 in the ResultsHTML and the NoResult attribute.

Listing 13.10   Include Statement That Brings in the Message title HTML

```
<@INCLUDE FILE="<@CGI><@APPFILEPATH>thread_disp.html">
```

The HTML that actually displays this is in Listing 13.11.

Listing 13.11   Display HTML for Listing a Thread by Title

```
<@ASSIGN NAME="forum" SCOPE="local"
VALUE=<@CREATEOBJECT OBJECTID="forum.tcf" TYPE="TCF">>
<@ASSIGN NAME="folderName" SCOPE="local" VALUE=<@CALLMETHOD OBJECT="forum"
SCOPE="local" METHOD="folder_name_from_ID(<@ARG folderID>)"
METHODTYPE="invoke">>
<@ASSIGN NAME="folderSecLevel" SCOPE="local" VALUE=<@CALLMETHOD OBJECT="forum"
SCOPE="local" METHOD="secLvl_from_ID(<@ARG folderID>)" METHODTYPE="invoke">>

<@ASSIGN NAME="user" SCOPE="local" VALUE=<@CREATEOBJECT
OBJECTID="user_sec.tcf" TYPE="TCF">>
<@ASSIGN NAME="currentUserLevel" SCOPE="local" VALUE=<@CALLMETHOD OBJECT="user"
SCOPE="local" METHOD="GetCurrentUserLevel()" METHODTYPE="invoke"> >
<@ASSIGN NAME="currentUser" SCOPE="local" VALUE=<@CALLMETHOD OBJECT="user"
SCOPE="local" METHOD="GetCurrentUserName()" METHODTYPE="invoke"> >

<HTML>
```

```
<HEAD>
  <TITLE>
    Forums
  </title>
</head>
<BODY bgcolor="#ffffff" text="#000000" link="#0000ff" alink="#ff0000"
vlink="#000088" topmargin=0>
  <HR>
  <FONT SIZE="+1" face="Verdana, Arial, Helvetica, sans-serif">
    <B>
      Thread:   @@local$folderName
    </B>
  </FONT>
  <HR>

  <table border=0 width=95%>
    <TR>
      <td>
        <FONT SIZE="1" FACE="Verdana, Arial, Helvetica, sans-serif">
          <@IF EXPR="<@VAR currentUserLevel> >=
          <@VAR folderSecLevel>" >
            Welcome <B>@@local$currentUser</B>, you are level
            @@local$currentUserLevel. Level @@local$folderSecLevel
            is required to post.<BR>
            <B>
              <A HREF="<@CGI><@APPFILE>?_function=
              post&folderID=<@ARG folderID>">Post</A>:
            </B>
            All registered users may post to this thread.
            <BR>
            <B>
              <A HREF="<@CGI><@APPFILE>?_function=listAllMsg&
              folderID=<@ARG folderID>">List All</A>:
            </B>
            Display all of the messages in this thread on one page.
          <@ELSEIF EXPR="<@VAR currentUserLevel> > 0">
            Welcome <B>@@local$currentUser</B>, you are level
            @@local$currentUserLevel.
            Level @@local$folderSecLevel is required to post.<BR>
          <@ELSE>
            You must be logged in to post to this thread.
          </@IF>
        </font>
      </td>
    </tr>
  </table>

  <table border=0 cellpadding=0 cellspacing=0 width="95%">
```

continues

Listing 13.11 (Continued)

```
<TR>
  <td bgcolor="#ffffff">
    <table border=0 cellpadding=4 border=0 cellspacing=1
    width=100%>
      <tr bgcolor="#777777">
        <td width=40>
           
        </td>
        <td >
          <FONT SIZE="1" FACE="Verdana, Arial, Helvetica,
          sans-serif" color="#ffffff">
            <B>
              Title
            </B>
          </FONT>
        </td>
        <td width=200>
          <FONT SIZE="1" FACE="Verdana, Arial, Helvetica,
          sans-serif" color="#ffffff">
            <B>
              Poster
            </B>
          </FONT>
        </td>
        <td width=200>
          <FONT SIZE="1" FACE="Verdana, Arial, Helvetica,
          sans-serif" color="#ffffff">
            <B>
              Date
            </B>
          </FONT>
        </td>
      </tr>

<@ROWS>
      <TR>
        <TD >
?
        </td>
        <TD >
          <A HREF="<@CGI><@APPFILE>?_function=showMessage&
          msgID=<@COLUMN 'forum_message.messageID'>">
          <@COLUMN 'forum_message.title'></A>
        </td>
        <td >
          <FONT SIZE="2" FACE="Verdana, Arial, Helvetica,
```

```
                    sans-serif">
                      <@COLUMN 'forum_message.poster'>
                    </FONT>
                  </td>
                  <td NOWRAP >
                    <FONT SIZE="2" FACE="Verdana, Arial, Helvetica,
                    sans-serif">
                      <@COLUMN 'forum_message.date'>
                    </FONT>
                  </td>
                </tr>
</@ROWS>

<@IF EXPR="<@NUMROWS>=0">
                <TR>
                  <TD >
                  </td>
                  <td >
                    <FONT SIZE="2" FACE="Verdana, Arial, Helvetica,
                    sans-serif">
                      <A HREF="<@CGI><@APPFILE>?_function=post&
                      folderID=<@ARG folderID>">Post</A>
                    </FONT>
                  </td>
                  <td NOWRAP >
                    <FONT SIZE="2" FACE="Verdana, Arial, Helvetica,
                    sans-serif">
                     There are no messages in this thread
                    </FONT>
                  </td>
                </tr>

</@IF>

          </table>
        </td>
      </tr>
    </table>
    <br>


    <table border=0 width=95%>
      <TR>
        <TD align=right>
         <FONT SIZE="2" FACE="Verdana, Arial, Helvetica, sans-serif">
          <@nextpages maxrows="<@MAXROWS>" totalrows="<@TOTALROWS>">
          </font>
```

continues

Listing 13.11 (Continued)

```
        </td>
      </tr>
    </table>
    <BR>
</font>
</body>
</html>
```

The first block of meta tags will look familiar. It is almost the same code that we used when displaying a folder, except that it uses `<@ARG folderID>` instead of the local variable `folderID`.

As you look through the HTML, you will find the same logic for limiting access to commands based on user level. The two available commands are Post, which calls back into this TAF to post a new message, and List All, which displays all the messages on the same page. The HTML is similar in appearance to the folder list. Also, the logic for displaying the messages is the same. Just as before, we loop through the rows and create new rows for the table, and we display a message and commands if there are no messages in the thread. Each row of the HTML table has three columns. In the first column is the title of the message as a hyperlink back into this TAF with `<@ARG_function>` equal to `showMessage`. The second column is the name of the person who posted the message. The last column is the date and time the message was posted.

The next `<@ARG_function>` case we want to handle is the `listAllMsg` case. Drag in an If action and configure it to check `_function`. The Search action we use will have the same Criteria tab entries as the list with just the title, but the Select tab will include all the columns in the table. The display HTML is in the file display_msg.html, which is `<@INCLUDE>` in the ResultsHTML attribute. Listing 13.12 contains the HTML.

Listing 13.12 Display HTML for Messages

```
<@ASSIGN NAME="forum" SCOPE="local" VALUE=<@CREATEOBJECT OBJECTID="forum.tcf"
TYPE="TCF">>
<@ASSIGN NAME="folderName" SCOPE="local" VALUE=<@CALLMETHOD OBJECT="forum"
SCOPE="local" METHOD="folder_name_from_ID(<@COLUMN 'forum_message.parentID'>)"
METHODTYPE="invoke">>
```

```
<@ASSIGN NAME="folderSecLevel" SCOPE="local" VALUE=<@CALLMETHOD OBJECT="forum"
SCOPE="local" METHOD="secLvl_from_ID(<@COLUMN 'forum_message.parentID'>)"
METHODTYPE="invoke">>

<@ASSIGN NAME="user" SCOPE="local" VALUE=<@CREATEOBJECT OBJECTID="user_sec.tcf"
TYPE="TCF">>
<@ASSIGN NAME="currentUserLevel" SCOPE="local" VALUE=<@CALLMETHOD OBJECT="user"
 SCOPE="local" METHOD="GetCurrentUserLevel()" METHODTYPE="invoke"> >
<@ASSIGN NAME="currentUser" SCOPE="local" VALUE=<@CALLMETHOD OBJECT="user"
SCOPE="local" METHOD="GetCurrentUserName()" METHODTYPE="invoke"> >

<HTML>
  <HEAD>
    <TITLE>
      Thread
    </title>
  </head>
  <BODY bgcolor="#ffffff" text="#000000" link="#0000ff" alink="#ff0000"
  vlink="#000088">
    <table border=0 width=95%>
      <TR>
        <td>
          <FONT SIZE="1" FACE="Verdana, Arial, Helvetica, sans-serif">
            <@IF EXPR="<@VAR currentUserLevel> >=
            <@VAR folderSecLevel>" >
              <B>
                <A HREF="<@CGI><@APPFILE>?_function=post&
                folderID=<@COLUMN 'forum_message.parentID'>">Post</A>:
              </B>
              All registered users may post to this thread.
              <BR>
            <@ELSEIF EXPR="<@VAR currentUserLevel> > 0">
              Welcome <B>@@local$currentUser</B>, you are
              level @@local$currentUserLevel.
              Level @@local$folderSecLevel is required to post.<BR>
            <@ELSE>
              You must be logged in to post to this thread.
            </@IF>
          </font>
        </td>
      </tr>
    </table>
    <FONT SIZE="2" FACE="Verdana, Arial, Helvetica, sans-serif">
      <table border=0 cellpadding=0 cellspacing=0 width="95%">
        <TR>
          <td bgcolor="#ffffff">
          <table width=100% border=0 cellspacing=1 cellpadding=4>
            <TR bgcolor="#777777">
```

continues

Listing 13.12 (Continued)

```
                        <TD valign=middle width=18%>
                          <FONT SIZE="1" face="Verdana, Arial,
                          Helvetica, sans-serif" color="#ffffff">
                            <B>
                              Author
                            </B>
                          </FONT>
                        </TD>
                        <TD valign=middle>
                          <FONT SIZE="1" face="Verdana, Arial,
                          Helvetica, sans-serif" color="#ffffff">
                            <B>
                              Thread:
                                <@ASSIGN NAME="forum"
                                SCOPE="local" VALUE=<@CREATEOBJECT
                                OBJECTID="forum.tcf" TYPE="TCF">>
                                <@CALLMETHOD OBJECT="forum"
                                SCOPE="local" METHOD="folder_name_from_ID
                                (<@COLUMN 'forum_message.parentID'>)"
                                METHODTYPE="invoke">

                            </B>
                          </FONT>
                        </TD>
                      </TR>
<@ROWS>
                      <tr >
                        <TD width=18% valign=top>
                          <FONT SIZE="2" face="Verdana, Arial,
                          Helvetica, sans-serif">
                            <B>
                             <@COLUMN 'forum_message.poster'>
                            </B>
                          </font>
                          <BR>
                          <FONT SIZE="1" face="Verdana, Arial,
                          Helvetica, sans-serif">
                            profile
                          </FONT>
                        </td>
                        <TD>
                            <TABLE BORDER="0" width=100%>
                              <TR>
                                <TD>
                                   <FONT SIZE="2"
                                   FACE="Verdana, Arial, Helvetica, sans-serif">
```

```
                                    <B><@COLUMN 'forum_message.title'></B>
                                        

                               </FONT>
                             </TD>
                             <TD align=right>
                               <FONT SIZE="2"
                               FACE="Verdana, Arial, Helvetica, sans-serif">
                                 <A HREF="<@CGI
<@APPFILE>?_function=post&folderID=<@COLUMN 'forum_message.parentID'>
&replyID=<@COLUMN 'forum_message.messageID'>&subject=RE:
<@COLUMN 'forum_message.title'>">Reply</A>
                                 <A HREF=""></A>
                               </FONT>
                             </TD>

                             <TD width=210>
                               <FONT SIZE="1"
                               color="#666666" face="Verdana, Arial,
                               Helvetica, sans-serif">
                                 posted
<@COLUMN 'forum_message.date'>    
                               </FONT>
                             </TD>
                           </TR>
                         </TABLE>
                         <HR>
                        <FONT SIZE="2" FACE="Verdana, Arial,
                        Helvetica, sans-serif">
                          <@COLUMN 'forum_message.message'
                          encoding=none>
                          </FONT>
                       </P>
                     </td>
                   </tr>
</@ROWS>
                 </table>
               </td>
             </tr>
           </table>
           <table border=0 width="95%">
             <TR>
               <TD valign=top align=left>
                 <FONT SIZE="1" FACE="Verdana, Arial, Helvetica,
                 sans-serif">
                   <P>
                   All times are CST (US)
```

continues

Listing 13.12   (Continued)

```
              </FONT>
            </td>
            <td align=right valign=top>
              <FONT SIZE="1" FACE="Verdana, Arial, Helvetica,
              sans-serif">
                 <A HREF="<@CGI><@APPFILE>
?_function=listThread&folderID=<@COLUMN 'forum_message.parentID'>">
List Thread Titles</A>
              </font>
            </td>
          </tr>
      </TABLE>
      <br>
  </font>
</body>
</html>
```

We start with the now familiar object meta tags to get our folder and user information. In this case, we are using the `<@COLUMN 'forum_message.parentID'>` tag to get the current folder's ID. Then we check the user level versus the security level to display the commands. A table is created for the messages to be displayed in and a `<@ROWS>` loop displays each found message. There is a fair bit of HTML here to make the page look cool, but you should be able to figure it out. Do notice that hidden in there is another `<@IF>` to display a reply command after each message. The link that the reply command uses includes the current message's message ID as the `replyID` parameter.

The next `<@ARG_function>` case we need to handle is the `showMessage` case. Create a new If action for this case and drag in a new Search action. The Search action needs all the forum_message table's columns, just as before, but the criteria are different. Instead of searching for the parentID, we look at the messageID. Configure your Criteria tab as shown in Figure 13.8.

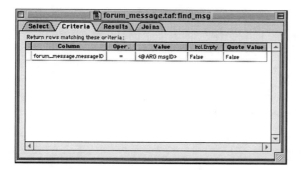

FIGURE 13.8 *Searching for a specific message.*

It turns out that we can reuse the display from the List All page. We will have only one row in our result set, so we will get only one message on the page. All the formatting and commands work the same. Include Listing 13.13 in the ResultsHTML attribute.

Listing 13.13   Including the Message Display Code for a Single Message

```
<@INCLUDE FILE="<@CGI><@APPFILEPATH>display_msg.html">
```

The next `<@ARG_function>` case to handle is for post. We want to enforce the rule that you must be logged in to post before we put up the form to enter a new message. Drag in the user_sec object and name the object variable user. Then drag the method GetCurrentUserName and assign the return value to a local variable named username. There are no parameters for this routine, so you don't need to do any other configuration.

To check for log in, we need an If/Else action set. Add an If action and have it determine whether `@@local$username` is empty. If it is, we need to put up an error message, so drag in a Results action and enter the error message HTML in Listing 13.14.

Listing 13.14   Error Message for Trying to Post When Not Logged In

```
<HR>
<FONT Color=Red>
You must be logged in to post.
</FONT>
<HR>
```

Drag in an Else action at the same level as the If action. There is a logged-in user now, so we can put up the form to enter a new message. That form is displayed by the HTML in Listing 13.15.

Listing 13.15 HTML for the Posting Form

```
<!DOCTYPE HTML PUBLIC "-//W3C//DTD HTML 3.2//EN">
<HTML>
<HEAD>
    <TITLE>Forums:New Message</TITLE>
</HEAD>
<BODY>

<FORM METHOD=POST ACTION="<@CGI><@APPFILE>?_function=insertMessage">

<TABLE border=1 width="372">
<TR VALIGN=TOP ALIGN=LEFT>
    <TD>
        Parent FolderID:
    </TD>
    <TD>
        <@ARG folderID>
        <INPUT TYPE=HIDDEN NAME="folderID"  VALUE="<@ARG folderID>">
    </TD>
</TR>

<TR VALIGN=TOP ALIGN=LEFT>
    <TD>
        Poster:
    </TD>
    <TD>
        @@local$username
        <INPUT TYPE=HIDDEN NAME="poster"  VALUE="@@local$username">
    </TD>
</TR>

<TR VALIGN=TOP ALIGN=LEFT>
    <TD>
        Message Title:
    </TD>
    <TD>
        <INPUT TYPE=TEXT MAXLENGTH=255 SIZE=50 NAME="title"
VALUE="<@ARG subject>">
        <INPUT TYPE=HIDDEN NAME="replyID"  VALUE="<@ARG replyID>">

    </TD>
</TR>

<TR VALIGN=TOP ALIGN=LEFT>
    <TD>
        Message:
```

```
    </TD>
    <TD>
        <TEXTAREA ROWS=10 COLS=70 WRAP=VIRTUAL NAME="msg_body"></TEXTAREA>
    </TD>
</TR>
<TR VALIGN=TOP ALIGN=LEFT>
    <TD>
    </TD>
    <TD>
<INPUT TYPE=SUBMIT NAME="Submit" VALUE="Submit">
    </TD>
</TR>

</FORM>

</BODY>
</HTML>
```

The posting form is a straightforward HTML form with only a couple of special features. Its data will be passed back to this TAF with <@ARG_function> set to insertMessage. There are three hidden fields; the name of the current user as poster, and the folderID and replyID arguments are passed on.

The last <@ARG_function> case is insertMessage. This is where we will actually insert the message into the database. Every message needs a unique ID, so you need to drag in the Utility object and configure it with the variable name utility. Then drag in the GetNextID method and configure it as shown in Figure 13.9.

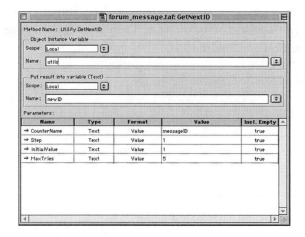

forum_message.taf: GetNextID

Method Name: Utility.GetNextID

Object Instance Variable
Scope: Local
Name: utils

Put result into variable (Text)
Scope: Local
Name: newID

Parameters:

Name	Type	Format	Value	Incl. Empty
→ CounterName	Text	Value	messageID	true
→ Step	Text	Value	1	true
→ InitialValue	Text	Value	1	true
→ MaxTries	Text	Value	5	true

FIGURE 13.9   *The method call to get a new ID for the message.*

As we did for the insert of a new folder, we want to check our parameters to make sure they are valid. Drag in an If action and configure it as shown in Figure 13.10.

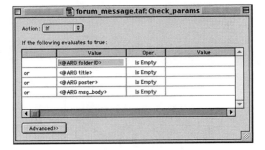

FIGURE 13.10   *An If action that checks the parameter for a new message.*

If this action fails, we need to display an error and return. Drag in a Results action and put the code in Listing 13.16 into it. Drag in a Return action to exit the TAF.

Listing 13.16   Parameter Error Message

```
<HR>
<FONT Color=Red>
Missing parameters
</FONT>
<HR>
```

Now that we're sure we have valid parameters for every column in the table, we need to do the insert of the message. Drag in an Insert action and configure it as shown in Figure 13.11.

Column	Value	Quote Value
messageID	@@local$newID	False
parentID	<@ARG folderID>	False
title	<@ARG title>	True
poster	<@ARG poster>	True
date	<@CURRENTTIMESTAMP>	True
repliedID	<@ARG replyID>	False
message	<@ARG msg_body>	True

Insert the following row into the table: forum_message

FIGURE 13.11   *Adding a message to the database.*

It would be good to display the thread with the new message added, just as we did after the insert of a new folder. Because we don't have a fall-through to the listing, we must add actions to make it happen. The easiest way to do this is to make a copy of the earlier Search action that listed the messages by title. Copy that action right under the insert.

These two TAFs give you a complete system for discussion on your Web site. You have the flexibility to create various folders and put individual discussion threads inside those folders. You can limit posting to people who are logged in and set the minimum user level needed to modify the folder.

Admin TAFs

The only admin tasks we need to do are deleting a folder or message. We will create a separate TAF to perform these functions and modify the user TAFs to expose the delete command to users with a level higher than 8.

Let's go ahead and add the commands to the user TAFs first. We really don't have to add anything to the TAFs, we just need to add delete links to the pages as they are displayed. That can be done by modifying the HTML include files for the two message lists. Listing 13.17 is the file folders_disp.html with the commands added in a column after the description.

Listing 13.17   Folder Display HTML Modified to Allow Admin Deletion of Folders

```
<@ASSIGN NAME="forum" SCOPE="local" VALUE=<@CREATEOBJECT OBJECTID="forum.tcf"
TYPE="TCF">>
<@ASSIGN NAME="folderName" SCOPE="local" VALUE=<@CALLMETHOD OBJECT="forum"
SCOPE="local" METHOD="folder_name_from_ID(@@local$folderID)" METHODTYPE=
"invoke">>
<@ASSIGN NAME="folderSecLevel" SCOPE="local" VALUE=<@CALLMETHOD OBJECT="forum"
SCOPE="local" METHOD="secLvl_from_ID(@@local$folderID)" METHODTYPE="invoke">>

<@ASSIGN NAME="user" SCOPE="local" VALUE=<@CREATEOBJECT OBJECTID="user_sec.tcf"
TYPE="TCF">>
<@ASSIGN NAME="currentUserLevel" SCOPE="local" VALUE=<@CALLMETHOD OBJECT="user"
SCOPE="local" METHOD="GetCurrentUserLevel()" METHODTYPE="invoke"> >
<@ASSIGN NAME="currentUser" SCOPE="local" VALUE=<@CALLMETHOD OBJECT="user"
SCOPE="local" METHOD="GetCurrentUserName()" METHODTYPE="invoke"> >

<HTML>
  <HEAD>
```

continues

Listing 13.17   (Continued)

```
    <TITLE>
      Forums: @@local$folderName
    </title>
  </head>
  <BODY bgcolor="#ffffff" text="#000000" link="#0000ff" alink="#ff0000"
  vlink="#000088" topmargin=0>
    <HR>
    <FONT SIZE="+1" face="Verdana, Arial, Helvetica, sans-serif">
      <B>
        Folder:   @@local$folderName
      </B>
    </FONT>
    <HR>
    <table border=0 width=95%>
      <TR>
        <td>
         <FONT SIZE="1" FACE="Verdana, Arial, Helvetica, sans-serif">
            <@IF EXPR="<@VAR currentUserLevel> >=
            <@VAR folderSecLevel>" >
              Welcome <B>@@local$currentUser</B>,
              you are level @@local$currentUserLevel.
              Level @@local$folderSecLevel is required to add folders
              or threads.<BR>
              <B>
                <A HREF="<@CGI><@APPFILE>?_function=
                add_folder&folderID=@@local$folderID">
New Folders</A>:
              </B>
              All registered users may add new folder to this folder.
              <BR>
              <B>
                <A HREF="<@CGI><@APPFILE>?_function=
                add_thread&folderID=@@local$folderID">New Thread</A>:
              </B>
              All registered users may add a new discussion
              thread to this folder.
            <@ELSEIF EXPR="<@VAR currentUserLevel> > 0">
              Welcome <B>@@local$currentUser</B>, you are
              level @@local$currentUserLevel. Level @@local$folderSecLevel
              is required to post.<BR>
            <@ELSE>
              You must be logged in to post to this thread.
            </@IF>
          </font>
        </td>
      </tr>
    </table>

    <table border=0 cellpadding=0 cellspacing=0 width="95%">
```

```
<TR>
  <td bgcolor="#ffffff">
    <table border=0 cellpadding=4 border=0 cellspacing=1
    width=100%>
      <tr bgcolor="#777777">
        <td width=40>
           
        </td>
        <td width=200>
          <FONT SIZE="1" FACE="Verdana, Arial,
          Helvetica, sans-serif" color="#ffffff">
            <B>
              Topic
            </B>
          </FONT>
        </td>
        <td>
          <FONT SIZE="1" FACE="Verdana, Arial,
          Helvetica, sans-serif" color="#ffffff">
            <B>
              Description
            </B>
          </FONT>
        </td>
        <@IF EXPR="<@VAR currentUserLevel> >= 8" >
          <td width=40>
            <FONT SIZE="1" FACE="Verdana, Arial,
            Helvetica, sans-serif" color="#ffffff">
              <B>
                Admin
              </B>
            </FONT>
          </td>
        </@IF>
      </tr>

<@ROWS>
      <TR>
        <TD >
          <@IF EXPR="<@COLUMN 'forum_folder.isThread'> = 0">
            <IMG SRC="folder.gif" ALIGN=LEFT ALT="folder">
          <@ELSE>
            Thread
          </@IF>
        </td>
        <td >
          <FONT SIZE="2" FACE="Verdana, Arial, Helvetica, sans-serif">
            <@IF EXPR="<@COLUMN 'forum_folder.isThread'> = 0">
              <A HREF="<@CGI><@APPFILE>?_function=
              listFolder&folderID=<@COLUMN 'forum_folder.folderID'>">
```

continues

Listing 13.17 **(Continued)**

```
                        <@COLUMN 'forum_folder.name'></A>
                    <@ELSE>
                      <A HREF="<@CGI
<@APPFILEPATH>forum_message.taf?_function=listThread&folderID=
<@COLUMN 'forum_folder.folderID'>"><@COLUMN 'forum_folder.name'></A>
                    </@IF>
                  </FONT>
                </td>
                <td NOWRAP >
                  <FONT SIZE="2" FACE="Verdana, Arial, Helvetica, sans-serif">
                    <@COLUMN 'forum_folder.description'>
                  </FONT>
                </td>
                <@IF EXPR="<@VAR currentUserLevel> >= 8" >
                  <TD WIDTH="40">
                    <A HREF="<@CGI><@APPFILEPATH>forum_admin.taf?_
                    function=deleteFolder&folderID=<@COLUMN
                    'forum_folder.folderID'>">delete</A>
                  </TD>
                </@IF>
              </tr>
</@ROWS>

<@IF EXPR="<@NUMROWS>=0">
              <TR>
                <TD >
                </td>
                <td >
                  <FONT SIZE="2" FACE="Verdana, Arial, Helvetica, sans-serif">
                    <A HREF="<@CGI><@APPFILE>?_function=
                    add_folder&folderID=@@local$folderID">New Folder</A><BR>
                    <A HREF="<@CGI><@APPFILE?_function=
                    add_thread&folderID=@@local$folderID">New Thread</A>
                  </FONT>
                </td>
                <td NOWRAP >
                  <FONT SIZE="2" FACE="Verdana, Arial, Helvetica, sans-serif">
                    There are no folders or threads
                  </FONT>
                </td>
              </tr>

</@IF>

          </table>
```

```
        </td>
      </tr>
    </table>
    <br>


    <table border=0 width=95%>
      <TR>
        <TD align=right>
         <FONT SIZE="2" FACE="Verdana, Arial, Helvetica, sans-serif">
          <@nextpages maxrows="<@MAXROWS>" totalrows="<@TOTALROWS>">
          </font>
        </td>
      </tr>
    </table>
    <BR>
</font>
</body>
</html>
```

The code in italics is the change. The first set of italic code adds the column to the header with the admin title. The second set of italic code adds links to our admin TAF with the folder ID as a parameter.

The display_msg.html must change as well. Listing 13.18 shows the changed file.

Listing 13.18   Message Display HTML Modified to Allow an Admin to Delete a Message

```
<@ASSIGN NAME="forum" SCOPE="local" VALUE=<@CREATEOBJECT OBJECTID="forum.tcf"
 TYPE="TCF">>
<@ASSIGN NAME="folderName" SCOPE="local" VALUE=<@CALLMETHOD OBJECT="forum"
SCOPE="local" METHOD="folder_name_from_ID(<@COLUMN 'forum_message.parentID'>)"
 METHODTYPE="invoke">>
<@ASSIGN NAME="folderSecLevel" SCOPE="local" VALUE=<@CALLMETHOD OBJECT="forum"
 SCOPE="local" METHOD="secLvl_from_ID(<@COLUMN 'forum_message.parentID'>)"
METHODTYPE="invoke">>

<@ASSIGN NAME="user" SCOPE="local" VALUE=<@CREATEOBJECT OBJECTID="user_sec.tcf"
 TYPE="TCF">>
<@ASSIGN NAME="currentUserLevel" SCOPE="local" VALUE=<@CALLMETHOD OBJECT="user"
```

continues

Listing 13.18   (Continued)

```
SCOPE="local" METHOD="GetCurrentUserLevel()" METHODTYPE="invoke"> >
<@ASSIGN NAME="currentUser" SCOPE="local" VALUE=<@CALLMETHOD OBJECT="user"
SCOPE="local" METHOD="GetCurrentUserName()" METHODTYPE="invoke"> >

<HTML>
  <HEAD>
    <TITLE>
      Thread
    </title>
  </head>
  <BODY bgcolor="#ffffff" text="#000000" link="#0000ff" alink="#ff0000"
  vlink="#000088">
    <table border=0 width=95%>
      <TR>
        <td>
          <FONT SIZE="1" FACE="Verdana, Arial, Helvetica, sans-serif">
            <@IF EXPR="<@VAR currentUserLevel> >=
            <@VAR folderSecLevel>" >
              <B>
                <A HREF="<@CGI><@APPFILE>?_function=post&
                folderID=<@COLUMN 'forum_message.parentID'>">Post</A>:
              </B>
              All registered users may post to this thread.
              <BR>
            <@ELSEIF EXPR="<@VAR currentUserLevel> > 0">
              Welcome <B>@@local$currentUser</B>, you are
              level @@local$currentUserLevel.
              Level @@local$folderSecLevel is required to post.<BR>
            <@ELSE>
              You must be logged in to post to this thread.
            </@IF>
          </font>
        </td>
      </tr>
    </table>
    <FONT SIZE="2" FACE="Verdana, Arial, Helvetica, sans-serif">
        <table border=0 cellpadding=0 cellspacing=0 width="95%">
          <TR>
            <td bgcolor="#ffffff">
              <table width=100% border=0 cellspacing=1 cellpadding=4>
                <TR bgcolor="#777777">
                  <TD valign=middle width=18%>
                    <FONT SIZE="1" face="Verdana, Arial, Helvetica,
                    sans-serif" color="#ffffff">
                      <B>
                        Author
                      </B>
                    </FONT>
```

```
                  </TD>
              <TD valign=middle>
                <FONT SIZE="1" face="Verdana, Arial, Helvetica,
                sans-serif" color="#ffffff">
                  <B>
                    Thread:
                      <@ASSIGN NAME="forum" SCOPE="local" VALUE=
                      <@CREATEOBJECT OBJECTID="forum.tcf" TYPE="TCF">>
                      <@CALLMETHOD OBJECT="forum" SCOPE="local"
                      METHOD="folder_name_from_ID (<@COLUMN
                      'forum_message.parentID'>)" METHODTYPE="invoke">

                  </B>
                </FONT>
              </TD>
            </TR>
<@ROWS>
              <tr >
                <TD width=18% valign=top>
                 <FONT SIZE="2" face="Verdana, Arial, Helvetica, sans-serif">
                   <B>
                    <@COLUMN 'forum_message.poster'>
                   </B>
                 </font>
                 <BR>
                 <FONT SIZE="1" face="Verdana, Arial, Helvetica, sans-serif">
                   profile
                 </FONT>
                </td>
                <TD>
                    <TABLE BORDER="0" width=100%>
                      <TR>
                        <TD>
                          <FONT SIZE="2" FACE="Verdana, Arial,
                            Helvetica, sans-serif">
                    <B><@COLUMN 'forum_message.title'></B>
                                

                          </FONT>
                        </TD>
                        <TD align=right>
                          <FONT SIZE="2" FACE="Verdana, Arial,
                          Helvetica, sans-serif">
                           <@IF EXPR="<@VAR currentUserLevel> >=
                           <@VAR folderSecLevel>" >
                              <A HREF="<@CGI><@APPFILE>?_
                              function=post&folderID=<@COLUMN
                              'forum_message.parentID'>
                              &replyID=<@COLUMN 'forum_message.messageID'>
```

continues

Listing 13.18 (Continued)

```
                                      &subject=RE:<@COLUMN 'forum_message.title'>
                                      ">Reply</A>
                                  </@IF>
                                  <@IF EXPR="<@VAR currentUserLevel> >= 8" >
                                      <A HREF="<@CGI><@APPFILEPATH>forum_admin.taf?_
                                      function=deleteMessage&msgID=
                                      <@COLUMN 'forum_message.messageID'>">Delete</A>
                                  </@IF>
                                  </FONT>
                              </TD>

                              <TD width=210>
                                  <FONT SIZE="1" color="#666666" face="Verdana,
                                  Arial, Helvetica, sans-serif">
                                      posted
<@COLUMN 'forum_message.date'>    
                                  </FONT>
                              </TD>
                          </TR>
                      </TABLE>
                      <HR>
                      <FONT SIZE="2" FACE="Verdana, Arial,
                      Helvetica, sans-serif">
              <@COLUMN 'forum_message.message' encoding=none>
                      </FONT>
                  </P>
                </td>
              </tr>
</@ROWS>
            </table>
          </td>
        </tr>
      </table>
      <table border=0 width="95%">
        <TR>
          <TD valign=top align=left>
            <FONT SIZE="1" FACE="Verdana, Arial, Helvetica, sans-serif">
              <P>
              All times are CST (US)
            </FONT>
          </td>
          <td align=right valign=top>
            <FONT SIZE="1" FACE="Verdana, Arial, Helvetica, sans-serif">
                <A HREF="<@CGI><@APPFILE>?_function=listThread&folderID=
                <@COLUMN 'forum_message.parentID'>">List Thread Titles</A>
```

```
                </font>
              </td>
            </tr>
          </TABLE>
          <br>
      </font>
  </body>
</html>
```

The only change made to the file was to add a Delete link right after the Reply link that is next to each message title. We check to make sure that the user level is higher than 8 before we display the link. The Delete links to our admin TAF with <@ARG_function> equal to deleteFolder.

Forum_admin.taf

Create a new TAF named forum_admin.taf. At the top of this TAF, we want to make sure that the user can delete items, just in case he found a way to this TAF by accident.

Sometimes you want to keep a few actions together in a TAF because they perform a certain piece of functionality, but you don't want them cluttering up the hierarchy and making your TAF hard to read. What you'd like to do is put these items inside another action that could be collapsed. Tango provides this functionality with the Group action. We will use it to group the check for user level at the top of the TAF.

> *You can also drag or copy a Group action and get all the items under it, which makes it useful for moving around chunks of code. You can even create a dummy TAF that contains a number of Group actions with commonly used actions inside them, and copy those Group actions to the TAFs that need them. This gives you a way of adding action snippets.*

Drag in a new Group action at the top of the TAF. We need to get the current user's user level, so drag in the user_sec object and configure its name to be user. Then drag in the GetCurrentUserLevel method and put its return value in a local variable called userlevel. Now add an If action to determine whether @@local$userlevel is less than 8. If it is, we need to put up an error message and exit the routine. Drag in a Results action and put Listing 13.19 into it. Then add a Return action to end execution. All this should be inside the Group action. You could drag this Group action into another TAF to check user level any time you want.

Listing 13.19 Error Message for Accessing a TAF with Too Low a User Level

```
<HR>
<FONT Color=Red>
Your user level is too low to do this.
</FONT>
<HR>
```

You can now collapse this Group and go on to the rest of the TAF without having to look at the five actions we just added.

This TAF has to handle two functions: deleteMessage and deleteFolder. We must set up an If/ElseIf block to handle these two values of _function.

First, we'll handle deleting a message. Drag in an If action and have it check whether <@ARG_function> is equal to deleteMessage. Under this If, drag in a Delete action. When deleteMessage is called, there is another argument called msgID, whose value is the messageID of the message to be deleted. All we have to do is configure the Delete action to check the forum_message.messageID column for this argument. Figure 13.12 shows how this should look.

FIGURE 13.12 *Deleting a specific message.*

Deleting a folder is only a little more complicated. Drag in an If action and configure it to check whether <@ARG_function> is equal to deleteFolder. When you delete a folder, you not only have to delete the folder from the folder table, but you also must delete all the messages and subfolders in that folder for their folder and message tables.

Because messages are at the bottom of the tree, let's delete them first. Drag in a Delete action and configure it as shown in Figure 13.13. This deletes all rows where the parentID column is the same as the `folderID` argument.

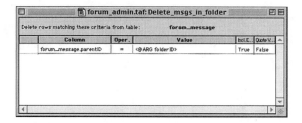

FIGURE 13.13   *Deleting all the messages in a folder.*

Next, we need to delete the actual folder and all its subfolders. We can do this in one Delete action by telling it to delete all rows where the folderID column or the parentID column is equal to the passed in `folderID`. The Delete action looks like Figure 13.14 when done.

FIGURE 13.14   *Deleting a folder and its child folders.*

An admin can now delete messages that contain inappropriate material or that they just don't like. Whole threads can be deleted when they become cold and stale. Your Web site now has a flexible forum module.

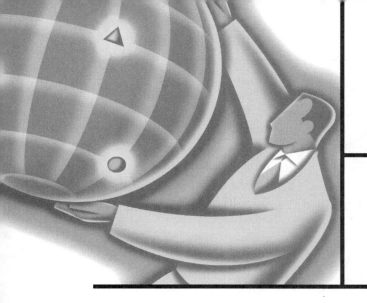

Store Front

What We'll Learn

- How to use the Store Front demo that comes with Tango 2000

Purpose

You will learn how to use the e-commerce application that comes with Tango 2000.

Planning

Database Schema

When Tango 2000 installs, it normally installs the tables that go with its demos, including these Store Front demo tables. Don't be overwhelmed by the number of tables. Creating an e-commerce application can be very complex, and Store Front is a feature-rich e-commerce application.

You can either delve into these tables and get a feel for the data behind the application, or you can skip ahead and try to understand how the application works and come back to study how it saves its data.

Database Table Name: Basket

Column Name	Data Type	Description
ShopperID	INTEGER	ID of basket owner
ProductID	INTEGER	ID of product in basket
ItemNumber	INTEGER	Line item number
Quantity	INTEGER	Quantity of product

```
CREATE TABLE Basket
(
    CONSTRAINT FK_B_ShopperID FOREIGN KEY (ShopperID)
REFERENCES Shopper ON DELETE CASCADE,
    CONSTRAINT FK_B_ProductID FOREIGN KEY (ProductID)
REFERENCES Product ON DELETE CASCADE,
    CONSTRAINT UK_Record UNIQUE (ShopperID, ProductID),
    ShopperID INTEGER,
    ProductID INTEGER,
    ItemNumber INTEGER,
    Quantity INTEGER
)
```

Database Table Name: Counters

Column Name	Data Type	Description
Name	CHAR(100)	Name
Value	INTEGER	Current value
Locked	BIT	Locked state

```
CREATE TABLE Counters
(
    CONSTRAINT UK_Name UNIQUE (Name),
    Name CHAR(100) CASE,
    Value INTEGER,
    Locked BIT
)
```

Database Table Name: Country

Column Name	Data Type	Description
Country	CHAR(2)	Country abbreviation
Name	CHAR(100)	Name
Disabled	BIT	Disabled flag

```
CREATE TABLE Country
(
    CONSTRAINT PK_Country PRIMARY KEY (Country),
    Country CHAR(2),
    Name CHAR(100),
    Disabled BIT
)
```

Database Table Name: Department

Column Name	Data Type	Description
ID	IDENTITY	Unique ID
ParentID	INTEGER	ID of parent
Name	CHAR(255)	Name
ItemNumber	INTEGER	Line item number
SelectionList	BIT	Product menu display flag
SelectionItem Number	INTEGER	Product menu line item number
Attribute0	CHAR(100)	Extra attribute
Attribute1	CHAR(100)	Extra attribute
Attribute2	CHAR(100)	Extra attribute
Attribute3	CHAR(100)	Extra attribute
Attribute4	CHAR(100)	Extra attribute
Disabled	BIT	Disabled flag
Description	LONGVARCHAR	HTML-capable description

```
CREATE TABLE Department
(
    CONSTRAINT PK_ID PRIMARY KEY (ID),
    ID IDENTITY,
    ParentID INTEGER,
    Name CHAR(255),
    ItemNumber INTEGER,
    SelectionList BIT,
    SelectionItemNumber INTEGER,
    Attribute0 CHAR(100),
    Attribute1 CHAR(100),
    Attribute2 CHAR(100),
    Attribute3 CHAR(100),
    Attribute4 CHAR(100),
    Disabled BIT,
    Description LONGVARCHAR
)
```

Database Table Name: DepartmentProducts

Column Name	Type	Description
DepartmentID	INTEGER	ID of department
ProductID	INTEGER	ID of product to display in department
ItemNumber	INTEGER	Line item number

```
CREATE TABLE DepartmentProducts
(
    CONSTRAINT FK_DP_DepartmentID FOREIGN KEY (DepartmentID)
REFERENCES Department ON DELETE CASCADE,
    CONSTRAINT FK_DP_ProductID FOREIGN KEY (ProductID)
REFERENCES Product ON DELETE CASCADE,
    CONSTRAINT UK_Record UNIQUE (DepartmentID, ProductID),
    DepartmentID INTEGER,
    ProductID INTEGER,
    ItemNumber INTEGER
)
```

Database Table Name: DepartmentRelations

Column Name	Data Type	Description
DepartmentID	INTEGER	ID of department
RelatedID	INTEGER	ID of related department
ItemNumber	INTEGER	Line item number

```
CREATE TABLE DepartmentRelations
(
    CONSTRAINT FK_DR_DepartmentID FOREIGN KEY (DepartmentID)
REFERENCES Department ON DELETE CASCADE,
    CONSTRAINT FK_DR_RelatedID FOREIGN KEY (RelatedID)
REFERENCES Department ON DELETE CASCADE,
    CONSTRAINT UK_Record UNIQUE (DepartmentID, RelatedID),
    DepartmentID INTEGER,
    RelatedID INTEGER,
    ItemNumber INTEGER
)
```

Database Table Name: MethodShippingRules

Column Name	Data Type	Description
ShippingMethodID	INTEGER	ID of shipping method
ShippingRuleID	INTEGER	ID of rule type
JavaScriptRule	LONGVARCHAR	JavaScript code for rule

```
CREATE TABLE MethodShippingRules
(
    CONSTRAINT FK_MSR_ShipMethID FOREIGN KEY (ShippingMethodID)
REFERENCES ShippingMethod ON DELETE CASCADE,
    CONSTRAINT FK_MSR_ShipRuleID FOREIGN KEY (ShippingRuleID)
REFERENCES ShippingRule ON DELETE CASCADE,
    CONSTRAINT UK_Record UNIQUE (ShippingMethodID, ShippingRuleID),
    ShippingMethodID INTEGER,
    ShippingRuleID INTEGER,
    JavaScriptRule LONGVARCHAR
)
```

Database Table Name: OrderStatus

Column Name	Data Type	Description
ID	IDENTITY	Unique ID
Name	CHAR(100)	Name
Description	LONGVARCHAR	Description

```
CREATE TABLE ProductShippingRules
(
    CONSTRAINT FK_PSR_ProductID FOREIGN KEY (ProductID)
REFERENCES Product ON DELETE CASCADE,
    CONSTRAINT FK_PSR_ShipMethID FOREIGN KEY (ShippingMethodID)
REFERENCES ShippingMethod ON DELETE CASCADE,
    CONSTRAINT FK_PSR_ShipRuleID FOREIGN KEY (ShippingRuleID)
REFERENCES ShippingRule ON DELETE CASCADE,
    CONSTRAINT UK_Record UNIQUE (ProductID, ShippingMethodID,
ShippingRuleID),
    ProductID INTEGER,
    ShippingMethodID INTEGER,
    ShippingRuleID INTEGER,
    JavaScriptRule LONGVARCHAR
)
```

Database Table Name: Product

Column Name	Data Type	Description
ID	IDENTITY	Unique ID
ParentID	INTEGER	Reserved for future use
Name	CHAR(255)	Name
ItemNumber	INTEGER	Reserved for future use
SKU	CHAR(100)	Unique product SKU
Code	CHAR(255)	Code

continues

Database Table Name: Product   (Continued)

Column Name	Data Type	Description
Type	CHAR(255)	Type
Weight	FLOAT	Weight
ListPrice	CURRENCY	List price
SalePrice	CURRENCY	Sale price
SaleStart	TIMESTAMP	Sale start date
SaleEnd	TIMESTAMP	Sale end date
OnSaleMessage	LONGVARCHAR	HTML-capable sales message
ImageFile	CHAR(255)	Image file
ImageWidth	INTEGER	Image width
ImageHeight	INTEGER	Image height
ImageAlt	CHAR(100)	Image alt
ImageHREF	CHAR(255)	Image href
Attribute0	CHAR(100)	Extra attribute
Attribute1	CHAR(100)	Extra attribute
Attribute2	CHAR(100)	Extra attribute
Attribute3	CHAR(100)	Extra attribute
Attribute4	CHAR(100)	Extra attribute
Disabled	BIT	Disabled flag
Description	LONGVARCHAR	HTML-capable description

```
CREATE TABLE Product
(
    CONSTRAINT PK_ID PRIMARY KEY (ID),
    CONSTRAINT UK_SKU UNIQUE (SKU),
    ID IDENTITY,
    ParentID INTEGER,
    Name CHAR(255),
    ItemNumber INTEGER,
    SKU CHAR(100),
    Code CHAR(255),
    Type CHAR(255),
    Weight FLOAT,
    ListPrice CURRENCY,
    SalePrice CURRENCY,
    SaleStart TIMESTAMP,
    SaleEnd TIMESTAMP,
    OnSaleMessage LONGVARCHAR,
    ImageFile CHAR(255),
    ImageWidth INTEGER,
    ImageHeight INTEGER,
```

```
        ImageAlt CHAR(100),
        ImageHREF CHAR(255),
        Attribute0 CHAR(100),
        Attribute1 CHAR(100),
        Attribute2 CHAR(100),
        Attribute3 CHAR(100),
        Attribute4 CHAR(100),
        Disabled BIT,
        Description LONGVARCHAR
)
```

Database Table Name: ProductRelations

Column Name	Data Type	Description
ProductID	INTEGER	ID of product
RelatedID	INTEGER	ID of related product
ItemNumber	INTEGER	Line item number

```
CREATE TABLE ProductRelations
(
    CONSTRAINT FK_PR_ProductID FOREIGN KEY (ProductID)
REFERENCES Product ON DELETE CASCADE,
    CONSTRAINT FK_PR_RelatedID FOREIGN KEY (RelatedID)
REFERENCES Product ON DELETE CASCADE,
    CONSTRAINT UK_Record UNIQUE (ProductID, RelatedID),
    ProductID INTEGER,
    RelatedID INTEGER,
    ItemNumber INTEGER
)
```

Database Table Name: ProductShippingRules

Column Name	Type	Description
ProductID	INTEGER	ID of product
ShippingMethodID	INTEGER	ID of shipping method
ShippingRuleID	INTEGER	ID of rule type
JavaScriptRule	LONGVARCHAR	JavaScript code for rule

```
CREATE TABLE ProductShippingRules
(
    CONSTRAINT FK_PSR_ProductID FOREIGN KEY (ProductID)
REFERENCES Product ON DELETE CASCADE,
    CONSTRAINT FK_PSR_ShipMethID FOREIGN KEY (ShippingMethodID)
REFERENCES ShippingMethod ON DELETE CASCADE,
    CONSTRAINT FK_PSR_ShipRuleID FOREIGN KEY (ShippingRuleID)
```

continues

```
REFERENCES ShippingRule ON DELETE CASCADE,
    CONSTRAINT UK_Record UNIQUE (ProductID, ShippingMethodID,
ShippingRuleID),
    ProductID INTEGER,
    ShippingMethodID INTEGER,
    ShippingRuleID INTEGER,
    JavaScriptRule LONGVARCHAR
)
```

Database Table Name: SalesOrder

Column Name	Data Type	Description
ID	IDENTITY	Unique ID
OrderNumber	CHAR(100)	Unique order number
RefundOrderNumber	CHAR(100)	Refund order number
ShopperID	INTEGER	ID of shopper
ShippingMethodID	INTEGER	ID of shipping method
OrderStatusID	INTEGER	ID of order status
SubTotal	CURRENCY	Sub total
Shipping	CURRENCY	Shipping costs
Handling	CURRENCY	Handling costs
Tax	CURRENCY	Tax
Total	CURRENCY	Total
OrderDate	TIMESTAMP	Order date
ShipDate	TIMESTAMP	Ship date
CreditCardRef	CHAR(4)	Credit card reference
CreditCardType	CHAR(4)	Credit card type
BillToName	CHAR(100)	Bill to name
BillToCompany	CHAR(100)	Bill to company
BillToAddressLine1	CHAR(100)	Bill to address line 1
BillToAddressLine2	CHAR(100)	Bill to address line 2
BillToAddressLine3	CHAR(100)	Bill to address line 3
BillToCity	CHAR(100)	Bill to city
BillToState	CHAR(2)	Bill to state
BillToCounty	CHAR(100)	Bill to county
BillToZip	CHAR(100)	Bill to ZIP
BillToCountry	CHAR(2)	Bill to country
BillToPhone	CHAR(100)	Bill to phone
ShipToName	CHAR(100)	Ship to name

Column Name	Data Type	Description
ShipToCompany	CHAR(100)	Ship to company
ShipToAddressLine1	CHAR(100)	Ship to address line 1
ShipToAddressLine2	CHAR(100)	Ship to address line 2
ShipToAddressLine3	CHAR(100)	Ship to address line 3
ShipToCity	CHAR(100)	Ship to city
ShipToState	CHAR(2)	Ship to state
ShipToCounty	CHAR(100)	Ship to county
ShipToZip	CHAR(100)	Ship to ZIP
ShipToCountry	CHAR(2)	Ship to country
ShipToPhone	CHAR(100)	Ship to phone
TrackingNumber	CHAR(100)	Order tracking number
ReferenceNumber	CHAR(100)	Order reference number
Comments	LONGVARCHAR	Order comments
ConfirmationEmail	LONGVARCHAR	Copy of order confirmation email

```
CREATE TABLE SalesOrder
(
    CONSTRAINT PK_ID PRIMARY KEY (ID),
    CONSTRAINT FK_SO_DR_ShopperID FOREIGN KEY (ShopperID)
REFERENCES Shopper ON DELETE RESTRICT,
    CONSTRAINT FK_SO_UR_ShopperID FOREIGN KEY (ShopperID)
REFERENCES Shopper ON UPDATE RESTRICT,
    CONSTRAINT FK_SO_DR_ShipMethID FOREIGN KEY (ShippingMethodID)
REFERENCES ShippingMethod ON DELETE RESTRICT,
    CONSTRAINT FK_SO_UR_ShipMethID FOREIGN KEY (ShippingMethodID)
REFERENCES ShippingMethod ON UPDATE RESTRICT,
    CONSTRAINT FK_SO_DR_OrdrStatID FOREIGN KEY (OrderStatusID)
REFERENCES OrderStatus ON DELETE RESTRICT,
    CONSTRAINT UK_OrderNumber UNIQUE (OrderNumber),
    ID IDENTITY,
    OrderNumber CHAR(100),
    RefundOrderNumber CHAR(100),
    ShopperID INTEGER,
    ShippingMethodID INTEGER,
    OrderStatusID INTEGER,
    SubTotal CURRENCY,
    Shipping CURRENCY,
    Handling CURRENCY,
    Tax CURRENCY,
    Total CURRENCY,
    OrderDate TIMESTAMP,
    ShipDate TIMESTAMP,
    CreditCardRef CHAR(4),
```

continues

```
    CreditCardType CHAR(4),
    BillToName CHAR(100),
    BillToCompany CHAR(100),
    BillToAddressLine1 CHAR(100),
    BillToAddressLine2 CHAR(100),
    BillToAddressLine3 CHAR(100),
    BillToCity CHAR(100),
    BillToState CHAR(2),
    BillToCounty CHAR(100),
    BillToZip CHAR(100),
    BillToCountry CHAR(2),
    BillToPhone CHAR(100),
    ShipToName CHAR(100),
    ShipToCompany CHAR(100),
    ShipToAddressLine1 CHAR(100),
    ShipToAddressLine2 CHAR(100),
    ShipToAddressLine3 CHAR(100),
    ShipToCity CHAR(100),
    ShipToState CHAR(2),
    ShipToCounty CHAR(100),
    ShipToZip CHAR(100),
    ShipToCountry CHAR(2),
    ShipToPhone CHAR(100),
    TrackingNumber CHAR(100),
    ReferenceNumber CHAR(100),
    Comments LONGVARCHAR,
    ConfirmationEmail LONGVARCHAR
)
```

Database Table Name: SalesOrderDetail

Column Name	Data Type	Description
SalesOrderID	INTEGER	ID of sales order
ProductID	INTEGER	ID of product
ShippingMethodID	INTEGER	ID of shipping method
OrderStatusID	INTEGER	ID of order status
ShipDate	TIMESTAMP	Line item ship date
ItemNumber	INTEGER	Line item number
Quantity	INTEGER	Quantity of product
Price	CURRENCY	Price at point of sale
Tax	CURRENCY	Line item tax
Discount	CURRENCY	Line item discount
TrackingNumber	CHAR(100)	Line item tracking number
ReferenceNumber	CHAR(100)	Line item reference number

```
CREATE TABLE SalesOrderDetail
(
    CONSTRAINT FK_SOD_DR_SaleOrdrID FOREIGN KEY (SalesOrderID)
REFERENCES SalesOrder ON DELETE RESTRICT,
    CONSTRAINT FK_SOD_UR_SaleOrdrID FOREIGN KEY (SalesOrderID)
REFERENCES SalesOrder ON UPDATE RESTRICT,
    CONSTRAINT FK_SOD_DR_ProductID FOREIGN KEY (ProductID)
REFERENCES Product ON DELETE RESTRICT,
    CONSTRAINT FK_SOD_UR_ProductID FOREIGN KEY (ProductID)
REFERENCES Product ON UPDATE RESTRICT,
    CONSTRAINT FK_SOD_DR_ShipMethID FOREIGN KEY (ShippingMethodID)
REFERENCES ShippingMethod ON DELETE RESTRICT,
    CONSTRAINT FK_SOD_UR_ShipMethID FOREIGN KEY (ShippingMethodID)
REFERENCES ShippingMethod ON UPDATE RESTRICT,
    CONSTRAINT FK_SOD_DR_OrdrStatID FOREIGN KEY (OrderStatusID)
REFERENCES OrderStatus ON DELETE RESTRICT,
    CONSTRAINT UK_Record UNIQUE (SalesOrderID, ProductID),
    SalesOrderID INTEGER,
    ProductID INTEGER,
    ShippingMethodID INTEGER,
    OrderStatusID INTEGER,
    ShipDate TIMESTAMP,
    ItemNumber INTEGER,
    Quantity INTEGER,
    Price CURRENCY,
    Tax CURRENCY,
    Discount CURRENCY,
    TrackingNumber CHAR(100),
    ReferenceNumber CHAR(100)
)
```

Database Table Name: ShippingCategory

Column Name	Data Type	Description
ID	IDENTITY	Unique ID
Name	CHAR(100)	Name
ItemNumber	INTEGER	Line item number
ForReturns	BIT	Category for return ship methods flag
Disabled	BIT	Disabled flag
Description	LONGVARCHAR	Description

```
CREATE TABLE ShippingCategory
(
    CONSTRAINT PK_ID PRIMARY KEY (ID),
    ID IDENTITY,
    Name CHAR(100),
    ItemNumber INTEGER,
```

```
ForReturns BIT,
Disabled BIT,
Description LONGVARCHAR
)
```

Database Table Name: ShippingMethod

Column Name	Data Type	Description
ID	IDENTITY	Unique ID
ShippingCategoryID	INTEGER	ID of shipping category
ItemNumber	INTEGER	Line item number
Name	CHAR(100)	Name
ShortDescription	LONGVARCHAR	HTML-capable short description
ImmedFullfillment	BIT	Method can be immediately fulfilled flag
DefOrderStatusID	INTEGER	Default order status ID for method
Attribute0	CHAR(100)	Extra attribute
Attribute1	CHAR(100)	Extra attribute
Attribute2	CHAR(100)	Extra attribute
Attribute3	CHAR(100)	Extra attribute
Attribute4	CHAR(100)	Extra attribute
Disabled	BIT	Disabled flag
Description	LONGVARCHAR	Description

```
CREATE TABLE ShippingMethod
(
    CONSTRAINT PK_ID PRIMARY KEY (ID),
    CONSTRAINT FK_SM_ShipCatgID FOREIGN KEY (ShippingCategoryID)
REFERENCES ShippingCategory ON DELETE CASCADE,
    CONSTRAINT FK_SM_OrdrStatID FOREIGN KEY (DefOrderStatusID)
REFERENCES OrderStatus ON DELETE RESTRICT,
    ID IDENTITY,
    ShippingCategoryID INTEGER,
    ItemNumber INTEGER,
    Name CHAR(100),
    ShortDescription LONGVARCHAR,
    ImmedFullfillment BIT,
    DefOrderStatusID INTEGER,
    Attribute0 CHAR(100),
    Attribute1 CHAR(100),
    Attribute2 CHAR(100),
    Attribute3 CHAR(100),
```

```
        Attribute4 CHAR(100),
        Disabled BIT,
        Description LONGVARCHAR
)
```

Database Table Name: ShippingRule

Column Name	Data Type	Description
ID	IDENTITY	Unique ID
Name	CHAR(255)	Name
AggregateParameters	CHAR(255)	Aggregate parameters
GeneralMethodRule	LONGVARCHAR	JavaScript for general method code
GeneralProductRule	LONGVARCHAR	JavaScript for general product code

```
CREATE TABLE ShippingRule
(
    CONSTRAINT PK_ID PRIMARY KEY (ID),
    ID IDENTITY,
    Name CHAR(255),
    AggregateParameters CHAR(255),
    GeneralMethodRule LONGVARCHAR,
    GeneralProductRule LONGVARCHAR
)
```

Database Table Name: Shopper

Column Name	Data Type	Description
ID	IDENTITY	Unique ID
Created	TIMESTAMP	Creation date
LastLogin	TIMESTAMP	Last login date
Name	CHAR(100)	Name
Password	CHAR(20)	Password
Company	CHAR(100)	Company
Email	CHAR(100)	Email
AddressLine1	CHAR(100)	Address line 1
AddressLine2	CHAR(100)	Address line 2
AddressLine3	CHAR(100)	Address line 3
City	CHAR(100)	City
State	CHAR(2)	State

continues

Database Table Name: Shopper (Continued)

Column Name	Data Type	Description
County	CHAR(100)	County
Zip	CHAR(100)	ZIP
Country	CHAR(2)	Country
Phone	CHAR(100)	Phone
Attribute0	CHAR(100)	Extra attribute
Attribute1	CHAR(100)	Extra attribute
Attribute2	CHAR(100)	Extra attribute
Attribute3	CHAR(100)	Extra attribute
Attribute4	CHAR(100)	Extra attribute
Admin	BIT	Administrator flag
Disabled	BIT	Disabled flag

```
CREATE TABLE Shopper
(
    CONSTRAINT PK_ID PRIMARY KEY (ID),
    CONSTRAINT UK_Email UNIQUE (Email),
    ID IDENTITY,
    Created TIMESTAMP,
    LastLogin TIMESTAMP,
    Name CHAR(100),
    Password CHAR(20),
    Company CHAR(100),
    Email CHAR(100),
    AddressLine1 CHAR(100),
    AddressLine2 CHAR(100),
    AddressLine3 CHAR(100),
    City CHAR(100),
    State CHAR(2),
    County CHAR(100),
    Zip CHAR(100),
    Country CHAR(2),
    Phone CHAR(100),
    Attribute0 CHAR(100),
    Attribute1 CHAR(100),
    Attribute2 CHAR(100),
    Attribute3 CHAR(100),
    Attribute4 CHAR(100),
    Admin BIT,
    Disabled BIT
)
```

Database Table Name: State

Column Name	Data Type	Description
Country	CHAR(2)	Country abbreviation
State	CHAR(2)	State abbreviation
Name	CHAR(100)	Name
Disabled	BIT	Disabled flag

```
CREATE TABLE State
(
    CONSTRAINT FK_S_Country FOREIGN KEY (Country)
REFERENCES Country ON DELETE CASCADE,
    CONSTRAINT UK_Record UNIQUE (Country, State),
    Country CHAR(2),
    State CHAR(2),
    Name CHAR(100),
    Disabled BIT
)
```

Database Table Name: Themes

Column Name	Data Type	Description
Name	CHAR(100)	Name
Description	LONGVARCHAR	Description
ExampleImage	CHAR(255)	Example image
ItemNumber	INTEGER	Line item number
System	BIT	System flag
Disabled	BIT	Disabled flag
Settings	LONGVARCHAR	Theme settings

```
CREATE TABLE Themes
(
    CONSTRAINT UK_Name UNIQUE (Name),
    Name CHAR(100),
    Description LONGVARCHAR,
    ExampleImage CHAR(255),
    ItemNumber INTEGER,
    System BIT,
    Disabled BIT,
    Settings LONGVARCHAR
)
```

Database Table Name: VariableCategories

Column Name	Data Type	Description
ID	IDENTITY	Unique ID
Name	CHAR(255)	Name
ItemNumber	INTEGER	Line item number
Scope	CHAR(100)	Variable scope
System	BIT	System flag
Disabled	BIT	Disabled flag
Description	LONGVARCHAR	Description

```
CREATE TABLE VariableCategories
(
    CONSTRAINT PK_ID PRIMARY KEY (ID),
    ID IDENTITY,
    Name CHAR(255),
    ItemNumber INTEGER,
    Scope CHAR(100),
    System BIT,
    Disabled BIT,
    Description LONGVARCHAR
)
```

Database Table Name: Variables

Column Name	Data Type	Description
CategoryID	INTEGER	ID of variable category
Name	CHAR(100)	Name
Value	LONGVARCHAR	Value
Type	LONGVARCHAR	Type
ItemNumber	INTEGER	Line item number
System	BIT	System flag
Disabled	BIT	Disabled flag
Description	LONGVARCHAR	HTML-capable description

```
CREATE TABLE Variables
(
    CONSTRAINT FK_V_CategoryID FOREIGN KEY (CategoryID)
REFERENCES VariableCategories ON DELETE CASCADE,
    CONSTRAINT UK_Name UNIQUE (Name),
    CategoryID INTEGER,
    Name CHAR(100),
    Value LONGVARCHAR,
    Type LONGVARCHAR,
```

```
    ItemNumber INTEGER,
    System BIT,
    Disabled BIT,
    Description LONGVARCHAR
)
```

Creating the TAFs

Every copy of Tango 2000 ships with a number of demo applications. These apps are there primarily to show you examples of Tango programming, but they are fully functional apps in and of themselves. One of these apps is called Store Front and it helps you deploy your own online store. Although it teaches you a bunch of things about programming Tango, if you take the time to work through all the TAFs, you don't have to fully understand Store Front to use it. Store Front is currently in use as Pervasive's own online store.

One thing to note about this app is that there are some Tango 3.5-isms in the code. The task of creating the Store Front was started immediately after Pervasive bought Everyware, the originators of Tango. But Tango 2000 didn't exist then, so the application was written using Tango 3.5. That means the Store Front doesn't make extensive use of all the new features of Tango 2000, such as objects and TCFs.

Installing the Store Front is easy. Run the provided StoreFront.sql file if your installation of Tango didn't already create the database tables. Then drag the StoreFront folder out of the Tango Demos folder and to your working location. Now you are ready to start configuring the application. Let's do a quick overview of how the Store Front works from a user's perspective.

User TAF

E-Commerce Process Flow

The process for placing an order in the Store Front demo consists of these standard steps:

1. Checking in
2. Finding a product
3. Adding the product to the shopping basket

4. Proceeding to checkout

5. Selecting the shipping method

6. Entering shipping information

7. Reviewing the order

8. Entering billing information

9. Purchasing the order

The Store Front keeps track of a user's information, including what items he has in his basket between sessions. Therefore, the user has to log in when he first comes into the store. This happens whenever he enters the site and is supposed to be simple. A side effect of having to check in is that checkout is faster because all a user's information is already stored in the database.

After a user is checked in, he needs to find products. He can do this in a number of ways. One is to perform a find operation on the products in the store. Another is to navigate through the departments in the store and the subfolders in the departments. There is also a dynamic popup menu available by clicking the Choose Product button located at the bottom of the screen. Last, a user might get to a product by clicking in a Related Product link on another product's page.

After the user finds the product he wants, he adds the product to his shopping basket by clicking the Add to Basket button. The system automatically adds the item to the user's basket with a quantity of one and takes the user to the shopping basket screen.

The user may go through this process a number of times to add items to his basket, but eventually he actually needs to buy the products. This is done by going to the checkout screen, which is accessed from the Basket screen via the Proceed to Checkout button.

After the user starts checking out, he must select the shipping method he wants to use. The administrator of the site might have defined multiple shipping methods and these methods will be displayed for the user to choose from.

After the user selects a shipping method, he goes to a screen where he can enter shipping information. This information tells the user where to send the ordered items.

Now we have all the information we need to calculate the total cost. Store Front displays the review screen, which shows all the items ordered and the total price, including shipping charges and taxes.

If the user confirms the reviewed items, he is prompted for payment information. Store Front gathers the information on how the user wants to pay.

Now the user can click Purchase. He will then get a screen confirming his order and giving him a unique order number.

Navigation Toolbar

When the user comes to any page in the Store, he finds a toolbar of buttons at the top of the page. These buttons provide the functionality for six common tasks.

The first button is About, which takes the user to a TAF that displays an about message. That message is in a separate HTML file called AboutMessage.html, and is located in the Common/Include folder of the Store Front.

The next button is Lobby, which is the home button of the store. It always brings the user back to the top page of the site; that is, the default location a user goes to when he enters the site.

The Find button enables the user to search the Store Front. The Find operation only searches the products in the store front.

The Basket button shows the user what he currently has in his shopping basket. The shopping basket contains items the user has selected, but hasn't committed to by checking out.

The Pay button takes the user to the checkout, allowing him to commit to buying the items in his basket and giving information about how he wants to pay.

The History button is where a user can check on previously ordered items. The user is shown every item he bought on the site and each order's current status.

Admin TAFs

As with most of our modules, the Store Front has an administrator back end. When you go to the admin.taf, you are presented with a page with two frames. The frame on the left contains links to the administrator functions, and the frame on the right displays the current function you are working with.

View Store Lobby

This takes you to the lobby page of the Store Front. It is your link to the main part of the site, enabling you to quickly go to the site and see what has changed as a result of other admin functions.

Select Site Theme

One of the really cool features of the Store Front is themes. These are different looks that a Web site can have. Themes change everything from the graphics to the font and background color. On the Theme configuration page, you will see pictures of the themes that come with the demo. You can also create your own themes by configuring the theme variables and saving them from this screen.

Maintain Department

After going through the user experience of the Store Front, the first thing you will probably be interested in is how to add products. All products in the Store Front are in departments, so we must learn how to add departments as well.

When you bring up the Maintain Department window, you can define a department by using the form provided. A description of each field is included in Table 14.1.

Table 14.1 Department Details

Field	Description
Name	This defines the name of the department and will appear as a hyperlink in the department hierarchy.

Field	Description
Parent Department	This defines the parent of the department. If the department should be a root department, select Root Department from the list. If the department should be used only in the product menu, select Selection List Only from the list.
Item Number	This number defines the order in which the department appears according to its parent department.
Selection List	Check this box if you want this department to be used in the product menu. Only departments that contain products should be included in the product menu.
Selection Item Number	If department is to be used in the product menu, this number defines its order there.
Attribute 0–4	These extra fields enable you to describe special attributes about the department and may be used for querying, tracking, or shipping rules.
Disabled	Check this box if you want to keep a department and its selected products intact, but prevent it from being displayed.
Description	This defines the description of a department. This description can contain HTML and meta tags. Note that only the departments containing products will ever show this description.

Maintain Product

Products are independent of departments. One product can be in a number of departments, so you enter each product separately and later associate it with a department. Table 14.2 describes the data associated with a product.

Table 14.2   Product Details

Field	Description
Name	Defines the name of the product as will appear in the system.
SKU	Defines the SKU used to identify the product when placing an order.

continues

Table 14.2 (Continued)

Field	Description
Code	This field is for end user use. Its intention was to capture any special information about the product that might be used during the purchase process or for post-sales tracking.
Type	The Type field's intention is to identify which products are available for download. Although ultimately for end-user use, the Store Front defines products using this field as either downloadable or ship only, and the sample shipping rules that come with the system look for this.
Weight	Defines the weight of a product. This field can be used when defining the rules that govern the shipping and handling costs of an order.
ListPrice	The list price of the product.
SalePrice	The sale price of the product, if any.
SaleStart	When to begin using the sale price.
SaleEnd	When to stop using the sale price.
OnSaleMessage	Any special message to display when product is on sale. This message can contain HTML.
ImageFile	The product image. This image should be located in the image path defined for the system. This could also be an advertisement for a related product.
ImageWidth	The width of the product image.
ImageHeight	The height of the product image.
ImageAlt	The alternate description or tooltip for the image.
ImageHREF	If clicking on the image should take the user to another screen, define that URL here.
Attribute 0–4	These extra fields enable you to describe special attributes about the product. They may be used for querying or tracking, and are especially useful for shipping rules.
Disabled	Check this box if you want to keep the product, but prevent it from being displayed.
Description	This defines the description for the product. This description can contain HTML and meta tags.

Reload All System Variables

One of the features of the Store Front is the capability to keep, or persist, the values of all the system variables event if you restart your Tango server. Normally, Tango variables are only stored in memory, which means that if you stop the server, your variables go away. To persist these variables, the Store Front saves them to the database. You can have the variables reloaded from the database by following this link.

System Configuration

As an admin, you can set a number of options for the application. These options are application-scope variables that are stored in a database table so that they persist through restarts of the server. An application-scope variable is related to a particular application, which is all the Tango files in a particular folder. This folder is set in the config.taf application file. The configuration variables for the Store Front are grouped into four categories.

General

The general variable category defines variables such as the store title, the contact email for the site, as well as any variables that do not quite fit into another category. Table 14.3 describes each of the general variables.

Table 14.3   General Variables

Variable	Description
Title	Name of the store that appears in the title
TitleMessage	Brief store purpose that should appear in the lobby
ContactEmail	Email address for information about the store
StoreClosed	Determines whether store is open or closed
GeneralShippingMethod	Shipping message that appears on shipping method selection screen; typically describes delivery information
ShowOrderStatus	Enables display of the order status column throughout the site
ShowProductSelector	Enables display of the product select menu
ShowProductWeight	Enables display of product weight on product detail screen

System

System variables control the store's behavior and integration within its environment. Table 14.4 describes all the system variables.

Table 14.4   System Variables

Variable	Description
CGI	Defines any needed CGI prefix required by your system
RedirectPrefix	Defines any prefix needed by your Web server to perform HTTP redirections
EmailEnabled	Enables email actions throughout system
ImagePath	Path to the images used by the store
IncludePath	Path to the include files used by the store
ScriptPath	Path to the script files used by the store
ThemePath	Path to the theme folders used by the store
TimeStamp	Display format for timestamps used throughout the system
Currency	Display format for currency used throughout the system
ShippingEnabled	Enables the display and calculation of shipping costs
HandlingEnabled	Enables the display and calculation of handling costs
DisplayLineItemTax	Enables the display of tax amounts at a line item level

Appearance

Appearance variables control the look and feel of the site. These variables are what change for each theme. Table 14.5 lists some of the more relevant appearance variables, excluding all the color variables because they are relatively self-explanatory.

Table 14.5   Appearance Variables

Variable	Description
Theme	Defines the current theme in use by the site
ThemeHeader	Path to the header used by the current theme
ThemeFooter	Path to the footer used by the current theme

Variable	Description
DefaultFont	Font that is used throughout the system
BodyAttributes	Attributes used for all HTML page bodies throughout the site

Credit Card

Credit card variables exists for dealing with credit card purchases within the Store Front demo.

Table 14.6   Credit Card Variables

Variable	Description
CreditCards	Defines the list of credit cards that will be accepted by the store
TestMode	Places the credit card functionality of the site in test mode
TestCCNum	The credit card number that is provided when the site is in test mode
TestCCExpYear	The credit card expiration year that is provided when the site is in test mode
TestCCExpMonth	The credit card expiration month that is provided when the site is in test mode

Close Store/Open Store

This area enables you, as admin, to close the store, which gives users a message saying that they can't come in.

This gives you a broad overview of how the Tango 2000 Store Front demo works. You can use it as the basis of your own e-commerce Web site.

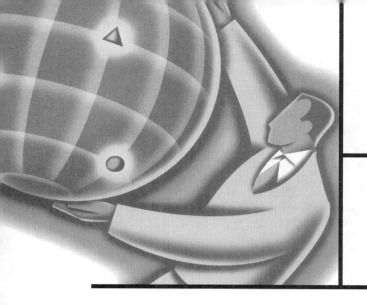

Auctions

What We'll Learn

- Automated execution of URLs
- <@DAYS> meta tag
- <@DATEDIFF> meta tag
- <@TSTOSECS> and <@SECSTOTS> meta tags

Purpose

We are going to create a set of TAFs that implement a simple auction site. It will allow people to post items for sale, others to post bids, and everyone concerned to be notified when the auction is over.

Planning

Feature List

- Allow the posting of an item for sale. The information needed for an item is the username of the seller, the date posted, the date the auction is over, starting price, and a description of the item.

- Display an item for sale, listing all the information about the item from the seller, as well as displaying the time left and the current high bid.

- Allow a buyer to enter a bid on a specific item.

- Track and display bid history.

- Periodically check auction items to see if they are closed. If they are, send emails to winning bidder and seller.

- Automatically remove bids on auctions that closed more than 30 days ago.

Database Schema

Only two database tables are needed for this auction module: one to hold the items for sale and one to hold the bids for various items. Each item will have a unique ID that will be a foreign key in the bid table.

Database Table Name: auction_item

Column Name	Data Type	Size
itemID	int	
title	char	100
seller_name	char	30
time_posted	timestamp	
time_finished	timestamp	
starting_price	int	
description	blob	
state	char	10

```
CREATE TABLE auction_item (
    itemID          int PRIMARY KEY,
    title           char(100),
    sellername      char(30),
    time_posted     timestamp,
    time_finished   timestamp,
    starting_price  int,
    description     blob,
    state           char(10)
)
```

Database Table Name: auction_bid

Column Name	Data Type	Size
itemID	int	
buyer_name	char	30
time_bid	timestamp	
bid_price	int	

```
CREATE TABLE auction_bid (
    itemID        int,
    buyer_name    char(30),
    time_bid      timestamp,
    bid_price     int
)
```

Creating the TAFs

Auctions are a very popular part of e-commerce today, as eBay has proven. They are being added to more traditional e-commerce sites like Amazon.com. We will create a number of TAFs that have the basic functionality of an auction.

A little auction terminology needs to be defined up front in this chapter. A thing that is being sold is called an *item*. The person selling an item is the *seller*. The person bidding on the item is a *bidder*.

TCF

auction.tcf

We will be using a number of functions from other parts of the auction site that need to be consolidated in a TCF. These functions will give us the current high bid for an item, the minimum someone has to bid on an item, the time left in an item's auction, and a function to clean up old auctions.

Create a new TCF named auction.tcf and add to it a new method called high_bid_for_itemID, with one In parameter called itemID. Keep the default return value of the local variable called returnValue.

high_bid_for_itemID

The first method we will implement allows you to pass in an itemID and retrieve the amount of the highest bid associated with that item. Doing this only takes one Search action. All the bids for all the items are in one table, so we just need to search for all the items with the passed in itemID. With that criteria, we can use the Select tab's capability to summarize and obtain the maximum value of the items we find.

Set the Criteria tab to select items in which the table column auction_bid.itemID is equal to the method variable itemID.

In the Select tab, you might have noticed the pop-up menu with the title Search Type. We've always used the default value for this pop-up, which is Normal. For this search, we want to retrieve the maximum value of all the rows selected. Change the popup to Summary of All Rows. When you do this, the whole window will change. The Select Columns panel looks different, but it works the same. Drag the auction_bid.bid_price column into the panel. At this point, the window will resemble Figure 15.1, with the summary function being MAX. MAX is the function we want, but you might want to look at some of the other available functions.

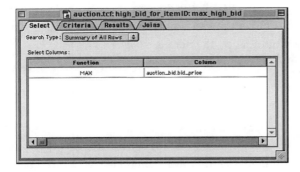

FIGURE 15.1 *Search action to get the maximum bid price.*

The result of this search is a little different from the searches we have done previously, in that it only returns one value. This value is in the resultSet array, so we have to get it out of that array and return the value. Do this by using the array notation to get the first row and column of the resultset. Put this assignment statement into the ResultsHTML attribute of the Search action:

```
<@ASSIGN NAME="returnValue" VALUE="@@local$resultSet[1,1]" SCOPE="method">
```

That is all this function needs to do; so add a Return action and save.

minimum_bid_for_ItemID

The next method we need to add is one to obtain the minimum bid for a given item. Usually the minimum bid is the same as the high bid, unless there are no bids. In which case, the minimum bid is the starting price. Create the new method and configure with an `itemID` parameter and return value in the `returnValue` variable.

The first piece of information we need to retrieve is the current high bid. We could do this by duplicating the Search we did in the `high_bid_for_itemID` method, but there is a better way. Drag in the `high_bid_for_itemID` method from the Object tab of the workspace window. This will allow us to call that method. Tango knows this method is in this TCF, so we don't have to create a CreateObject action. We want to pass on the `itemID` we were passed in, so configure the CallMethod action as shown in Figure 15.2.

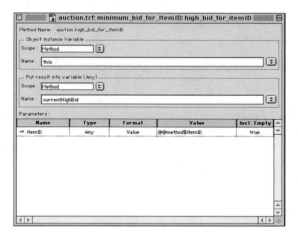

FIGURE 15.2   *Getting the current high bid.*

After this call returns, we need to find out if there was a high bid. If no one has bid on this item yet, the value returned will be empty. Drag in an If action and configure it to check whether `@@local$currentHighBid` is empty. If it is empty, there is no high bid, and we need to retrieve the starting price of the item. We do this by dragging in a Search action and setting its criteria to find rows in which the auction_item.itemID column is equal to the passed-in `itemID`. In the Select tab, we add the `auction_item.itemID` and `auction_item.starting_price`. Because the `itemID` column is the primary key of the auction_item table, we will get back only one row. We need to return the value of the starting_price column as our return value, which we do by adding this assign statement to the ResultsHTML attribute of the Search action:

```
<@ASSIGN NAME="returnValue" VALUE="<@COLUMN 'auction_item.starting_price'>
" SCOPE="method">
```

If there is a high bid, we just need to return its value. Drag an Else action into the TAF. Below it, put a Result action with this assignment in it:

```
<@ASSIGN NAME="returnValue" VALUE="@@local$currentHighBid" SCOPE="method">
```

timeleft

Another utility function we are going to need for our auctions is the ability to get the time left in the auction. We could do this based on an `itemID`, but it would require a database search to get the ending time of the item. In most cases, we will only be calling the method when we already know all the item's information, so we'll configure the method to take the ending time as a parameter.

Create a new method called `timeleft` and configure it as shown in Figure 15.3.

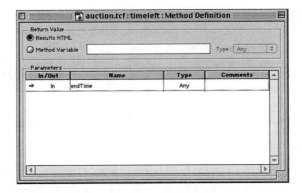

FIGURE 15.3 *The timeleft method call.*

We will be doing quite a bit of time math in this routine. Tango provides the means of subtracting two dates and retrieving the number of days between them via the <@DAYS> tag. Unfortunately, it doesn't have a similar <@TIME> tag, but it does give us the tools to do it. In Tango, you can convert any given time to the number of seconds since 1/1/1970 at midnight. You can then convert those seconds back to a textual date. We will use this to calculate the difference between now and the end of the auction.

Drag in an Assign action and configure it to resemble Figure 15.4. Inside this assign, we make the calculations to determine the difference between the two times. We need to have the current time and the end time in seconds. We use the meta tag <@TSTOSECS> to do this. <@TSTOSECS> takes a timestamp and converts it to seconds. In the first assignment, we convert the current timestamp to seconds and assign it to the local variable curtimeInSecs. In the second assignment, we convert the end time, which was passed into our method, into seconds and assign it to endInSecs. The last calculation we do is to subtract one from the other and assign the result to the secsDiff variable.

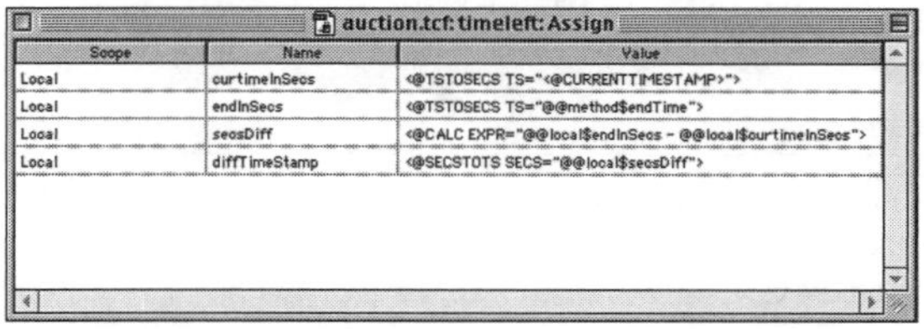

Scope	Name	Value
Local	curtimeInSecs	<@TSTOSECS TS="<@CURRENTTIMESTAMP>">
Local	endInSecs	<@TSTOSECS TS="@@method$endTime">
Local	secsDiff	<@CALC EXPR="@@local$endInSecs - @@local$curtimeInSecs">
Local	diffTimeStamp	<@SECSTOTS SECS="@@local$secsDiff">

FIGURE 15.4 *Calculating the seconds until the auction is over.*

Now we know the number of seconds between now and the end of the auction, but what if the auction is already over? We need to return the value we want displayed as the time left, so if the auction is over, we'll return a message that says the auction is closed. We need to determine if it is over by comparing our two sets of seconds. If there are more seconds in the current time than in the end time, the auction is over. Drag in an If action and configure it as shown in Figure 15.5.

FIGURE 15.5   *Is the auction over?*

If this If action evaluates to true, we need to return a message saying the auction is over. We configured our return value to be ResultsHTML so that we can just add a Result action and put whatever message we want in it. You will probably want to keep the message short because it might be output inline in the final Web page. My message was just the statement "Auction is closed" with some HTML to bold it.

Now we need to handle the case in which there is still time in the auction. Drag in an Else action and put a Result action under it. Listing 15.1 shows the HTML and meta tags we need to display the time left.

Listing 15.1   Time Left Results

```
<@IF EXPR="<@DATEDIFF DATE1=' <@SECSTOTS SECS="@@local$secsDiff"
  FORMAT='%m/%d/%Y'>' DATE2=' 1/1/1970'> > 0" >
<@DATEDIFF DATE1=' <@SECSTOTS SECS="@@local$secsDiff"
  FORMAT='%m/%d/%Y'>' DATE2=' 1/1/1970'> days,
</@IF>

<@SECSTOTS SECS="@@local$secsDiff" FORMAT="%H hours, %M minutes,
%S seconds." >
```

We want to display the time left in this format: "1 days, 06 hours, 37 minutes, 45 seconds." The time display isn't too complicated, but calculating the days takes a little doing. Remember I mentioned Tango can calculate the number of days between two dates? That's what we do in the <@DATEDIFF> tags in Listing 15.1. We use these tags twice: once to find out whether there are any days remaining in the auction, and, if so, once to display the days. The <@SECSTOTS> meta tag takes our difference in seconds and converts it to a date. This date is the number of seconds since 1/1/1970. So if we want to find the number of days, we convert to a date and calculate the number of days since the beginning of 1970. Notice the FORMAT attribute in the <@SECSTOTS> tag. If we pass a straight timestamp to the <@DATEDIFF> tag, we get an invalid date error. It can only handle dates, not time. So we use the format attribute to configure the output to only display the date.

After we've output the date, we use the <@SECSTOTS> with special FORMAT attributes to output the time. All this is passed back to the calling routine for display.

remove_item_by_itemID

Removing an item requires that we delete from two different tables. First we must delete all the bids for an item, and then we must delete the item itself. Do this using two delete actions, which will delete the table's itemID columns for the passed-in @@method$itemID value.

clear_old_auctions

One of our requirements is to remove old auctions. We also need to periodically change the state of auction item records to closed so that they don't show up in the list. We are going to put that functionality into this TCF.

Create a new method called clear_old_auctions. It has no parameter and returns nothing.

The first task we'll do is the updating of closed items. Drag in an Update action and configure it as shown in Figure 15.6.

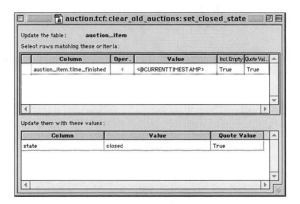

FIGURE 15.6 *Closing finished auctions.*

After this, we'll delete those items that have been closed for over a month. This is a two step process: first we need to find all the records that are too old, and then we need to loop through this array and delete each item. Add a Search action and drag in the auction_item.itemID and auction_item.time_finished columns. The Criteria tab needs to be configured as shown in Figure 15.7. We only delete closed auctions that are older than 30 days. We use the <@DAYS> tag to get the date that is 30 days earlier than the current date.

FIGURE 15.7   *Finding old items for removal.*

Now we have a list of items that need to be deleted. We can loop through the list and call the remove_item_by_itemID method with each itemID. Do this by inserting Listing 15.2 into the Results attribute of the Search action.

Listing 15.2   Removing Old Items

```
<@ROWS >
<@CALLMETHOD OBJECT="this"  METHOD="remove_item_by_itemID(
   <@COLUMN 'auction_item.itemID'>)" METHODTYPE="invoke">
</@ROWS>
```

This code calls the remove_item_by_itemID method of "this" object. "This" is a special keyword that refers to the same object from which you are calling. It is only valid inside a TCF method.

User TAF

auction_items.taf

Create a new TAF called auction_items.taf, which will handle all the functionality dealing with items. An auction is useless if nothing is being sold, so the first thing we want to do is implement a way of getting items into the auction database. We're going to use the <@ARG _function> methodology in this TAF, and the <@ARG _function> you'll need to configure is an If action for new_item_form.

All we have to do for the form is display it. As we did in the forums, we are going to put most of our display code in separate HTML files. The one for the new item form is called item_form.html, the contents of which are in Listing 15.3.

Listing 15.3   HTML for Displaying the New Item Form

```
<@ASSIGN NAME="user" SCOPE="local" VALUE=<@CREATEOBJECT
  OBJECTID="user_sec.tcf" TYPE="TCF">>
<@ASSIGN NAME="currentUserLevel" SCOPE="local" VALUE=<@CALLMETHOD
  OBJECT="user" SCOPE="local" METHOD="GetCurrentUserLevel()"
  METHODTYPE="invoke"> >
<@ASSIGN NAME="currentUser" SCOPE="local" VALUE=<@CALLMETHOD
  OBJECT="user" SCOPE="local" METHOD="GetCurrentUserName()"
  METHODTYPE="invoke"> >

<HTML>
  <HEAD>
    <TITLE>
      New Auction Item
    </TITLE>
  </HEAD>
  <BODY BGCOLOR="#ffffff" TEXT="#000000" LINK="#0000ff"
   ALINK="#ff0000" VLINK="#000088">
<@IFEMPTY VALUE="@@local$currentUser">
<HR>
<FONT COLOR=red>
You cannot add an item unless you are logged in.
</FONT>
<HR>
<@ELSE>
    <TABLE BORDER=0 WIDTH=95%>
      <TR>
        <TD>
          <FONT SIZE="1" FACE="Verdana, Arial, Helvetica, sans-serif">
            <B>
              Commands
            </B>
            any commands go here.
            <BR>
          </FONT>
        </TD>
```

continues

Listing 15.3 (Continued)

```
</TR>
    </TABLE>
    <FONT SIZE="2" FACE="Verdana, Arial, Helvetica, sans-serif">
        <TABLE BORDER=0 CELLPADDING=0 CELLSPACING=0 WIDTH="95%">
          <TR>
            <TD BGCOLOR="#ffffff">
              <TABLE WIDTH=100% BORDER=0 CELLSPACING=1
                CELLPADDING=4>
                <TR BGCOLOR="#777777">
                  <TD VALIGN=MIDDLE WIDTH=18%>
                    <FONT SIZE="1" FACE="Verdana, Arial,
                    Helvetica, sans-serif" COLOR="#ffffff">
                      <B>
                        @@local$currentUser
                      </B>
                    </FONT>
                  </TD>
                  <TD VALIGN=MIDDLE>
                    <FONT SIZE="1" FACE="Verdana, Arial,
                    Helvetica, sans-serif" COLOR="#ffffff">
                      <B>
                        Adding a new Item.
                      </B>
                    </FONT>
                  </TD>
                </TR>
                <TR >
                  <TD WIDTH=18% VALIGN=TOP>
                    <FONT SIZE="2" FACE="Verdana, Arial,
                    Helvetica, sans-serif">
                      <B>
                        Time:
                      </B>
                    </FONT>
                    <BR>
                    <FONT SIZE="1" FACE="Verdana, Arial,
                    Helvetica, sans-serif">
                      <@CURRENTTIMESTAMP>
                    </FONT>
                  </TD>
                  <TD>
                    <FORM ACTION="<@CGI><@APPFILE>?
                    function=item_insert" METHOD=POST>
                      <TABLE BORDER="0">
                        <TR>
                          <TD>
```

```
                           <FONT SIZE="2" FACE=
                           "VERDANA, ARIAL,
                           HELVETICA, SANS-SERIF">
                           Item Title:
                              <TD ALIGN=LEFT>
                            <INPUT TYPE="text" NAME=
                            "title" SIZE=50>
                                 </TD>
                               </FONT>
                            <INPUT TYPE="hidden" NAME=
                            "sellername" VALUE=
                            "@@local$currentUser">
                               </TD>
                         </TR>
                         <TR>
                            <TD>
                         <FONT SIZE="2" FACE="VERDANA,
                            ARIAL, HELVETICA,
                            SANS-SERIF">
                              Starting price:
                                <TD ALIGN=LEFT>
                                   <INPUT
                                    TYPE="text"
                                    NAME=
                                    "start_price"
                                    SIZE=10><BR>
                                   </TD>
                                  </FONT>
                                </TD>
                         </TR>
                         <TR>
                            <TD>
                               <FONT SIZE="2" FACE=
                               "VERDANA, ARIAL,
                               HELVETICA, SANS-SERIF">
                               Auction Length:
                                  <TD ALIGN=LEFT>

<SELECT NAME="auction_end">
<OPTION LABEL="1 Day" Value="<@days date=<@currentdate> days=1>
 <@CURRENTTIME>">
<OPTION LABEL="3 Days" Value="<@days date=<@currentdate> days=3>
 <@CURRENTTIME>">
<OPTION LABEL="1 Week" Value="<@days date=<@currentdate> days=7>
 <@CURRENTTIME>">
</SELECT>

                                  </TD>
                                  </FONT>
```

continues

Listing 15.3   (Continued)

```
                                </TD>
                              </TR>
                              <TR>
                                <TD>
                                  <FONT SIZE="2" FACE=
                                  "VERDANA, ARIAL,
                                  HELVETICA,
                                  SANS-SERIF">
                                    Description:
                                    <TD ALIGN=LEFT>
                                     <TEXTAREA NAME=
                                      "description"
                                     ROWS=10 COLS=80>
                                     </TEXTAREA>
                                    </TD>
                                  </FONT>
                                </TD>
                              </TR>
                            <TR>
                              <TD></TD>
                              <TD ALIGN=right>
                                <INPUT TYPE=SUBMIT NAME=
                                "Submit"
                                 VALUE="Submit">
                              </TD>
                            </TR>
                          </TABLE>
                        </FORM>
                    </td>
                  </tr>
                </table>
              </td>
            </tr>
          </table>
          <table border=0 width="95%">
            <TR>
              <TD valign=top align=left>
                <FONT SIZE="1" FACE="VERDANA, ARIAL, HELVETICA,
                                     SANS-SERIF">
                 <P>
                 All times are CST (US)
                </FONT>
              </td>
              <td align=right valign=top>
```

```
            </TD>
          </TR>
        </TABLE>
        <BR>
    </FONT>
</@IF>
</BODY>
</HTML>
```

Much of this form is familiar to you, but let's look at the features specific to the new item form, which we used `<@include>` to include it in the TAF. First, we don't want people who aren't logged in to add items. So we create an `<@IFEMPTY><@ELSE>` block that encompasses most of the file. At the top of the page, it checks to see if the currentUsername is empty and if it is, it just displays an error message. The actual HTML for the form is inside of the `<@ELSE>` portion.

Our auction site will limit how long an auction can go on with three options: 1 day, 3 days, or a week. We display these three options as a pop-up menu, whose values for each item are calculated. The value we want to send on for the ending time needs to be a date and time. Using the `<@DAYS>` tag, we can calculate a date easily, but that doesn't give us a time. Because our durations are all even days, we can end the auction at the current time on the ending day. By putting the `<@CURRENTTIME>` tag after the `<@DAYS>` tag, we get a complete timestamp.

When the user hits the Submit button, the data is passed back to our TAF with `<@ARG _function>` equal to `item_insert`. Configure another If action to handle the `item_insert` `<@ARG _function>` value.

As we did for the forums, we want to check the parameters before doing an insert. Drag an If action under the `item_insert` If and configure it to check parameters as shown in Figure 15.8. Inside it add a Result action with the error message of your choice and a Return action.

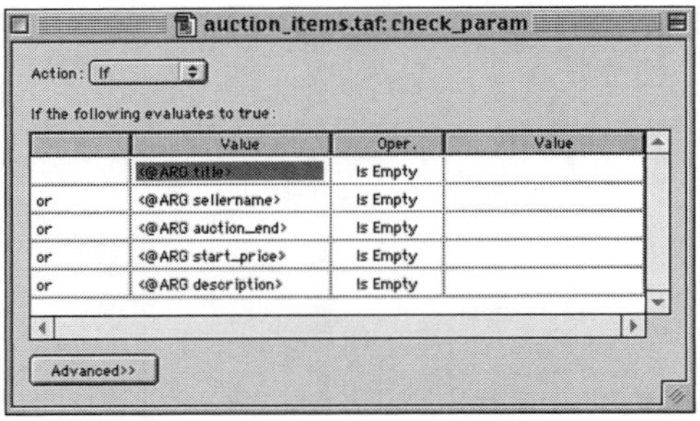

FIGURE 15.8 *Checking the input parameters for a new auction item.*

Now that we are sure we've got good data, let's generate a new ID for this item. Drag in a Utility object and configure it like all the previous ones. Drag in a `GetNextID` method and configure it like all the others except with the counter name of `auction_itemID`. When you are done, an executing TAF at this point will hold a new ID in the `newID` variable.

The last thing you need to do is configure the actual Insert action to resemble Figure 15.9.

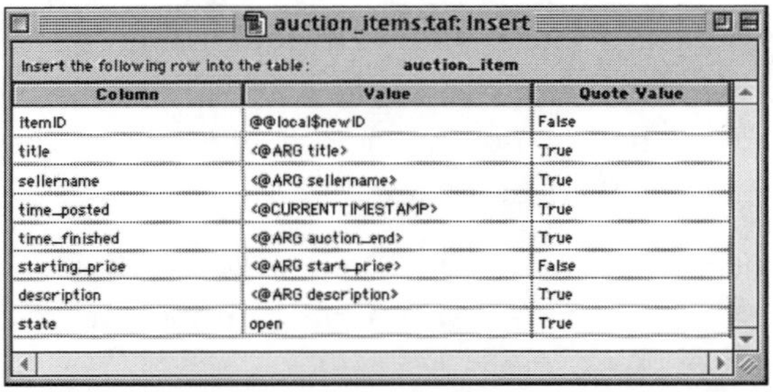

FIGURE 15.9 *Inserting a new item in the database.*

You need to tell the user that the insert happened. We hard code the state of all new items to be open. I used the HTML in Listing 15.4, which also provides a link back to the list of auction items.

Listing 15.4   Inserted OK Message

```
The item <@ARG title> was successfully added at <@CURRENTTIMESTAMP>.
  The auction will end at <@ARG auction_end>.
<P>
<A HREF="<@CGI><@APPFILEPATH>auction_items.taf?_function=items_list">

  Back to list.</A>
```

Notice the link in Listing 15.4 sets `<@ARG _function>` to `items_list`? That's a hint for you to create a new If action in your TAF.

In this listing of items, we want to display a table of items that are available for bidding. Each row needs to have the closing time, the item title, the time it was posted, a link to bid on it, and the time left in the auction. Providing this information is easy, except for the time left. Well, actually that is easy too, but we need to add an action before we do the Search for the items. Drag in the Auction object from your object palette. This will create an instance we can use later. Name the object instance `auction`.

Now do the search. Create a new Search action and configure the Select tab to resemble Figure 15.10. The Criteria tab needs to be configured to find items whose auction_items.state is equal to open.

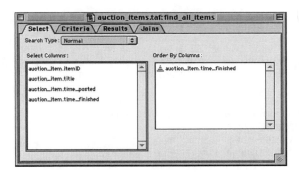

FIGURE 15.10   *Columns needed to display the item list.*

The Result attribute of this Search needs to contain an `<@INCLUDE>` meta tag that includes a file named auction_list.html, the contents of which are in Listing 15.5.

Listing 15.5   HTML to Display the List of Auction Items

```
<@ASSIGN NAME="user" SCOPE="local" VALUE=<@CREATEOBJECT
 OBJECTID="user_sec.tcf" TYPE="TCF">>
<@ASSIGN NAME="currentUserLevel" SCOPE="local" VALUE=<@CALLMETHOD
 OBJECT="user" SCOPE="local" METHOD="GetCurrentUserLevel()"
 METHODTYPE="invoke"> >
<@ASSIGN NAME="currentUser" SCOPE="local" VALUE=<@CALLMETHOD
 OBJECT="user" SCOPE="local" METHOD="GetCurrentUserName()"
 METHODTYPE="invoke"> >

<HTML>
```

continues

Listing 15.5   (Continued)

```html
<HEAD>
    <TITLE>
      Auction items for sale.
    </TITLE>
  </HEAD>
  <BODY BGCOLOR="#ffffff" TEXT="#000000" LINK="#0000ff"
ALINK="#ff0000" VLINK="#000088">
    <TABLE BORDER=0 WIDTH=95%>
      <TR>
        <TD>
         <FONT SIZE="1" FACE="Verdana, Arial, Helvetica, sans-serif">
              <B>
              <A HREF="<@CGI><@APPFILE>?_function=new_item_form">
               Add new Item</A>
              </B>
              Any logged in user can add an item to the auction.
              <BR>
          </FONT>
        </TD>
      </TR>
    </TABLE>
    <FONT SIZE="2" FACE="Verdana, Arial, Helvetica, sans-serif">
        <TABLE BORDER=0 CELLPADDING=0 CELLSPACING=0 WIDTH="95%">
          <TR>
            <TD BGCOLOR="#ffffff">
              <TABLE WIDTH=100% BORDER=0 CELLSPACING=1>
                <TR BGCOLOR="#777777">
                  <TD VALIGN=MIDDLE WIDTH=18%>
                    <FONT SIZE="1" FACE="Verdana, Arial,
                    Helvetica, sans-serif" COLOR="#ffffff">
                      <B>
                        Close Time
                      </B>
                    </FONT>
                  </TD>
                  <TD VALIGN=MIDDLE>
                    <FONT SIZE="1" FACE="Verdana, Arial,
                    Helvetica, sans-serif" COLOR="#ffffff">
                      <B>
                        Item
                      </B>
                    </FONT>
                  </TD>
                  <TD VALIGN=MIDDLE>
                    <FONT SIZE="1" FACE="Verdana, Arial,
                    Helvetica, sans-serif" COLOR="#ffffff">
                      <B>
```

```
                    Time left
                  </B>
                </FONT>
              </TD>
            </TR>
<@ROWS>

          <TR >
            <TD WIDTH=18%>
              <FONT SIZE="2" FACE="Verdana, Arial,
                Helvetica, sans-serif">
                <B>
                  <@COLUMN 'auction_item.time
                  _finished'>
                </B>
              </FONT>
              <BR>
              <FONT SIZE="1" FACE="Verdana, Arial,
                Helvetica, sans-serif">

              </FONT>
            </TD>
            <TD>
                <TABLE BORDER="0" WIDTH=100%>
                  <TR>
                    <TD width=200>
                      <FONT SIZE="2"
                      FACE="Verdana,
                       Arial, Helvetica,
                       sans-serif">
              <A HREF="<@CGI><@APPFILE>?_function=
              list_an_item&itemID=
              <@COLUMN 'auction_item.itemID'>">
              <@COLUMN 'auction_item.title'></A>
              (#<@COLUMN 'auction_item.itemID'> )
                      </FONT>
                    </TD>
                    <TD ALIGN=RIGHT>
                      <FONT SIZE="2" FACE=
                      "Verdana, Arial,
                       Helvetica, sans-serif">
              <A HREF="<@CGI>
<@APPFILEPATH>auction_bids.taf?
_function=bid_form&itemID=
 <@COLUMN 'auction_item.itemID'>">Bid</A>
                      </FONT>
                    </TD>
                    <TD align=right>
                      <FONT SIZE="1"
                      color="#666666"
```

continues

Listing 15.5   (Continued)

```
                                    face="VERDANA, ARIAL,
                                    HELVETICA,
                                    SANS-SERIF">
                                 posted <@COLUMN
                            'auction_item.time_posted'>
                                    </FONT>
                                   </TD>
                                 </TR>
                               </TABLE>
                        </td>
                               <TD>
                                  <FONT SIZE="1" color="Red"
                                   face="VERDANA, ARIAL,
                            HELVETICA, SANS-SERIF">
                                     <@CALLMETHOD OBJECT=
                                     "auction"
                                     SCOPE="local"
                                     METHOD= "timeleft(
                                      <@COLUMN
                            'auction_item.time_finished'>)"
                                        METHODTYPE=
                                     "invoke" encoding=none>
                                      </FONT>
                                     </TD>
                         </tr>
</@ROWS>
                          </table>
                     </td>
                  </tr>
               </table>
<HR>
         <table border=0 width="95%">
           <TR>
             <TD valign=top align=left>
               <FONT SIZE="1" FACE="VERDANA, ARIAL, HELVETICA,
                                SANS-SERIF">
                  <P>
                  All times are CST (US)
                 </FONT>
               </td>
               <td align=right valign=top>
                </TD>
             </TR>
          </TABLE>
```

```
        <BR>
      </FONT>
    </BODY>
  </HTML>
```

Most of this is just there to look good and make navigation easy. We provide a link for each item to allow a new bid. In the last column of each row, we display the time left by calling the timeleft method of the auction object we created earlier. Notice that inside the <@CALLMETHOD> meta tag we set the encoding attribute to none. This keeps Tango from changing any HTML tags you might put in there into text.

We display the title of each item as a link back to our file to the <@ARG _function> case list_an_item. Drag in a new If action for this new function. We need to display all the relevant information about a single item in this page. That means we need to get the current high bid for the item. So drag in another instance of the auction object. Configure it just like the others. Now drag in the high_bid_for_item method and configure it as shown in Figure 15.11.

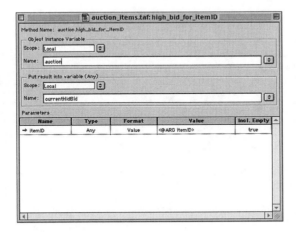

FIGURE 15.11   *Getting an item's current high bid.*

The rest of the information we want to display requires a Search action. Drag one in and add all the columns in the auction_item table in it. Configure the criteria to find the `itemID` we were passed. This will give you back one item's data. Add a result attribute with a single `<@INCLUDE>` for the file auction_item.html. The HTML to display a single item is in Listing 15.6.

Listing 15.6 Displaying a Single Item

```
<@ASSIGN NAME="user" SCOPE="local" VALUE=<@CREATEOBJECT
 OBJECTID="user_sec.tcf" TYPE="TCF">>
<@ASSIGN NAME="currentUserLevel" SCOPE="local" VALUE=<@CALLMETHOD
 OBJECT="user" SCOPE="local" METHOD="GetCurrentUserLevel()"
 METHODTYPE="invoke"> >
<@ASSIGN NAME="currentUser" SCOPE="local" VALUE=<@CALLMETHOD
 OBJECT="user" SCOPE="local" METHOD="GetCurrentUserName()"
 METHODTYPE="invoke"> >

<HTML>
  <HEAD>
    <TITLE>
      Auction Item #<@COLUMN 'auction_item.itemID'>:
       <@COLUMN 'auction_item.title'>
    </TITLE>
  </HEAD>
  <BODY BGCOLOR="#ffffff" TEXT="#000000" LINK="#0000ff"
    ALINK="#ff0000" VLINK="#000088">
    <TABLE BORDER=0 WIDTH=95%>
      <TR>
        <TD>
    <FONT SIZE="1" FACE="Verdana, Arial,
             Helvetica, sans-serif">
             <B>
               <A HREF="<@CGI><@APPFILEPATH>auction_bids.taf?
                         function=bid_form&
                  itemID=<@COLUMN 'auction_item.itemID'>">
                     Bid</A>
             </B>
           Any logged in user can bid on an item to the auction.
           <BR>
           <B>
             <A HREF="<@CGI>
             <@APPFILEPATH>
             auction_bids.taf?_function=bid_history&
```

```
                        itemID=<@COLUMN 'auction_item.itemID'>">
                            Bid History</A>
                    </B>
                Any logged in user can bid on an item to the auction.
                    <BR>
                </FONT>
            </TD>
        </TR>
    </TABLE>
    <FONT SIZE="2" FACE="Verdana, Arial, Helvetica, sans-serif">
        <TABLE BORDER=0 CELLPADDING=0 CELLSPACING=0 WIDTH="95%">
            <TR>
                <TD BGCOLOR="#ffffff">
                <TABLE WIDTH=100% BORDER=0 CELLSPACING=1 CELLPADDING=4>
                    <TR BGCOLOR="#777777">
                        <TD VALIGN=MIDDLE>
                            <FONT SIZE="2" FACE="Verdana, Arial,
                            Helvetica, sans-serif" COLOR="#ffffff">
                                <B>
                            Item #<@COLUMN 'auction_item.itemID'>:
                                <@COLUMN 'auction_item.title'>
                                </B>
                            </FONT>
                        </TD>
                    </TR>
                    <TR >
                        <TD>
                            <TABLE BORDER="0" WIDTH=100%>
                                <TR>
                                    <TD>
                                    <FONT SIZE="2" FACE="Verdana,
                                    Arial, Helvetica,
                                    sans-serif">
                                        <B>Seller:</B>
                                    <@COLUMN
                                    'auction_item.sellername'>
                                    </FONT>
                                    <P>
                                        <FONT SIZE="1" color=
                                        "#666666"
                                         face="VERDANA,
                                         ARIAL, HELVETICA,
                                         SANS-SERIF">
                            Opened: <@COLUMN
                            'auction_item.time_posted'><BR>
                            Closed: <@COLUMN
                            'auction_item.time_finished'><BR>
                            Current Time: <@CURRENTTIMESTAMP><BR>
```

continues

Listing 15.6   **(Continued)**

```
                              <FONT COLOR=RED>
                       Time Left: <@CALLMETHOD OBJECT=
                            "auction"
                        SCOPE="local" METHOD="timeleft(
                        <@COLUMN 'auction_item.time_
                        finished'>)"
                       METHODTYPE="invoke" encoding=none>
                              </FONT>
                            </FONT>
                            <P>
                            <FONT SIZE="1" face="VERDANA,
                       ARIAL, HELVETICA, SANS-SERIF">
                            Start price: <@COLUMN
                       'auction_item.starting_price'><BR>

                       <@IFEMPTY VALUE=
                          "@@local$currentHidBid">
                          <@ELSE>
                       <B>High bid:
                          @@local$currentHidBid</B>
                            </@IF>
                          </FONT>
                        </TD>
                      </TR>
                    </TABLE>
                  </td>
                </tr>
                <TR>
                  <TD>
                  <HR>
                  <B>Description:</B><BR>
                  <@COLUMN 'auction_item.description'
                  encoding=multilinehtml>
                  </TD>
</TR>
                </table>
              </td>
            </tr>
        </table>
<HR>
        <table border=0 width="95%">
          <TR>
            <TD valign=top align=left>
              <FONT SIZE="1" FACE="VERDANA, ARIAL,
```

```
              HELVETICA, SANS-SERIF">
            <P>
            All times are CST (US)
          </FONT>
        </td>
        <td align=right valign=top>
          <FONT SIZE="1" FACE="VERDANA, ARIAL, HELVETICA, SANS-SERIF">
            <A HREF="<@CGI><@APPFILEPATH>auction_items.taf?_
            function=items_list">
            Back to list.</A>
          </FONT>
        </TD>
      </TR>
    </TABLE>
    <BR>
  </FONT>
</BODY>
</HTML>
```

All the functionality here should be clear at this point. We call the auction object to get the time left for display. We put the high bid in by using the variable we set in the Call Method action before the Search.

This TAF now lets us do all the things we want to with an item, except bid on it. That functionality is in another TAF.

auction_bids.taf

There are three tasks we need for bids. We need to be able to enter a new bid on a specific item, check the bid for validity and insert it into the database, and list the bid history. Each of these will have their own <@ARG _function> If action.

The first If action needs <@ARG _function> to equal bid_form. When you display the form for a user to enter a new bid you are going to need to display the minimum bid. Therefore you need to create an instance of the auction object, by dragging in the object and configuring it with the name auction. Next drag in a minimum_bid_for_item method and configure it as shown in Figure 15.12.

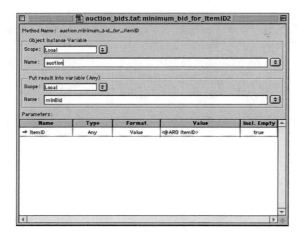

FIGURE 15.12 *Getting the minimum bid needed to win the auction.*

We are ready to display the form now. Drag in a new Result action and put an <@INCLUDE> tag in it to include the file bid_form.html. The form HTML resembles Listing 15.7.

Listing 15.7   Form for Entering a New Bid on an Item

```
<@ASSIGN NAME="user" SCOPE="local" VALUE=<@CREATEOBJECT
 OBJECTID="user_sec.tcf" TYPE="TCF">>
<@ASSIGN NAME="currentUserLevel" SCOPE="local" VALUE=<@CALLMETHOD
 OBJECT="user" SCOPE="local" METHOD="GetCurrentUserLevel()"
 METHODTYPE="invoke"> >
<@ASSIGN NAME="currentUser" SCOPE="local" VALUE=<@CALLMETHOD
 OBJECT="user" SCOPE="local" METHOD="GetCurrentUserName()"
 METHODTYPE="invoke"> >

<HTML>
  <HEAD>
    <TITLE>
      New Bid
    </TITLE>
  </HEAD>
  <BODY BGCOLOR="#ffffff" TEXT="#000000" LINK="#0000ff"
    ALINK="#ff0000" VLINK="#000088">
    <TABLE BORDER=0 WIDTH=95%>
      <TR>
        <TD>
        </TD>
      </TR>
    </TABLE>
```

```
<FONT SIZE="2" FACE="Verdana, Arial, Helvetica, sans-serif">
    <TABLE BORDER=0 CELLPADDING=0 CELLSPACING=0 WIDTH="95%">
<TR>
            <TD BGCOLOR="#ffffff">
              <TABLE WIDTH=100% BORDER=0
                  CELLSPACING=1 CELLPADDING=4>
                <TR BGCOLOR="#777777">
                  <TD VALIGN=MIDDLE WIDTH=18%>
                    <FONT SIZE="1" FACE="Verdana, Arial,
                        Helvetica, sans-serif"
                        COLOR="#ffffff">
                      <B>
                         @@local$currentUser
                      </B>
                    </FONT>
                  </TD>
                  <TD VALIGN=MIDDLE>
                    <FONT SIZE="1" FACE="Verdana, Arial,
                        Helvetica, sans-serif"
                        COLOR="#ffffff">
                      <B>
                         Bidding on item: <@ARG itemID>
                      </B>
                    </FONT>
                  </TD>
                </TR>
                <TR >
                  <TD WIDTH=18% VALIGN=TOP>
                    <FONT SIZE="2" FACE="Verdana, Arial,
                        Helvetica, sans-serif">
                      <B>
                         Time:
                      </B>
                    </FONT>
                    <BR>
                    <FONT SIZE="1" FACE="Verdana, Arial,
                        Helvetica, sans-serif">
                      <@CURRENTTIMESTAMP>
                    </FONT>
                  </TD>
                  <TD>
                    <FORM ACTION="<@CGI><@APPFILE>
                    ?_function=bid_insert"
                      METHOD=POST>
                      <TABLE BORDER="0">
                      <TR>
                        <TD>
                          <FONT SIZE="2" FACE="VERDANA,
```

continues

Listing 15.7 (Continued)

```
                             ARIAL, HELVETICA,
                             SANS-SERIF">
                            Minimum Bid: $@@local$minBid
                            <BR>
                             </FONT>
                           </TD>
                         </TR>
                         <TR>
                          <TD>
                          <FONT SIZE="2" FACE="VERDANA,
                           ARIAL, HELVETICA, SANS-SERIF">
                            Bid amount:      <INPUT TYPE=
                                       "text"
                             NAME="bid"> (in USD)<BR>
                             </FONT>
                           </TD>
                         </TR>
                         <TR>
                          <TD ALIGN=right>
                          <FONT SIZE="2" FACE="VERDANA,
                           ARIAL, HELVETICA, SANS-SERIF">
                   <INPUT TYPE="hidden" NAME="itemID" VALUE=
                   "<@ARG itemID>">
                   <INPUT TYPE="hidden" NAME="bidder"
                    VALUE="@@local$currentUser">
                   <INPUT TYPE=SUBMIT NAME="Submit"
                    VALUE="Submit">
                            </FONT>
                          </TD>
                        </TR>
                        </TABLE>
                      </FORM>
                 </td>
               </tr>
             </table>
          </td>
        </tr>
      </table>
      <table border=0 width="95%">
        <TR>
          <TD valign=top align=left>
            <FONT SIZE="1" FACE="VERDANA, ARIAL, HELVETICA,
            SANS-SERIF">
              <P>
              All times are CST (US)
```

```
            </FONT>
          </td>
          <td align=right valign=top>
            <FONT SIZE="1" FACE="VERDANA, ARIAL, HELVETICA, SANS-SERIF">
                <A HREF="<@CGI><@APPFILEPATH>
                auction_items.taf?_function= list_an_item&itemID=<@ARG
                itemID>">Back to item</A><BR>
                <A HREF="<@CGI><@APPFILEPATH>auction_items.taf?_
                function=items_list">
                Back to list.</A>
            </FONT>
          </TD>
        </TR>
    </TABLE>
    <BR>
  </FONT>
</BODY>
</HTML>
```

All this page does is display the information we already have generated. When the user clicks the Submit button, auction_bid.taf will be called with <@ARG _function> set to bid_insert. Let's implement that functionality now.

Under the If for <@ARG _function> equals bid_insert, we need to retrieve the minimum bid so that we can verify the user bid at least the minimum amount. The easiest way to get that information is to select the CreateObject and CallMethod actions from the previous If and copy them into the new one. We now have the minimum bid in the variable minBid. We need to check it and display a message if the amount entered is too low. Add another If action that checks to see if <@ARG bid> is less than @@local$minBid. If this is true, we need to tell the user; so drag a Result action under the If and put an error message in it telling the bidder that his bid was too low.

Put in an Else action that will be executed if he bids more than the current high bid. We're almost ready to do the insert, but we need to check our parameters. Drag yet another If action in and configure it as shown in Figure 15.13.

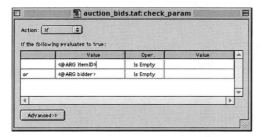

FIGURE 15.13 *Parameter checking If action.*

If this statement is true, the parameters are wrong. Tell the user there is a problem in a Result action under the If and add a Return to leave the TAF.

We've got good parameters; so we are ready to do the actual Insert action. Drag in an Insert action and configure it as shown in Figure 15.14.

Column	Value	Quote Value
itemID	<@ARG itemID>	False
buyer_name	<@ARG bidder>	True
time_bid	<@CURRENTTIMESTAMP>	True
bid_price	<@ARG bid>	False

FIGURE 15.14 *Inserting a new bid into the database.*

The last thing the bid TAF needs to do is display the bid history. The bid history is a listing of all the bids on a particular item sorted by price, from the highest to the lowest. Add an If action that checks if <@ARG _function> is bid_history. Under it drag a Search action. We're going to display the bidder name, the time the bid was placed, and the amount of the bid. Configure the Search action as shown in Figure 15.15.

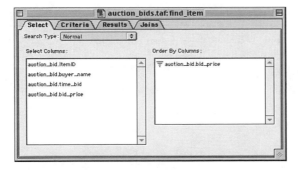

FIGURE 15.15   *Finding information for the bid history.*

The criterion for the search is that the `auction_bids.itemID` is equal to the `itemID` argument we are passed. After we have our list of bids, it is just a matter of displaying them. Do this by including the file bid_list.html in the Result attribute. Listing 15.8 contains the contents of the bid_list.html. You should already understand all the display code.

Listing 15.8   HTML for Displaying the Bid History

```
<@ASSIGN NAME="user" SCOPE="local" VALUE=<@CREATEOBJECT
 OBJECTID="user_sec.tcf" TYPE="TCF">>
<@ASSIGN NAME="currentUserLevel" SCOPE="local" VALUE=<@CALLMETHOD
 OBJECT="user" SCOPE="local" METHOD="GetCurrentUserLevel()"
 METHODTYPE="invoke"> >
<@ASSIGN NAME="currentUser" SCOPE="local" VALUE=<@CALLMETHOD
 OBJECT="user" SCOPE="local" METHOD="GetCurrentUserName()"
 METHODTYPE="invoke"> >

<HTML>
  <HEAD>
    <TITLE>
      Bid History for Item <@ARG itemID>
    </TITLE>
  </HEAD>
  <BODY BGCOLOR="#ffffff" TEXT="#000000" LINK="#0000ff"
  ALINK="#ff0000" VLINK="#000088">
    <TABLE BORDER=0 WIDTH=95%>
      <TR>
        <TD>
          <FONT SIZE="1" FACE="Verdana, Arial, Helvetica, sans-serif">
            <B>
```

continues

Listing 15.8   (Continued)

```
            <A HREF="<@CGI><@APPFILEPATH>auction_bids.taf?
            function=
               bid_form&itemID=<@ARG itemID>">Bid</A>
         </B>
         Any logged in user can bid on an item to the auction.
      </FONT>
   </TD>
</TR>
</TABLE>
<FONT SIZE="2" FACE="Verdana, Arial, Helvetica, sans-serif">
   <TABLE BORDER=0 CELLPADDING=0 CELLSPACING=0 WIDTH="95%">
      <TR>
         <TD BGCOLOR="#ffffff">
         <TABLE WIDTH=100% BORDER=0 CELLSPACING=1 CELLPADDING=4>
            <TR BGCOLOR="#777777">
               <TD VALIGN=MIDDLE WIDTH=18%>
                <FONT SIZE="1" FACE="Verdana, Arial,
                 Helvetica, sans-serif" COLOR="#ffffff">
                   <B>
                      Bid Amount
                   </B>
                </FONT>
               </TD>
               <TD VALIGN=MIDDLE>
                  <FONT SIZE="1" FACE="Verdana, Arial,
                  Helvetica, sans-serif" COLOR="#ffffff">
                     <B>
                        Bid time
                     </B>
                  </FONT>
               </TD>
              <TD VALIGN=MIDDLE>
                  <FONT SIZE="1" FACE="Verdana, Arial,
                  Helvetica, sans-serif" COLOR=
                  "#ffffff">
                     <B>
                        Bidder
                     </B>
                  </FONT>
              </TD>
            </TR>
<@ROWS>
            <TR >
              <TD WIDTH=18%>
                 <FONT SIZE="2" FACE="Verdana, Arial,
                 Helvetica, sans-serif">
                    <B>
                       <@COLUMN 'auction_bid.bid_price'>
```

```
                                  </B>
                                </FONT>
                              </TD>
                              <TD WIDTH=18%>
                                <FONT SIZE="2" FACE="Verdana, Arial,
                                Helvetica, sans-serif">
                                  <@COLUMN 'auction_bid.time_bid'>
                                </FONT>
                              </TD>
                              <TD>
                                <FONT SIZE="2" FACE="Verdana, Arial,
                                Helvetica, sans-serif">
                                  <@COLUMN 'auction_bid.buyer_name'>
                                </FONT>
                              </td>
                            </tr>
</@ROWS>
                        </table>
                      </td>
                    </tr>
                  </table>
<HR>
                  <table border=0 width="95%">
                    <TR>
                      <TD valign=top align=left>
                        <FONT SIZE="1" FACE="VERDANA, ARIAL,
                        HELVETICA, SANS-SERIF">
                          <P>
                          All times are CST (US)
                        </FONT>
                      </td>
                      <td align=right valign=top>
                        <FONT SIZE="1" FACE="VERDANA, ARIAL,
                        HELVETICA, SANS-SERIF">
                          <A HREF="<@CGI><@APPFILEPATH>auction_items.taf?
                          _function= list_an_item&itemID=
                          <@COLUMN 'auction_bid.itemID'>">
                            Back to item</A>
                        </FONT>
                      </TD>
                    </TR>
                  </TABLE>
                  <BR>
                </FONT>
              </BODY>
            </HTML>
```

Admin TAFs

auction_admin.taf

The code for the admin TAF is two actions. All it does is create an instance of the `auction` object and call its `clear_old_auctions` method. The method `clear_old_auctions` doesn't even have parameters or a return value. I'm going to leave the creation of this TAF as an exercise for the user.

Although this TAF doesn't do much, it is very important. It cleans old data out of our database. We need to run it periodically. We could just put a new reoccurring item in our Palm Pilot telling us to run this TAF, but there has to be a better way. Of course there is, or I wouldn't have started talking about it.

The Tango server duplicates the functionality of the UNIX cron utility all the way down to using the same file format. Cron allows you to configure tasks to be executed at specific intervals. Tango allows you to specify URLs to be executed at these times. The URL you want to specify will be our admin TAF.

The location of the file that defines the Tango periodic events is defined in the `crontabFile` configuration variable on your server. When you know where it is, you can open it in a text editor and configure it to execute the auction_admin.taf.

Before we get into configuring your crontab file, you need to know the URL of your auction_admin.taf file. If you put it somewhere you can access via browser, you can copy the URL out of the browser.

A crontab file is looked at continuously. Each line in the file has six fields, which you can specify, that are separated by spaces or tabs. The first five fields are time fields, and the sixth is the URL you want to execute. You can put an asterisk in any of the first five fields as a wildcard.

I'm only going to show you how to configure the file to execute our admin URL every day at midnight. You can find more information on how to configure the file in the documentation for cron or Tango. To configure it to check once a day, set a line in the file to Listing 15.9.

Listing 15.9   Cron Line to Check Once a Day

```
0 0 * * 0-6 http:/your.site.com/admin/auction_admin.taf
```

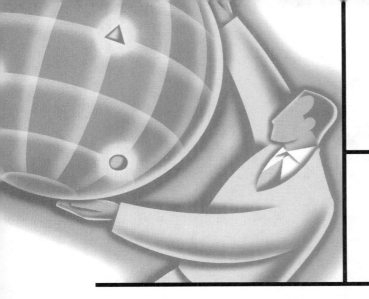

Find

What We'll Learn

- CDATA blocks in XML
- <@CHOICELIST>
- <@REPLACE>

Purpose

We will create a flexible, TCF-based search system that will enable us to
do finds on various databases on the site. Instead of doing a search on
the text generated by our TAFs, we will do searches on the data that generates the TAFs.

Planning

Feature List

- User must be able to search the entire site, or search specific areas
  of the site.
- Admin can add new areas by writing a new find handler for the
  area.

Database Schema

Find does not create any new databases, but does use the databases from other modules in the site. In this chapter, we write find handlers for the Web directory, the forums, and the user profiles created in previous chapters.

Creating the TAFs

According to Jakob Neilsen, the primary means of navigation in a Web site is the search box. People come to a site looking for a particular piece of information and they have learned the quickest way to find it is to do a search. So far, our Web site doesn't provide a means of searching any of the data it displays. It is time to change that.

We don't want to use the old static text means of searching a Web site. The text on our pages isn't the data of the site; instead, Tango is displaying the information stored in various database tables. We want to search these database tables. Sometimes the user will know what part of the site he wants to search and sometimes he will want to search the whole Web site. For instance, he might be looking for URLs containing a particular string, or he might just want to find that string wherever it occurs. We need to give the users a means of searching a particular area or the whole site. Because different areas of the site are being searched, we can display the results by area and not just as a jumble of text.

Different areas have different data and need to be searched differently, but all search results can be displayed in a similar manner. The data that a search returns for each found item are the name of the item found, a description of what was found, and a URL to go to the item found. For example, when searching a forum, you would return the message title, all or part of the message, and a URL that displays the message. When searching the Web directory, you would return the title of the URL found, the description, and the URL found.

What we want is an expandable search mechanism that can handle searching different kinds of data, but that will return the data in the same information format. We'll accomplish this by creating a TCF that has a different method for each type of data to search, which we'll call a find handler method. Each find handler method will return a list of found items with the three pieces of data we want. But we don't want to have to call all the find handler methods from every TAF that has a search box. Instead, we want one method call that will return our search. This single method must take into account the kind of search we want—either everything or a specific area search.

A search box is not something that goes on only one page; rather, its HTML is included on a number of pages. Therefore, for convenience, we will create a TCF method that returns the HTML for the search form. This form will include a pop-up menu that enables the user to select a specific area of the site or the whole site to search.

TCF

Create a new TCF called find.tcf. The On_Create and On_Destroy methods don't need to do anything.

DoFind

The first routine we will create is the DoFind routine. This will be a routine that actually handles the request from the form. Create a new method and configure it as shown in Figure 16.1.

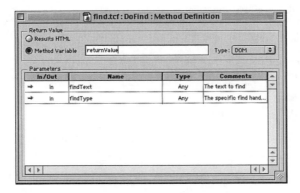

FIGURE 16.1 *Configuration of the DoFind method.*

DoFind will accept the text to be found, *findText*, and the area to be searched, findType. It will return a list of items found, grouped by the area in which they were found. This data is hierarchical, and when you see hierarchical data, the first storage mechanism you should think of is XML. We will return a DOM variable that contains the data generated by the search.

We could pass back the actual display HTML for the found results, but that is an inflexible approach because if we need to change the display of our results, we have to change it in every find handler. By passing back XML, we put all the display, or presentation, logic in the TAF, which enables us to change it there one time and have it changed for every found item. Also, you could avoid the display transformation by using XSL. XSL is an XML-related standard that creates style sheets for XML data. That means you can specify how an XML file is rendered in HTML and your browser will automatically handle rendering the HTML. Unfortunatly the only browser currently supporting this standard is Internet Explorer 5. For more information on XSL, check out the links in Appendix B, "Other Tango Resources."

The parameter findType contains a string that uniquely identifies the area to be searched. If we want to search all the find handlers, this value is ALL. If we want to search a specific area such as the Web directory, we put the string webDir in this parameter. Ultimately, this parameter is set from a pop-up menu in the search form.

The format of our data will be like Figure 16.2. Each node in this tree is an XML node. The XML tag for each node is shown. There can be multiple FOUNDSETs and multiple FOUNDITEMs.

```
Root <SEARCHRESULT>
  Area <FOUNDSET> with a name
    A single found item <FOUNDITEM> with a name
        The description of the item <DESCRIPTION>
        The URL for the item <URL>
```

FIGURE 16.2   *A diagram of search result data.*

The DoFind routine is always going to return a <SEARCHRESULT> with at least one <FOUNDSET>. The <FOUNDSET> may contain no <FOUNDITEM> nodes, if none are found. Based on the value of the findType parameter, we will search on either a particular area or the whole site.

Searching an area is accomplished by calling a find handler method in the TCF. For example, we will create a routine to search the Web directory database, called FH_WebDir. We're naming all these find handlers starting with FH_. By isolating the search of one area to its own method, we allow reuse and easy adding of new handlers. If we want to search all areas of the site, we call each find handler in turn and add its results to the DOM we will return. To search just one specific area, we call just that routine and add only its result.

That means the DoFind routine depends on the `find handler` methods being in place before we can fully create it. So, you must create the three `find handlers` we will be using, FH_UserProfiles, FH_Forums, and FH_WebDir. It doesn't matter whether they work at this point, but they must exist, so create the methods and configure them as shown in Figure 16.3. All the parameters are the same; only the names of the routines are different.

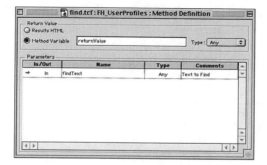

FIGURE 16.3   *The configuration for any find handler method.*

After you have these routines added to the TCF, save them and add them to your Objects panel.

Now we are ready to add actions to the DoFind method. The first thing we must do is to create the DOM root node for our return value. Drag a new Result action into DoFind and put the code in Listing 16.1 in it.

Listing 16.1   Creation of Root Node for the Return Value of DoFind

```
<@ASSIGN NAME="mainDOM" SCOPE="method" VALUE="<@DOM VALUE='
<SEARCHRESULT></SEARCHRESULT>'>">
```

This creates a temp variable to which we will add all the search results returned by the `find handlers`. Remember that in XML, there can be only one root tag; in our case, that root is <SEARCHRESULT>.

The first case we will handle is where the user wants to search all the Web site. Drag an If action into the DoFind method. Configure it to check whether @@method$findType is equal to ALL as shown in Figure 16.4.

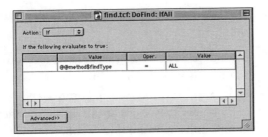

FIGURE 16.4 *Checking whether we want to search the whole site.*

Inside this If action, we will call all the `find handlers`. Let's do the Web directory first. From your Objects panel, drag in the FH_WebDir method and configure it as shown in Figure 16.5.

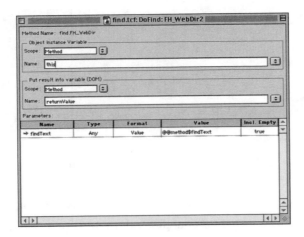

FIGURE 16.5 *Calling a* `find handler`.

We're just passing on the `findText` parameter to the `find handler` and assigning the search results, which are a DOM, to the local variable `returnValue`.

After this call is made, we'll have the value of a search in the `returnValue` DOM and we need to get it into our `mainDOM` variable so that it can later be returned. We do this in the ResultsHTML attribute of the Call Method action. Put Listing 16.2 into the ResultsHTML. This code does a simple insert of the returned DOM into the `mainDOM`.

Listing 16.2   Adding the `find` `handler`**'s Result to Our Return Variable**

```
<@DOMINSERT OBJECT="mainDOM" SCOPE="local" ELEMENT="root()" POSTION="append">
    @@local$returnValue
</@DOMINSERT>
```

All the calls to `find` `handlers` work in exactly the same way. Drag in the FH_UserProfiles and FH_Forums methods and configure them just as you did for FH_WebDir in Figure 16.5. Then add Listing 16.2 to their ResultsHTML as well.

Now, let's handle the specific search area cases. These all work exactly the same way, so I'll show you only the WebDir case. You should be able to duplicate the steps for the other `find` `handlers`, and in `find` `handlers` you create in the future. Drag in an If action and configure it to check `@@method$findType` for the type of a Web directory search, webDir. The mechanism for doing the search is the same we used in the ALL search, except that we use only one `find` `handler`. Given this, you can copy the Call Method action from under the IfAll action to under the IfWebDir action. That's all you have to do to search a specific area. Add in If actions for the other two `find` `handlers` now.

The last thing we have to do in DoFind is assign our accumulated DOM, mainDOM, to the return value variable. Do this by dragging a Result action into the TCF under all the other actions. Make sure that it doesn't end up inside the last If action—it needs to be under the root. Inside the Result action put Listing 16.3, which is a simple assign to the `returnValue` variable we specified in the configuration of the DoFind method.

Listing 16.3   Returning Our Accumulated Search Results

```
<@ASSIGN NAME="returnValue" VALUE="@@local$mainDOM" SCOPE="Method">
```

DoFind is now functional. Of course, it won't return any values because none of the `find` `handler` methods work. Let's create them now.

FH_WebDir

The actual search of the data is pretty straightforward for this handler. Drag in a Search action and select all the relevant columns from the weblinks table. Configure the Criteria tab to match the one shown in Figure 16.6.

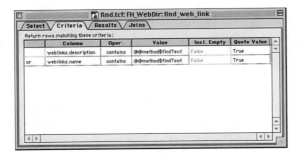

FIGURE 16.6   *Doing the actual find in the table.*

I want to point out a couple of points about this search. First, notice that the criteria are ORed together. We want to say something was found if any of these columns contains the search text. Secondly, notice our operator is contains. We want to say something was found if it is anywhere in the text of the field. If the user searches for Austin, we want to find it even if it is buried in the user's biography.

After we have the results of the search, we need to create the XML from it. We'll do this in the ResultsHTML of the Search action. Put Listing 16.4 into the ResultsHTML.

Listing 16.4   Building the XML for the Found Items

```
<@ASSIGN NAME='TEMPVAR' VALUE='<FOUNDSET NAME="Web Directory">
 </FOUNDSET>' SCOPE='method'>
<@ASSIGN NAME="returnValue" SCOPE="Method" VALUE="
 <@DOM VALUE='@@method$TEMPVAR'>">

<@ROWS>
<@DOMINSERT OBJECT="returnValue" SCOPE="Method"
 ELEMENT="root()" POSTION="append">
    <FOUNDITEM NAME="<@COLUMN 'weblinks.name'>"></FOUNDITEM>
</@DOMINSERT>

<@DOMINSERT OBJECT="returnValue" SCOPE="Method"
 ELEMENT="root().child(<@CURROW>)" POSTION="append">
    <DESCRIPTION><![CDATA[<@COLUMN 'weblinks.description'>]]></DESCRIPTION>
</@DOMINSERT>

<@DOMINSERT OBJECT="returnValue" SCOPE="Method"
 ELEMENT="root().child(<@CURROW>)" POSTION="append">
    <URL>
<![CDATA[<@COLUMN 'weblinks.url'>]]>
```

```
    </URL>
  </@DOMINSERT>
</@ROWS>
```

First, we create a root node for all the times found in the Web directory. This node is called <FOUNDSET>. It is created in a two-step process to avoid quote mismatch problems. The returnValue variable is the one we specified as the return value of the method. Also notice that we hardcode the name of the found set. This is the name that will be displayed as the area we searched.

Now we have a DOM variable to which we can assign nodes. Next, we loop through each row we found and build a <FOUNDITEM> node and add it to the returnValue DOM. One of the attributes of the <FOUNDITEM> is the name of the item, which in this case is the name of the item in the Web directory. Next, we create a <DESCRIPTION> node and put the item description as its value. Notice that the ELEMENT attribute of the <@DOMINSERT> tag points the child node at the index of the current row in our loop.

Have you thought about what would happen if you tried to put XML inside an XML tag pair? Or, for that matter, HTML because it has tags. Well, it wouldn't work because the parser would be confused about which tags were for the data and which were for the tags. Another problem is the ampersand. This can cause problems because the ampersand is what XML and HTML use to escape certain characters such as the greater-than and less-than characters. So, if your data contains one of these characters, you must do something to tell XML to ignore special characters inside of it. That is what CDATA does for you. It is part of the XML standard and specifies that any data between the starting <!CDATA[and the ending]]> is to be ignored by the parser. In our case, we aren't sure whether there is an ampersand in the title or the description, but there could be, so we surround it with a CDATA block.

After we insert the <DESCRIPTION>, we insert the stored URL. It is quite common for a URL to have an ampersand in it to delineate parameters, so we use CDATA again.

Now we have a DOM for all the items we found in the database. The function ends and it is returned to DoFind.

FH_Forums

After you've created one `find handler`, the others are easy. For FH_Forum, drag in another Search action and configure it to search the relevant columns in the forum_message table. Its Criteria tab should match the one shown in Figure 16.7.

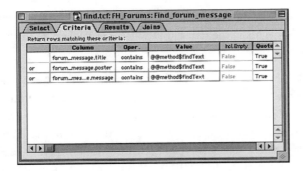

FIGURE 16.7 *The Criteria tab for searching forum messages.*

The meta tags inside the ResultsHTML (given in Listing 16.5) are almost the same as the meta tags for FH_WebDir.

Listing 16.5   Generating the XML for the Find in the Forums

```
<@ASSIGN NAME='TEMPVAR' VALUE='<FOUNDSET NAME="Forums"></FOUNDSET>'
 SCOPE='method'>
<@ASSIGN NAME="returnValue" SCOPE="Method" VALUE="
<@DOM VALUE='@@method$TEMPVAR'>">

<@ROWS>
<@DOMINSERT OBJECT="returnValue" SCOPE="Method" ELEMENT="root()"
POSTION="append">
    <FOUNDITEM NAME="<@COLUMN 'forum_message.title'>"></FOUNDITEM>
</@DOMINSERT>

<@DOMINSERT OBJECT="returnValue" SCOPE="Method" ELEMENT="root().child
(<@CURROW>)" POSTION="append">
    <DESCRIPTION><@LEFT STR="<@COLUMN 'forum_message.message'>" NUMCHARS="50">
... posted by: <@COLUMN 'forum_message.poster'></DESCRIPTION>
</@DOMINSERT>

<@DOMINSERT OBJECT="returnValue" SCOPE="Method" ELEMENT="root().child
(<@CURROW>)" POSTION="append">
    <URL>
<![CDATA[http://<@CGIPARAM SERVER_NAME>/TangoBook/chap13/forum_message.taf?
```

```
_function=showMessage&msgID=<@COLUMN 'forum_message.messageID'>]]>
      </URL>
</@DOMINSERT>
</@ROWS>
```

The parts of Listing 16.5 that are different are in italics. We change the name of the found set to Forums. The name of the found item is also changed to the message title. The description is generated from the first 50 characters of the message and who posted it. And the URL is generated as it was in Chapter 13, "Forums," to show a single message. Remember this pattern of change because you can reuse this code for any new handler just by changing these areas. As a matter of fact, let's do that with the user profiles handler.

FH_UserProfiles

We need to create a new Search action with the relevant columns selected. The criteria for the search are in Figure 16.8.

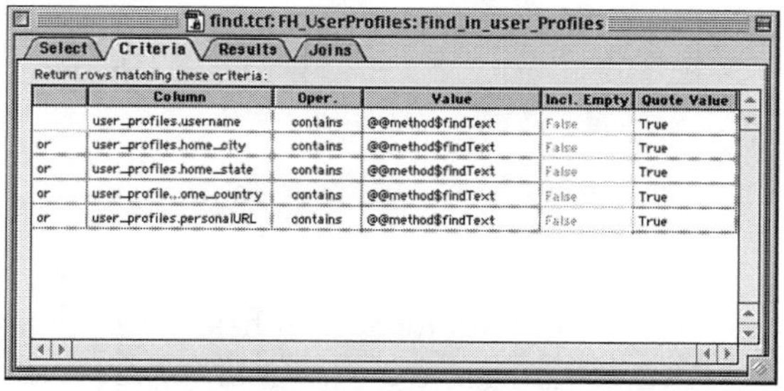

FIGURE 16.8 *Doing the find in the user_profiles table.*

The generation of the XML is described in Listing 16.6. It is the same pattern but with the found set name changed to User Profiles, the found item name changed to the user_profiles.username column, the description set to the first 50 characters of the user's biography, and the URL generated as shown in Chapter 9, "User Profiles."

Listing 16.6 Generating the XML for User Profiles

```
<@ASSIGN NAME='TEMPVAR' VALUE='<FOUNDSET NAME="User Profiles">
 </FOUNDSET>' SCOPE='method' >
<@ASSIGN NAME="returnValue" SCOPE="Method" VALUE="
 <@DOM VALUE='@@method$TEMPVAR'>">

<@ROWS>
<@DOMINSERT OBJECT="returnValue" SCOPE="Method"
ELEMENT="root()" POSITION="append">
    <FOUNDITEM NAME="<@COLUMN 'user_profiles.username'>"></FOUNDITEM>
</@DOMINSERT>

<@DOMINSERT OBJECT="returnValue" SCOPE="Method"
 ELEMENT="root().child(<@CURROW>)" POSITION="append">
    <DESCRIPTION><@LEFT STR="<@COLUMN 'user_profiles.biography'>"
      NUMCHARS="50">...</DESCRIPTION>
</@DOMINSERT>

<@DOMINSERT OBJECT="returnValue" SCOPE="Method"
  ELEMENT="root().child(<@CURROW>)" POSITION="append">
    <URL>
<![CDATA[http://<@CGIPARAM SERVER_NAME>/members/profile.taf?
_function=find_user&username=<@COLUMN 'user_profiles.username'>]]>
    </URL>
</@DOMINSERT>

</@ROWS>
```

GetAreaList

We need to be able to generate a pop-up menu that has a user-friendly name in it and sets its HTML parameter to the internal string for searching an area. Tango provides a means of generating this pop-up menu by using an array with two columns—one column is the visible name and the second column is the internal value. We will isolate the creation of this array to a method called GetAreaList. Create a new method and configure it as shown in Figure 16.9.

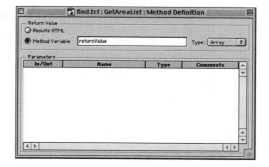

FIGURE 16.9   *Configuration of the GetAreaList method.*

All this method does is create an array and return it in the returnValue method variable. This is accomplished with the meta tag in Listing 16.7.

Listing 16.7   Creating the Name Array

```
<@ASSIGN NAME="returnValue" VALUE="<@ARRAY VALUE=
'Whole Site,ALL;Forums,forum;Web Directory,webDir;User Profiles,profiles;'>"
SCOPE="method">
```

Using standard array syntax, we create a two-dimensional array in which each column is delineated by a comma, and a semicolon delineates each row. To add a new item to this list, you just add a new pair to the list. It is also good to always put Whole Site first so that it will be the default value.

GetFindForm

The final method we want to add to the TCF is one that generates the HTML for the search box form. The search box form has two parts: a text field for entering the search string and a pop-up menu with the areas to search.

Create a new method named GetFindForm and set its return value to be ResultsHTML. By doing this, we'll be able to generate HTML just as we would in a TAF, and the results will be returned without having to add them to a variable. There are no parameters.

The first thing we want to do is get the array of values for the pop-up menu. We do this by calling the GetAreaList method. Drag it from the

Objects panel into the TCF. You might have to refresh the Find object in the Objects panel to get the new methods to show up. Configure GetAreaList as shown in Figure 16.10.

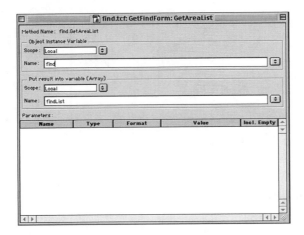

FIGURE 16.10 *Getting the array for the pop-up menu.*

Now drag in a Result action, where we will generate the HTML for the form. Use Listing 16.8 to create the form.

Listing 16.8   The Search Box HTML

```
<FORM METHOD=POST ACTION="<@CGI><@APPFILE>?_function=doFind">
Find:
<INPUT TYPE=TEXT MAXLENGTH=255 SIZE=25 NAME="findText" VALUE="">
<@CHOICELIST NAME=findType TYPE=select OPTIONS=@@local$findList[*,1]
 VALUES=@@local$findList[*,2] SELECTED="Whole Site">
<INPUT TYPE=SUBMIT NAME="Submit" VALUE="Submit">
</FORM>
```

Most of Listing 16.8 is straight HTML, but in the middle there is a new Tango tag called <@CHOICELIST>. This is a very flexible tag that will generate a pop-up menu or a group of radio buttons. It has more optional parameters than any other meta tag, but we will focus on the few we need for our pop-up menu.

The first attribute is the name of the parameter that will get the value of the pop-up when the user submits the form. We use findType because that describes the content of the pop-up. We want a pop-up, which is a select control in HTML, so we set TYPE to select. The options, which are the names that are displayed, are the first column of findList and the values, which are the actual strings passed in as findType, are in column two. Finally, we explicitly say that we want Whole Site shown.

That's it. You now have all the parts you need to do a find. The next section will put them into action.

User TAF

Doing a search is a two-step process. First, you put up the form and then you process the forum. The first step can be done on any page, but the second must be in a dedicated TAF. For the purposes of this chapter, we will put both steps in the same TAF.

Create a new TAF called find.taf. We'll use <@ARG _function> to determine which stage of the search we want. Drag in an If action to check <@ARG _function> for empty. The default case will be to put up the find form. Doing that is easy because we get the form from the TCF. Drag the find object from your object palette and configure the Create Object action to create a variable named find. Now drag in the method GetFindForm, and tell it to put its result into the variable result. In the ResultsHTML for this Call Method action, display the variable using an <@VAR> tag like this: <@VAR NAME=result encoding=none>. We have to use <@VAR> because we need to set the encoding to none to make our HTML work. This will display our form when the TAF is executed.

Now we are ready to handle the results of the form. Our search form is going to call back here with <@ARG _function> equal to doFind. Drag in an If action and configure it to handle the doFind case. We will use the find.tcf throughout, so we start off by creating the object. Drag the find object into the TCF and configure it to be named find.

Often, the results of a search won't be exactly what we want, so we'll want to do another search. The easiest way to do this is to put the find form at the top of your search results page. You can do this easily by copying the Call Method action from the first If to the new one.

If the user doesn't enter any text in the search field, we would get every record in the database, which would be bad. So, let's check our parameter first. Drag in an If action and configure it to check whether <@ARG findText>

is empty. Under the If action, drag in a Result action and put an error message in it. Then drag in a Return action to stop execution.

Now that we have a valid search string, let's do the search. Drag in the DoFind method from the Objects panel. Configure it as shown in Figure 16.11.

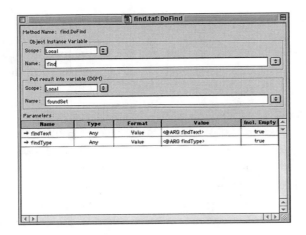

FIGURE 16.11 *Doing the find.*

After this call returns, we will have an XML structure that we need to display. Right off we can start finding out things about the XML. The first thing we'll do is create an array to hold the names of all the areas searched. We also want to keep the number of rows found. We do this by using Listing 16.9, which you should put in the ResultsHTML of the Call Method action.

Listing 16.9   Getting the Areas Searched

```
<@ASSIGN NAME="foundSets" VALUE="<@ELEMENTATTRIBUTE OBJECT='foundSet'
 SCOPE='local' ATTRIBUTE='NAME' ELEMENT='root().child(all)' TYPE=ARRAY>"
 SCOPE="local">

<@ASSIGN NAME="numFoundSets" VALUE="<@NUMROWS array='@@local$foundSets'>"

 SCOPE="local">
```

In this TAF, I have attempted always to put the display logic in its own actions. We are getting ready to loop through the rows of the array we created. We want to put each found set name in a row in an HTML table, but we need to start the table outside the loop. To do this, drag in a Result action and put <TABLE> into it.

Next, drag in a For action and configure it as shown in Figure 16.12. This will loop through the rows of our table.

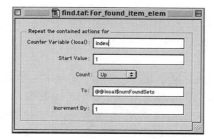

FIGURE 16.12   *Looping through the found sets.*

Next, we will create an array that has a list of the names of the items found. We do this by looking for the NAME attribute of the found set nodes. Drag a ResultsHTML inside the For action and put Listing 16.10 into it.

Listing 16.10   Finding the Found Set Names

```
<@ASSIGN NAME="foundItems" VALUE="<@ELEMENTATTRIBUTE OBJECT='foundSet'
 SCOPE='local' ATTRIBUTE='NAME'
 ELEMENT='root().child(@@local$index).child(all)' TYPE=ARRAY>" SCOPE="local">

<@ASSIGN NAME="numNodes" VALUE="<@NUMROWS ARRAY='foundItems'>" SCOPE="local">

<@IFEMPTY VALUE="@@local$numNodes">
<@ASSIGN NAME="numNodes" VALUE="0" SCOPE="local">
</@IF>
```

We also check to make sure something was found and set the number of nodes correctly. Now that we have our list of found items, we are ready to display the current found set. Drag in a Result action and insert Listing 16.11 into it.

Listing 16.11   Displaying the Name of the Current Found Set

```
<TR ALIGN=LEFT VALIGN=TOP>
<TD bgcolor="#777777" valign=middle>
    <FONT SIZE="1" face="Verdana, Arial, Helvetica, sans-serif"
     color="#ffffff">
        <B>
            @@local$foundSets[ @@local$index,1] (found: @@local$numNodes )
        </B>
    </FONT>
</TD>
</TR>
```

If no nodes were found, we want to put in a row with a message saying that we couldn't find anything in this search area. Drag in an If action and configure it to check whether @@local$numNodes is zero. Under that If action, drag in a ResultsHTML action and put Listing 16.12 into it.

Listing 16.12   No Results Row for a Found Set

```
<TR ALIGN=LEFT VALIGN=TOP>
<TD>
        <FONT SIZE="2" FACE="Verdana, Arial, Helvetica, sans-serif">
            No instances of "<@ARG findText>" found in
            @@local$foundSets[ @@local$index,1].
        </FONT>
</TD>
</TR>
```

Don't return, or you won't finish the table. Drag in a For action to loop through the found items, and configure it as shown in Figure 16.13. If there were no rows, and we put up the error message, this loop will do nothing.

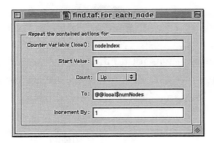

FIGURE **16.13**   *Looping through the found items.*

For each item found, we need to display a row. Drag in a Result action and put Listing 16.13 into it.

Listing 16.13 Displaying the Found Item

```
<@ASSIGN NAME="description" VALUE="<@ELEMENTVALUE OBJECT='foundSet'
 SCOPE='local' ELEMENT='root().child(@@local$index).child(
@@local$nodeIndex).child(1)'>"
 SCOPE="local">

<@ASSIGN NAME="URL" VALUE="<@ELEMENTVALUE OBJECT='foundSet'
 SCOPE='local' ELEMENT='root().child(@@local$index).child(
@@local$nodeIndex).child(2)'>"
 SCOPE="local">


<TR ALIGN=LEFT VALIGN=TOP>
<TD>
    <FONT SIZE="2" FACE="Verdana, Arial, Helvetica, sans-serif">

      <A HREF="@@local$URL">

          <@REPLACE STR="@@local$foundItems[@@local$nodeIndex,1]"
            FINDSTR="<@ARG findText>"
            REPLACESTR="<B><@ARG findText></B>" encoding=none>
      </A>
        -
          <@REPLACE STR="@@local$description"
            FINDSTR="<@ARG findText>"
            REPLACESTR="<B><@ARG findText></B>" encoding=none>


    </FONT>
</TD>
</TR>
```

The first thing we do is get the current found item's description and URL and assign them to local variables.

Inside the <TR> tags, we see some standard HTML and an interesting new meta tag, <@REPLACE>. We are bolding any instances of the search string in the display of the results. We do this by replacing every instance of the search string in the title and the description with the search string with HTML <B> tags around it. <@REPLACE> takes first the string to be changed, and then the string to be found, and the string to replace it.

When this For action ends, we've generated all the rows. Drag in a Result action, making sure that it is at the same level as the Result action that contains the start of the table tag, and put the end table tag </TABLE> into it.

This could all be avoided if you used XSL, but not all browsers support XSL.

Admin TAFs

There are no administration tasks for Find. An admin does need to write new handlers and add them to the DoFind and GetFindForm methods of the find.tcf.

There are very few steps to adding a new handler:

1. Create a new `find handler` method in find.tcf. Create the method name starting with FH_. The configuration of the method is the same as shown in Figure 16.5, with only the name being different.

2. Drag a new Search action into your `find handler` method and configure it to search the relevant columns. Remember to OR your criteria and use contains as your operator.

3. Using Listing 16.4 as a template, create the XML to pass back in the ResultsHTML attribute of your Search action. You need to change these things:

   - Change the found set's name.
   - Change the name of the found item.
   - Change the description.
   - Change the URL.

4. Add a method call to the DoFind method under the IfALL action to call the new `find handler`. In this Call Method action's Results attribute, add Listing 16.2.

5. Add a new If action to DoFind that checks `@@method$findType` for the new method's type string.

6. Copy the Call Method action created in step 2 under the new If action created in step 3.

7. Add your new area's display name and find type to the array in GetAreaList.

This is all you have to do to add a new find handler, making it fairly simple to search new database tables. Because all the presentation logic is handled in the TAF, you can easily change the look of all the search results from outside this TCF.

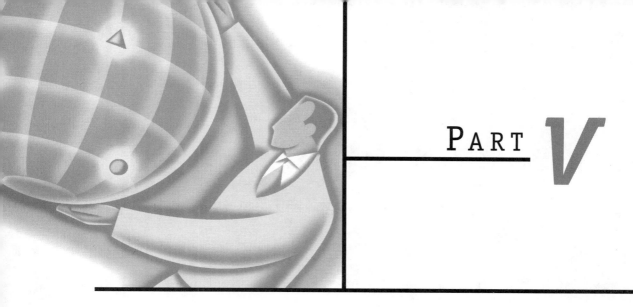

PART V

Appendixes

Tango Actions

Action Icon	ActionName	Description	Reference Chapter
	Search	Performs search on a data source	Introduced in Chapter 3. Criteria and joins are introduced in Chapter 6.
	Insert	Inserts rows into a data source	Introduced in Chapter 3.
	Update	Changes the values of rows from a data source	Introduced in Chapter 9.
	Delete	Removes rows from a data source	Introduced in Chapter 9.
	Direct DBMS	Sends entered SQL statements directly to a data source	Introduced in Chapter 7.
	Begin Transaction	Starts a database transaction on a data source	None.

continues

Action Icon	ActionName	Description	Reference Chapter
	End Transaction	End with commit or rollback all the database changes of the current transaction	None.
	Results	Inserts text or HTML into the Web page	Introduced in Chapter 3.
	Presentation	Inserts another document into the Web page	Introduced in Chapter 8.
	Email	Sends email message	Introduced in Chapter 3.
	File	Reads, writes, and deletes on a file	Introduced in Chapter 7.
	Script	Runs a server-side Javascript	None.
	External	Executes external code such as DLLs, AppleScript, Java, and command-line entries	None.
	Create Object	Creates a new object from a TCF, Java, or COM object	Introduced in Chapter 8.
	Call Method	Calls a method in a Tango object	Introduced in Chapter 8.
	Assign	Assigns values to a variable	Introduced in Chapter 6.
	Group	Groups a set of actions together	Introduced in Chapter 13.
	If	Creates an If conditional statement	Introduced in Chapter 3.

Action Icon	ActionName	Description	Reference Chapter
[??]	ElseIf	Creates an Else action that includes an If condition	Introduced in Chapter 3.
[↓]	Else	Creates an Else conditional statement	Introduced in Chapter 3.
[o]	While	Creates a While loop conditional action	Introduced in Chapter 6.
[↔]	For	Creates a For loop conditional action	Introduced in Chapter 7.
[o]	Object Loop	Iterates through a group of objects returned from an Object call	None.
[r]	Break	Breaks out of a conditional loop action	None.
[↔]	Branch	Moves execution to another action inside or outside of the current TAF	None. Branch actions should be avoided. In T2K, they can often be replaced with TCF methods.
[↩]	Return	Stops execution of the TAF and returns from any branches	Introduced in Chapter 8.
[🔍]	Search builder	Starts wizard for building multiaction searches	Introduced in Chapter 5.
[📄]	New Record builder	Starts wizard for creating Web pages to insert data from a form into a database	Introduced in Chapter 5.

Other Tango Resources

This appendix includes other resources you might want to check out after you have finished this book. These resources provide everything from help and tutorials to sample code.

Pervasive

Tango Developer's Journal

Tango Developer's Journal is a quarterly magazine for Tango and P.SQL developers. It contains useful articles specifically about the use of Tango and Pervasive's database product.

```
http://www.tangojournal.com
```

Manuals

Tango comes with an excellent set of manuals on the CD. You can also order hard copies of these books from Pervasive.

Tango User's Guide

This book discusses each part of the Tango application and tells you what each part does. It is useful for getting the big picture about an area of functionality you've never used.

Meta Tags and Configuration Variables

I live in this book when I'm creating a Tango app. The book lists alphabetically each Tango meta tag and how to use it.

Web Sites

`http://www.pervasive.com/`

The main page of Pervasive's Web site.

`http://componentzone.pervasive.com/`

The place to go to find sample code and Tango components for use in your projects.

Pervasive Developer Page

`http://www.pervasive.com/developerzone`

DevTalk Web Forums

`http://devtalk.pervasive.com/`

Archives of All Prior Issues of "PervasiveDevWire"

`http://www.pervasive.com/developerzone/techlibrary/devwirearchives/index.html`

"PervasiveDevWire" is an email newsletter for users of Pervasive products, including Tango.

Betas

`http://tango.pervasive.com/products/betas/`

Feedback

`http://www.pervasive.com/developerzone/feedback`

Tango Knowledge Base

`http://tango.pervasive.com/support/knowledge/tangokb.taf`

Product Updates and Service Packs

`http://www.pervasive.com/support/updates/index.html`

Product Enhancement Requests

http://www.pervasive.com/developerzone/feedback/suggestions.html

Technical Library

http://www.pervasive.com/developerzone/techlibrary

Where to Get Your Tango Application Hosted

http://www.pervasive.com/developerzone/thirdparty/tangohosting.html

Trial Downloads

http://www.pervasive.com/products/download/

White Papers on Pervasive Software

http://www.pervasive.com/support/technical/white

Tango Talk

This is Pervasive's Internet mailing list for Tango users. It is an invaluable resource for connecting with expert users and Pervasive employees. Most of the engineering team monitors this list.

To subscribe to the list, send a message with "SUBSCRIBE" in the subject to tango-talk@pervasive.com.

You can also subscribe on the Web at http://www.pervasive.com/developerzone/emailnews/.

Non-Pervasive Tango Web Sites

Cool Web-Building Resources

http://infomatters.com/im/freestuff

This site contains a number of snippets and sample code listings.

TangoZone

http://www.tangozone.com

A non-Pervasive Web site for Tango developers. It has its own version of the Tango-Talk mailing list.

XML

XML Journal

http://www.sys-con.com/xml/index2.html

XML.com

http://www.xml.com

The main site for all things XML.

The Annotated XML Specification

http://www.xml.com/axml/testaxml.htm

Xml.org

http://www.xml.org/

An XML portal.

Dr. Dobb's Journal

Has an excellent resource section devoted to XML and related tech stuff.

http://www.ddj.com/topics/xml/

XSL

The XSL standard.

http://www.w3.org/Style/XSL/

Miscellaneous

The Alertbox: Current Issues in Web Usability

A biweekly column by Dr. Jakob Nielsen. Dr. Nielsen provides many tips on how to make your Web site not suck.

http://www.useit.com/alertbox

Building High-Performing, Highly Reliable Tango Applications

In this appendix, I describe techniques and methods you can use to design, develop, and deploy reliable, high-performing Tango applications.

The information here focuses on using Tango in Windows NT and UNIX environments. Currently, the Mac OS version of Tango does not include the load splitting and failover features that play an important role in the deployment of Tango applications. However, many of the other solutions to performance issues described here are also applicable to Mac deployments.

Determine Your Requirements

If your Tango-based Web site must be available as close as possible to 24 hours a day, seven days a week, or if you have specific performance goals in mind, there is a wide variety of issues that you must consider while building and deploying your application. These issues will impact each stage of your application's life cycle. For example, high availability and high performance requirements place more demands on the hardware and software that run your application then they are capable of right out of the box. Knowing these requirements up front can ensure that appropriate purchasing and configuration decisions are made.

Often, the mission of your Web application will have the greatest impact on how you meet your requirements. Here are some examples of applications that share a high availability, high performance requirement, but that might use very different implementations to meet that requirement:

- A Web application used for five hours to collect votes during an election
- A stock-trading application
- An online-banking application
- A personal auction application
- A payment-processing application

Some of these applications require 100% availability and consistent performance during their relatively short life span (for instance, the vote collection system). Some require high availability during business hours as well as predictable performance delivery during peak usage times (stock trading), or must be available to users at all times with minimal downtime (online banking, personal auction site, payment processing). Each of these applications might employ different strategies for dealing with issues that affect availability, such as reliability and failover, periodic maintenance, and data backups.

In addition to determining your availability requirements, you should also make note of the anticipated load requirements and performance expectations. This information can help you to select the appropriate hardware and software you use to deploy your application. The anticipated load requirements and performance expectations will also impact many of the design decisions you make during development.

Usage and performance information is typically measured as the number of page views per minute or second. For a Web application, you should extend performance metrics to identify the nature of each page view. For example, in Tango, this includes determining how many actions are executed as part of each page view, how many database actions are executed, how long each database query takes to process, and the size of the rowset that your application will be retrieving from the database. Coincidentally, it's been my experience that the best-performing applications are usually the most reliable and, thus, most available. In large part, this is because these applications put the least amount of stress on the hardware and software resources available to them.

To assist you in determining your performance requirements, you might also want to utilize commercial services that provide performance statistics of comparable Web sites. Such services can benchmark your site against industry averages or your competitors. They can also provide baseline performance information that you can use while designing your site.

Last, but certainly not least, you need to consider what your budget allows. Many of the items described here have a price tag associated with them, in the form of capital purchases, development time, or expertise that you might not have in-house. You must evaluate each cost point to determine its return on investment in your situation. Even if you can't afford the ultimate solution right now, being aware of your options can help you make decisions today that you can grow with tomorrow.

Developing for Performance

The best way to end up with an application that performs well is to consider this requirement during the design and development of your application. That sounds easy, but with Tango providing many different ways to accomplish the same task, it can be difficult to find your way to this goal. Let's get started by describing some of the many techniques that you can employ in your applications.

Robust Error Handling

Runtime errors can be raised in your application for many reasons, such as a syntax error in your application, a database you use is unavailable, or an object that returns an error as part of its processing. Reducing the number of errors is an important part of a highly available solution. Errors typically take longer to process, and that processing consumes resources that could be used for requests from other users. Additionally, in some cases, external components you use in your application might not have had enough negative testing, and thus might be more susceptible to failure when an unexpected error occurs.

Tango provides several methods for trapping and reacting to errors, and they are detailed in the next few sections.

Error HTML

Error HTML can be associated with individual actions in your application files. The Error HTML can contain both HTML for presentation as well as Tango meta tags for processing. Use Error HTML if you anticipate an error with a specific action.

For example, if you use a Mail action to send an email message, your application should be able to react appropriately if the mail server is unavailable. Listing C.1 contains sample code to check for this problem in a Mail action's Error HTML.

Listing C.1

```
<@ERRORS>
    <@! "-321 is the error returned when the Tango cannot connect to the mail
        server">
    <@IF "<@ERROR part='number1'> = '-321'">
        <H1>Mail Server Unavailable</H1>
        <P>The desired email message could not be sent. </P>
    </@IF>
</@ERRORS>
```

The code in Listing C.1 displays a simple message if Tango cannot connect to your mail server. In your application, you might want to perform some other task, such as sending a message to a pager or writing a note to an error log file, instead of showing a message. Listing C.2 expands on the sample code to call a Tango class file to log the error to a text file. The log_error method in the TCF uses a single File Write action that writes out the error number, error name, TAF name, and action name parameters that were passed to the method.

Listing C.2

```
<@ERRORS>
    <@! "-321 is the error returned when the Tango cannot connect to the mail
        server">
    <@IF "<@ERROR part='number1'> = '-321'">
        <H1>Mail Server Unavailable</H1>
        <P>The desired email message could not be sent. </P>
        <@! "instantiate log object">
        <@ASSIGN NAME="errorlogObject" SCOPE="local" VALUE=<@CREATEOBJECT
         OBJECTID="LogError.tcf" TYPE="TCF">>
        <@! "call log_error method to write error to a text file">
```

```
        <@CALLMETHOD OBJECT="errorlogObject" SCOPE="local" METHOD="log_error
        (<@ERROR part='number1'>, <@ERROR part='name1'>,<@APPFILE>,
         <@CURRENTACTION>)" METHODTYPE="invoke">
    </@IF>
</@ERRORS>
```

Logging problems that occur in your application can provide you with the information you need to prevent the errors from happening in the first place.

If sending email is not a critical task to your application, you can use the <@CLEARERRORS> meta tag to resume processing with the next action in your TAF, or use an HTTP redirect to redirect the user to another TAF. Listing C.3 demonstrates using the <@CLEARERRORS> meta tag while still logging that an error occurred.

Listing C.3

```
<@ERRORS>
    <@! "-321 is the error returned when the Tango cannot connect to the mail
        server">
    <@IF "<@ERROR part='number1'> = '-321'">
        <@! "instantiate log object">
        <@ASSIGN NAME="errorlogObject" SCOPE="local" VALUE=<@CREATEOBJECT
         OBJECTID="LogError.tcf" TYPE="TCF">>
        <@! "call log_error method to write error to a text file">
        <@CALLMETHOD OBJECT="errorlogObject" SCOPE="local" METHOD="log_error
        (<@ERROR part='number1'>, <@ERROR part='name1'>,<@APPFILE>,
         <@CURRENTACTION>)" METHODTYPE="invoke">
        <@! "clear the error so that processing will continue with the next
             action">
        <@CLEARERRORS>
    </@IF>
</@ERRORS>
```

The Component Zone on Pervasive's Web site contains other sample error-reporting components that you can use in your applications.

Default Error File

Putting Error HTML with every action in your TAF or TCF can be time-consuming, particularly to handle unanticipated errors that occur infre-quently. Instead, Tango enables you to designate a file to be executed when the action that generated the error has no Error HTML, or if an error occurs before the processing of a TAF begins. To take advantage of this capability, use config.taf to set the Default Error HTML file.

The code samples in Listings C.1 through C.3 can also be used in the default Error HTML file to react to errors on a global basis.

Platform Independence

Tango provides you with the flexibility to deploy your solution on Mac, Windows, Solaris, and Linux. You might need to take advantage of this flexibility to achieve your performance and reliability goals. Also, the capability to deploy on a different platform might be a useful backup strategy should your primary system become unavailable.

While you build your application, be sure to keep in mind that UNIX systems are case sensitive. That means all filenames used in your applications—such as names of TAFs called from Branch actions, TCFs used in Call Method actions, files referenced using the @INCLUDE meta tag, images, and files used in the File action—must match exactly. Making it a habit to ensure that the filenames match during development is much less stressful than trying to correct this problem at the last minute.

Database Independence

Another technique to consider in your applications is to use variables for all deployment datasource parameters. Deployment datasource parameters are set in either the Properties window for the datasource in the Workspace window (to affect any future actions that use the data source) or in the Properties window of a database action (to affect existing actions).

By using variables for these parameters, your application can dynamically change the database with which it is communicating. This can be used to redirect your requests to a different database if your primary database becomes unavailable.

Caching Data

If you work with relatively static data from a database, such as lists of departments or states, caching that data inside Tango can reduce the number of database queries performed by your application. Using application-scope variables makes this convenient.

- Create a TAF that performs the database queries.

- Instead of formatting the data returned for display, use an Assign action to save the contents of the local scope resultSet variable (Tango always puts the results of a database action into this variable) into an application-scope array variable.

- Call this TAF manually when your application starts, or have Tango do this automatically by using the application-scope Startup URL. The Startup URL feature enables you to define TAFs that are executed when your Tango Server starts.

If your data is not static, you still might be able to take advantage of this technique. By using Tango's timed URL processing feature (also known as *cron*), you can have this application file executed periodically, keeping the cached data up to date.

After you have this data cached, you can use it in your application just as you use data returned directly from the database. The @ROWS and @COLS meta tags enable you to iterate over an array. Within these meta tags, you can use the @COL and @COLUMN meta tags to access individual values in the array. In cases in which you will be displaying the data on a form, the @CHOICELIST meta tag makes it very easy to create data-driven form elements using the cached data.

Caching HTML

There are also instances when it makes sense to cache HTML. For example, if you have a report that requires significant processing time to create, but the data used in the report changes infrequently, you can generate the report once, save the HTML to a variable, and then simply return the contents of the variable when the report is requested.

To save HTML to a variable, drag a Results action into your TAF after the actions that create the HTML you want to save. Place the meta tags shown in Listing C.4 into the Results action.

Listing C.4

```
<@! "Save the accumulated results HTML to a variable named savedHTML">
<@ASSIGN savedHTML <@RESULTS>>
<@COMMENT>
        Save the date the report was created in a separate variable
        You can use this date to determine if the reports is 'stale'
        and needs to be rebuilt
</@COMMENT>
<@ASSIGN savedHTMLdate <@CURRENTTIMESTAMP>>
<@! "If you want to clear the accumulated results HTML include the following
    meta tag">
<@PURGERESULTS>
```

When you save the HTML to a variable, it is helpful to also create another variable containing the date and time that the information was saved. If the data you saved is only valid for a day, you can use this information to decide when to regenerate the report or use the cached version.

Also, depending on your application, it might make sense to use Tango's timed URL processing feature to schedule automatic updates of the cached report.

To display the saved report using the saved HTML, use a Results action containing the meta tags shown in Listing C.5.

Listing C.5

```
<@COMMENT>
        Return the contents of the savedHTML variable.
        Use encoding=NONE so that any html in the variable is returned without
        Translation.
</@COMMENT>
<@VAR savedHTML encoding=NONE>
```

Application Partitioning

If your application has a function that requires significantly more time than the rest of the application, such as the payment-processing component of an e-commerce site, you might want to set up a separate server to handle the time-consuming process. This ensures that other users of your application are not affected by the extra resource requirements that the function imposes. Other examples of when you should consider partitioning your application include the creation of reports that aggregate a significant amount of data and interfacing with services that are outside your network.

Optimizing Database Queries

Usually, the SQL generated by Tango Search actions should execute in a reasonable amount of time, assuming that the appropriate indices are present. If you are using Direct DBMS actions to perform more sophisticated database queries, you might need to work with a trained database administrator to tune both the database and the SQL itself.

Many database systems provide a query analyzer or performance analysis tool to assist with this task. If you don't have these tools, Tango can help out. The @DATASOURCESTATUS meta tag reports the maximum processing time required to execute a database query. Additionally, reviewing Tango log files can point out actions that required abnormal amounts of time to complete. In one situation I was involved in, adding some hints to a query reduced its execution time from 30–40 seconds to 1–2 seconds. You shouldn't let opportunities to get that level of improvement pass by in your applications.

Avoiding Unneeded Work

First, when you use Tango's database actions, pay close attention to the value of the Include If Empty column in the criteria lists. If you're not familiar with this attribute of database actions, it is used to indicate whether a column is included in the criteria when its value is not present. If this attribute is not set appropriately, you might force the database into an unintentional table scan or to return many more rows than you intended. Either of these scenarios can have a significant impact on the resources used by your database and by Tango. If you notice database queries acting unexpectedly, this is an area that should be investigated.

Managing Database Connections

Tango pools users through shared database connections. For example, when you run a TAF that accesses a database, Tango opens a connection to the database, executes the query, and then keeps the connection open. If the same TAF is run again, Tango will reuse the connection for the second execution of the TAF. Because opening a connection can be a time-consuming process, this improves the performance of subsequent TAF executions. By default, if a connection is unused for 30 minutes, it is closed by Tango. However, if a request to use a database is received while the open connection is in use, Tango opens a second connection to the database. This can result in many database connections when your application is under a heavy load.

If you have a resource or license limitation on your database server, you should investigate Tango's `dsconfig` configuration variable, which enables you to limit the number of connections that Tango opens to a particular database. The `dsconfig` information can be set using the Advanced link in the data sources section of config.taf.

This feature can be used to ensure that Tango will not exceed the limitations of your database during periods of peak usage. If your database has a limit to the number of connections, this feature can also be used to keep several database connections reserved for administrative use. By the way, if Tango does reach the maximum number of database connections allowed, incoming requests for database services are still served, but only after a connection is freed.

Multiple Tango Servers

If you are deploying your site with multiple Tango Servers (described further in the next section, "Preparing to Deploy"), an issue you must contend with is tracking state information (that is, user variables) when a server is taken down. When a server is not running, Tango automatically routes a user to a different server, but any state information on the user's original server is lost. Currently, Tango Servers do not share state information between server processes.

The first step in dealing with this problem is making sure that your site reacts appropriately when user state information is lost while the user is still visiting your site. If your site has a login, the next hit received from the user should redirect him to the login page, rather than providing him with an error message.

In some applications you build, it might be practical to use the database to record state information. This will enable you to recover information in a failover situation. For example, in a commerce site, using the database to record items in the shopping basket will ensure that the user's selections are maintained if they are moved to a different server. Employing this technique might not even be noticeable to your users because many users expect the purchase process to take longer then the time they spend browsing for products. After the user identifies himself following a move to a different server, his shopping basket will be restored and, hopefully, his purchase intention will remain intact. The e-commerce template included with Tango 2000 contains a great example of using a database to manage items in a shopping cart. The application demonstrates that it is not necessary to keep all user data in the database. By keeping only what is critical and reconstructing the rest when the user logs back in to your application, the interruption to the user is minimized. Think about how this can be applied in your applications.

Preparing to Deploy

The first step to deployment is to make sure that your server is running with the most appropriate version of Tango. Starting with Tango 2000, there are more flavors of the Tango Application Server from which to choose. Here's a summary of the new license types:

License Type	Description
Small Business Edition	Single Tango Server process limited to 10 concurrent user sessions
Standard Edition	Single Tango Server process; no user session limitation
Professional Edition	Allows multiple Tango Server processes on a single machine
Corporate Edition	Allows multiple Tango Server processes running on multiple machines at a single location

This is an extremely brief summary of the different versions of Tango Server that are available. You should check with your sales person or the Pervasive Web site to get more details about each of these editions before deciding which one is right for you. However, if you're deploying a high-availability application, you will probably end up with the Professional Edition or Corporate Edition because those are the versions that enable you to run multiple servers.

Load Splitting

When running multiple Tango Servers, you use Tango's load-splitting feature to distribute load between the servers. After it is configured, there is very little you need to do to your application to take advantage of load splitting—Tango Server manages this process for you. The first time that a user visits your site, Tango randomly assigns that user to one of the servers. The next hit received from the user is sent automatically to the same server. This ensures that the user's state information is available.

How does this work? Tango encodes an identifier for the user's server, called his *user key* or *user reference*. If a server is taken down, Tango automatically routes the user's request to a different server. In that case, Tango generates a new user key for the user because the server identified in the user's original key is no longer valid.

To configure load splitting when Tango Server resides on the same machine as the Web server, you can use the config.taf application file to create and maintain load groups. If Tango Server resides on a separate machine, you must manually edit Tango's configuration files to identify the Tango Servers to which a Tango plug-in or cgi should send requests.

Before you deploy your site, you should perform testing on it to ensure that it operates as expected when under load. One way to do this testing is to call your friends and ask them to access the site. A simpler method is to take advantage of load-testing tools. These tools enable you to record a series of tasks in your Web browser, and then play them back as many users. Several commercial tools, as well as some freely downloadable ones, are available for this task.

Another option to consider is the use of your hardware vendor's performance lab. Many vendors, such as Sun and Dell, have labs available with the latest versions of their hardware for use in testing your application. These labs might prove to be useful, particularly in those cases when you are not sure how much horsepower to purchase.

Ensuring High Availability

After your application is up and running, you need to make sure that it stays that way.

Since version 3, Tango Server has attempted to recover from a fatal error and restart itself automatically. In Tango 2000, the Server Watcher was added to improve this process and ensure that a Tango Server is always running. The Server Watcher is an active-watching process that communicates with a Tango Server though shared memory. When the Server Watcher senses that a Tango Server is either not running or is not responding to user requests, the Server Watcher restarts the Tango Server. Each Tango Server process has its own Server Watcher.

The Server Watcher ensures that the Tango Servers that run your Web application are operational. Your site will probably contain other components that require similar monitoring. There are commercial tools available that perform this monitoring, such as SNMP tools. You can also use Tango to assist with this monitoring. Create an application file that uses the @URL meta tag to ping pages in your application. If there is a problem accessing these pages, the application file can send an email or page to an administrator.

When you set up tools to monitor your site, make sure that they hit each of the points of failure. Even the simplest application will consist of three different services: Web, application, and database. As you add functionality to your application, you are likely to introduce additional servers or services that must be monitored. Be sure that your monitoring utilities include these items.

External Factors

So far, we have focused on issues inside Tango that affect performance and reliability. Before you deploy your solution, it is extremely important to review the other components of your application, both hardware and software. When you first install the hardware and software that will run your application, chances are good that it is not configured in the most appropriate manner.

From a hardware perspective, there are issues such as uninterruptible power supplies (UPS), redundant power supplies, RAID drives, hot-swappable hardware, and so on, that must be considered if reliability is a concern. You should discuss your requirements with your hardware vendor to ensure that you have what is appropriate for your application and your budget.

A question that often arises is whether it is better to purchase one large machine or two less-capable machines. Although my usual response to this question is to suggest the purchase of two large machines, I know that real life interjects itself from time to time. There is no set answer to this question because I'm sure your situation is different from others. However, the following are some of the many merits of the purchase of two less-capable machines that have, in total, equal or greater horsepower than a single machine:

- You can partition your application, moving functions that require more resources to the second machine.

- In the event of a serious failure of one of the machines, you will have a second machine to put in its place with minimal turnaround time.

- Having two machines can also provide a separate machine to use for testing purposes.

- In those instances where additional horsepower is required, Tango's load splitting can send requests to servers running on multiple machines just as easily as it can to servers on a single machine.

From a software perspective, you must spend time to tune and configure your operating system, Web server, database server, and other components so that they operate appropriately. Most vendors will provide guides that describe how to tune their products for performance and availability. If you can't find this information in the user documentation, have a look in the knowledge base on the vendor's Web site. Additionally, books are available that describe how to tune Windows and UNIX-based systems. Seek out, read, implement, and test the suggestions in these guides.

If you are expecting a lot of activity, it is important to ensure that your Web server is up to the task. Performing the load testing described earlier helps identify problems in this area. If a high degree of concurrency will be commonplace with your application, you must investigate using either multiple physical Web servers or multiple Web server processes on your machine. When you use multiple Web servers, you probably need to consider a load-balancing software or hardware solution to distribute the load between these servers.

Last, your database poses several challenges. You must ensure that backups occur regularly and don't disrupt usage of your application. If failover of your database is required, you might want to investigate mirroring or replication solutions. The solution you select here will be based on how up to date you need your data to be if a failover occurs.

Conclusion

Deploying your application in a high-availability environment poses many unique challenges. By considering this requirement during the design and development of your application and incorporating the suggestions in this appendix, your application will be more than up to this challenge.

INDEX

Symbols

A

X-Y-Z